THE LOST WORLD OF COMMUNISM

This book is dedicated to the memory of my late parents, Molly and Jack

THE LOST WORLD OF COMMUNISM

An Oral History of Daily Life Behind the Iron Curtain

PETER MOLLOY

BBC BOOKS

Published to accompany the BBC television series *The Lost World of Communism* first broadcast on BBC2 in 2009.

1 3 5 7 9 10 8 6 4 2

First published in 2009 by BBC Books, an imprint of Ebury Publishing
A Random House Group Company.

The Random House Group Limited Reg. No. 954009.
Addresses for companies within the Random House Group can be found at www.randomhouse.co.uk

A CIP catalogue record for this book is available from the British Library

ISBN 978 1 846 07616 9

Commissioning editor: Albert DePetrillo
Project editor: Christopher Tinker
Copy-editors: Karen Farrington and Julian Flanders
Designer: Jonathan Baker at Seagull Design
Production controller: Phil Spencer

Printed and bound in Great Britain by Clays of St Ives PLC

The Random House Group Limited supports The Forest Stewardship Council (FSC), the leading international forest certification organisation. All our titles that are printed on Greenpeace approved FSC certified paper carry the FSC logo. Our paper procurement policy can be found at www.rbooks.co.uk/environment

CONTENTS

INTRODUCTION

'A spectre is haunting Europe – the spectre of Communism.'

First line of the *Communist Manifesto* (1848) by Karl Marx and Friedrich Engels

IN 1989 A WAY of life ended for millions of people behind the Iron Curtain. The Berlin Wall came down, communism collapsed in Eastern Europe and the Cold War ended. It was a year of revolution to rank alongside 1789 or 1917.

But what was life really like for East Europeans, effectively imprisoned in the Eastern bloc? The headlines of Cold War spies and secret police surveillance, of political repression and dissident activism do not tell the whole story. After the end of the Cold War, some remembered their lives as 'perfectly ordinary', others hankered for the security and certainty of life under communism while still more missed the camaraderie or the privileges attendant on power.

This book gathers unique personal testimony from those who lived in communist East Germany, Czechoslovakia and Romania. Their recollections evoke the moods, preoccupations and experiences of a lost world of communism. The three societies were very different, experiencing very different kinds of rule.

In East Germany people lived under the collective leadership of a one-party dictatorship. In Romania they experienced life under a one-family dictatorship during the rule of Nicolae and Elena Ceauşescu. In Czechoslovakia, where the Communist Party tried to break away from its Stalinist past, they briefly experienced a more democratic form of communist rule. The failure of those reforms following invasion on 21 August 1968 consigned Czechoslovaks to two further decades of dictatorship and stagnation known as 'the era of forgetting'.

During the Second World War, the world's first communist state, the Soviet Union, had borne the brunt of Nazi aggression with over 27 million dead. It is unsurprising that as victory approached its leader, Josif Vissarionovich Stalin, was determined to secure his country's western boundaries. To many on the left, despite his arbitrary reign of terror Marshal Stalin remained an iconic figure associated with liberation from Nazi tyranny.

Communist rule in Eastern Europe rolled in behind waves of Soviet tanks as the Red Army 'liberated' countries soon termed the 'Eastern bloc'. Largely speaking, these were Czechoslovakia, Romania, Poland, Hungary, Bulgaria and, initially, Albania. Militarily, they ultimately all joined the Warsaw Pact, designed to defend international socialism against capitalist powers. Yugoslavia under Marshal Josip Tito, although a socialist country, broke away from the USSR in 1948.

INTRODUCTION

Following conferences at Yalta and Potsdam between the Soviet Union and the Western allies in 1945 Europe had been effectively divided into two spheres of influence. Occupied Germany was divided into four zones and Berlin was separated into four sectors. The scene was set for the Cold War.

It was, in essence, an ideological conflict between a capitalist West and a communist East that included the Soviet Union and the countries of Eastern Europe. Winston Churchill presciently observed the new European political landscape in a speech delivered in America in March 1946. 'From Stettin in the Baltic to Trieste in the Adriatic, an iron curtain has descended across the Continent. Behind that line lie all the capitals of the ancient states of Central and Eastern Europe. Warsaw, Berlin, Prague, Vienna, Budapest, Belgrade, Bucharest and Sofia, all these famous cities and the populations around them lie in what I must call the Soviet sphere, and all are subject in one form or another, not only to Soviet influence but to a very high and, in many cases, increasing measure of control from Moscow... The Communist parties, which were very small in all these Eastern States of Europe, have been raised to pre-eminence and power far beyond their numbers and are seeking everywhere to obtain totalitarian control... Whatever conclusions may be drawn from these facts – and facts they are – this is certainly not the liberated Europe we fought to build up.'

Support for communism and the Soviet Union varied greatly between nations. In Czechoslovakia communism was already a significant political force prior to the arrival of the Red Army. Historically, the Czechs and the Slovaks looked upon the Soviet Union as a friend. A successful Soviet-backed Communist Party existed in pre-war Czechoslovakia. In 1938, the Soviet Union was the only power to declare iself ready to aid Czechoslovakia. When Soviet troops entered Prague in May 1945, they were welcomed as liberators. In the free elections of 1946, the Communist Party won 38 per cent of the vote. It was the largest showing of support for communism ever expressed in Eastern Europe in a democratic ballot. The communists were the largest party in parliament and had a key role in a coalition government.

The Czech writer Pavel Kohout, although from a bourgeois background, was an ardent young communist at the end of the Second World War. The reasons for his conversion to communism echo those of many Czechoslovaks of the time. He was disillusioned with capitalism, dismayed with Britain and France's abandonment of their country to Hitler's mercies in the Munich Agreement of September 1938 and supported the Soviets in 1945. 'My father found no protection in his bourgeois origin nor in his knowledge of seven languages against a four-year period of unemployment, so my first significant life experience was the world economic crisis, which in this country was perceived as a total failure of capitalism. We wanted to prevent Czechoslovakia, which ranked among the ten most advanced countries, from going through the same crisis it had experienced in the 1930s.

'The second reason, which I felt even more strongly about, was the Munich Treaty. It was seen in Czechoslovakia as a total failure of the Western democracies. The English and French left us out on a limb in 1938 when Neville Chamberlain came home with the famous statement about "peace with honour". And when the country was liberated by the Red Army, the seeds were sown for the majority of inhabitants to change the system and the protector.'

Communism was about sharing a revolutionary vision of a more just world. Industrialization and collectivization would transform the economy. A new type of socialist personality with a collective sense of values would transform society. The guiding principle would be, 'from each according to his ability, to each according to his need'.

What Eastern Europeans actually experienced in those post-war years, however, had little to do with such a utopian vision and everything to do with an extraordinary level of social and political control, modelled on Stalin's Soviet Union.

Communism's official ideology in this Stalinized Eastern Europe was Marxist-Leninism, a mixture of the theories of Marx, Engels, Lenin and Stalin himself. Marxist theory claimed that as the people experienced a 'false consciousness', a condition where they were not able to appreciate what was best for them, the party had to adopt a 'leading role'. Accordingly, the party had to be in the 'vanguard', acting for the real interests of the people even if party policy was against the people's will.

That 'leading role' meant that the party sought to control every aspect of its citizens' lives. Another guiding principle was the idea of 'democratic centralism'. In practice, it meant that every level within the party had to accept and carry out decisions made at the level above it. This system invested those leading the party in the Political Bureau (or Politburo) with an extraordinary degree of power.

Yet, along with the party's power went paranoia. Since all the communist regimes of Eastern Europe were imposed from without and within, the rulers always felt insecure. They never enjoyed the support of the majority of their electorates, even at the best of times. That's why communist states were also police states.

One of the first communist regimes to be established in Eastern Europe was in Romania where the Communist Party had been a tiny organization before the Second World War, with less than a thousand members. During the war Romania had been an ally of Hitler's but on 23 August 1944 the pro-Nazi goverment of Marshal Ion Antonescu was overthrown at the instigation of King Michael supported by, among others, the communists. The Romanians changed sides and their troops, vanquished at Stalingrad, now took up arms against Hitler's forces. In February 1945 Stalin sent his foreign minister to Bucharest to organize Romania's new government. In fraudulent elections the communist-dominated Front of Popular Democracy won an overwhelming victory. Two years later, King Michael was forced to leave Romania at gunpoint. The country was now in the hands of a small group of communists, erstwhile fascists and opportunists. From 1952 onwards, communist Romania was controlled by two dictators, Gheorghe Gheorghiu Dej and Nicolae Ceauşescu.

As a socialist country Romania had the dubious distinction of never undergoing the process of de-Stalinization that affected most Eastern bloc countries at some point after the dictator's death. Under Nicolae Ceauşescu and his wife Elena it became a one-family dictatorship. What Romanians experienced during these years was a type of dynastic communism fuelled by narcissism, paranoia and a North Korean-style megalomania.

In Germany after the Second World War, the Soviets controlled the country's centre except for part of Berlin, which came under British, American and French jurisdiction. To the east, areas that had formerly been German were assigned to Poland. To the west was the larger region that became the Federal Republic of Germany (West Germany), with its capital in Bonn.

Everywhere, Germany was facing a host of difficulties. Thousands of people were homeless after Allied bombing destroyed as much as a quarter of the housing. The people were hungry and their misery was compounded by rampant inflation, reducing the value of what little money they had in their pockets. Psychologically, they were coming to terms with the defeat of Hitler's Nazi regime. The crimes carried out in his name weighed heavily. Most families were also bruised by bereavements.

The German Democratic Republic (GDR or in German DDR, *Deutsche Demokratische Republik*) was formally established on 7 October 1949 with its seat of government in East Berlin. Now Germany was formally divided into a capitalist West and a communist East. The new country's national anthem was entitled, 'Resurrected from Ruins'. But initial efforts at resurrection were hampered as the Soviets removed much of what remained of Germany's industry to the motherland by way of wartime reparations. The economy was further damaged by an exodus of people seeking the additional wealth and freedom of life in West Germany.

The divided city of Berlin had city administrations, one for East Berlin and one for West Berlin. In many ways, though, Berlin still functioned as one city. Despite checkpoints and other restrictions, the people of Berlin could move reasonably freely around the city. Telephone lines, sewage and transport were shared. Many people lived in one half of the city and had family, friends and jobs in the other. Even when East Germany closed the borders between East and West Germany in 1952 to stop people fleeing the DDR, they did not seal off West Berlin until the advent of the Berlin Wall in August 1961.

By 1952 the 1,381-kilometre inner German border had been constructed with its fearsome wire fences and armed guards. The defences faced inwards to keep East Germans at bay. In 1961 fortifications were upgraded and the Wall was built to further stem East Germany's brain drain. The crime of escaping was considered so grave by the East German authorities as to merit the death sentence.

Throughout virtually its entire existence, East Germany was ruled by one party, the Socialist Unity Party of Germany (*Sozialistiche Einheitspartei Deutschland* or SED), modelled along Soviet lines. Both party and country, primarily, had two leaders: Walter Ulbricht and, from 1971, Erich Honecker. Of all the East European nations, it was a country that was defined by its ideology. It saw itself as socialist, anti-fascist and morally superior to its Western counterpart. Its position as the western outpost of the Soviet imperium, on the front line of the Cold War in a divided Germany, also made it unique among the communist states of Eastern Europe.

Communism in Czechoslovakia swung between extremes, from Stalinism to attempts to reform the system. These were crushed in 1968 when troops from five Warsaw Pact countries invaded. To prevent casualties, Czechoslovakian leader Alexander Dubček ordered domestic troops not to resist. He was swiftly replaced by Gustáv Husák and a purge of reformers meant all significant jobs went to hard-line communists and opportunists. Soviet troops squatted on Czech territory until 1991.

The bitterness felt among swathes of society was slow to abate. In 1969 student Jan Palach burnt himself to death in Wenceslas Square, Prague, in protest at the Warsaw Pact intervention. He was the first of three students to die in this manner.

Of course, while the regimes in Eastern Europe can accurately be decribed as communist, what people experienced was not communism but various forms of state socialism, en route, the regimes claimed, to a communist utopia.

After the failed attempts to reform Soviet-style socialism in Czechoslovakia, any significant change from within the Communist Party had to wait for Mikhail Gorbachev, the Soviet leader from 1985, with his reform agenda of *glasnost* (openness) and *perestroika* (restructuring).

The collapse of communism in Europe in 1989 was unexpected and sudden. The end came with the end of the Soviet empire but a variety of internal factors within each socialist state contributed to its demise. In East Germany widespread public anger over rigged local government elections was one factor. Other more significant contributory causes were a poorly performing economy and frustration at travel restrictions imposed by the government.

Reactions to communism's demise also varied from country to country. It was clear in the DDR that many of those who took to the streets in Berlin and other cities in a series of mass demonstrations did not want the end of East Germany, but the establishment of a different kind of socialism. In Romania, a major balance of payments crisis had occurred after substantial loans from the West were squandered in mismanaged industrial ventures. Ceauşescu then exported the country's major commodities in order to pay back what was owed. Once the breadbasket of Europe, Romanian farm workers and their families went hungry as successive harvests were assigned for export. As the economy became increasingly exhausted so the levels of hardship rose and spread. For his own part, Ceauşescu and his family lived well in a series of villa-style residences or 'palaces'.

Still it was unclear whether Ceauşescu's downfall had been brought about by a party coup rather than a people's revolution, leaving Romanians wondering how much had really changed. In Czechoslovakia, it was people power that in a ten-day revolution swept away one-party rule.

In the end, communism proved to be an intellectual and moral failure. The secret police's treatment of former party members is but one illustration of the moral bankruptcy of the system. In 1977 Pavel Kohout, the former Stalinist who had arranged his wedding to coincide with the day of Stalin's birthday, written poems in praise of the Soviet leader and supported Czechoslovakia's Stalinist show trials of the 1950s, joined Charter 77, the human rights group. In the following years he became prominent in the movement and the target of an StB (secret police) assassination plan.

'The secret police tried to talk two traffic policemen from Kutná Hora into creating a traffic accident in which I would die,' he recalls. 'The two men drove back home in silence. When they got to Kutná Hora they wondered what they were going to do about it. One of them asked, "Was it an order?" The other said, "It was a recommendation." And the first one said, "Sod it, it stinks." After that they were never promoted and I was not killed.'

Above all, it is the fall-out from the moral devastation that communism wreaked across Eastern Europe that lingers longest. As Václav Havel says elsewhere in this book, 'Two new generations will have to grow up to wash away the footprints of communism'.

1
PARTY PEOPLE

Oh the Party, the Party is always right
And comrade, may it ever be so;
For who fights for the right
He is always right
Against lies and exploitation
Whoever insults life is stupid or bad
Whoever defends humanity
Is always right
Grown from the spirit of Lenin
Welded by Stalin
The Party, the Party, the Party

Song of the Party, 1950

MOSCOW, 30 APRIL 1945. At 6 a.m. a bus pulled up to the side entrance to the Hotel Lux on Tverskaya Street. Ten German communists climbed aboard and headed for the airport where an American DC3 transport plane was waiting. The party comprised some of the leading lights of the future East German administration, including Walter Ulbricht, the future leader of East Germany.

WOLFGANG LEONHARD

ANOTHER OF THE men on board was 23-year-old Wolfgang Leonhard. 'As the plane took off, we knew we were flying to Germany, but not where, how, or what would be required of us. No one told us whether it would be a brief visit or whether it would be for ever. One was not told anything; this was one of the most essential elements of the Soviet dictatorship. If people are too well informed, then it is hopeless. You must not be informed.'

While the military conflict of the Second World War was drawing to a close, the political battle for post-war Europe was just beginning. Leonhard and his colleagues had been trained, organized and funded by Stalin. Their mission was to assist the Red Army in setting up a new political system in eastern Germany. They were the first German émigrés to return to the Soviet-occupied part of Germany at the end of the war. Leonhard, the youngest member of the group, was a committed communist and fluent Russian speaker. 'During the flight, my concern and hope was that things in Germany, under the Soviet occupation, would be different than in the Soviet Union. That there would be greater opportunities for an independent development of socialism, that things would be better, more peaceful, more tolerant.'

After they landed they headed for Berlin and witnessed the fearful devastation brought about under Hitler's rule. Anti-fascism was a powerful impetus for the establishment of communist regimes across this part of the continent. It would also become a constant alibi for the dictatorial behaviour of these communist regimes. 'The closer we came to Berlin, the more appalling the destruction. In Lichtenberg and towards the centre of the city everything was full of smoke. It was unbelievable, like a vision from hell. The scale of the destruction was grim. People looked absent-minded, as if they couldn't see or understand anything any more. They stood there with small buckets next to the water pumps. But there was another side as well.

'White flags were hung out everywhere. Hanging white flags on 1 May was a test of courage as well as an opinion: I surrender; I don't want to have anything to do with war any more. People with white armbands walked the streets, a clear expression of the citizens' opinion. It was very encouraging for us to see how people had turned away from the Nazi system and how they expressed their feelings.

'The unity of Germany at that time was an absolute certainty. In the early days all the occupying powers worked closely together. In the beginning, there was a feeling of togetherness. We hoped we might work together for the future. That hope did not survive very long.'

As a 13-year-old, Leonhard had fled Nazi Germany with his communist mother, Susanne, and spent his adolescence in the Soviet Union. There he witnessed Stalin's harshest purges. Although a staunch communist, his mother was sentenced to ten years in Siberia. Despite all this, Leonhard was dedicated to the communist cause. 'I was Walter Ulbricht's secretary, so I saw him every day from early in the morning until very late. I translated for him too. We had a Soviet driver and a Soviet officer who looked after us. I could travel anywhere. No one but the Ulbricht group could do that.

'Ulbricht wanted everything to be controlled from the top. He didn't want initiative and enthusiasm; he wanted conformists, apple-polishers. Ulbricht's favourite statement was, "It has to look democratic; but we must have everything in our control."'

To look democratic, Ulbricht introduced a 'regime of deputies'. This meant that a figurehead from any party was appointed as, for example, a mayor, but that their deputies were communists. When Ulbricht needed a mayor for a middle-class suburb he sent Leonhard out on to the streets to find one. Leonhard approached every man wearing a necktie until a suitable frontman could be found.

Another of Ulbricht's favourite sayings was, 'To learn from the Soviet Union is to learn victory'. And he meant it. Ulbricht was a loyal servant of Stalin. He took his instructions from General Ivan Serov who was the senior NKVD (People's Commissariat for Internal Affairs – the secret police) 'political officer' in the Soviet Zone. Ulbricht's task was to transform a popular front of anti-fascist groups in the Soviet Zone of Occupied Germany into one overwhelmingly dominant party.

The two most popular political parties in the Soviet Zone were the Social Democrats (SPD) and the Communists (KPD). The problem for the communists was that the SPD was by far the more popular party. Accordingly, the communists decided on a merger between the two parties, so as to control their rivals.

On 21 and 22 April 1946 the new Socialist Unity Party of Germany (SED) was formed at a meeting in the German State Opera House in East Berlin. To a great extent it was a shotgun wedding. Afterwards, many of the bride's family were sidelined, incarcerated or suffered a worse fate. Meanwhile, the SED transformed itself into a Stalinist party. Leonhard recalls, 'What was becoming increasingly evident was our subordination to the Soviet Union. All essential things were imported from the Soviet Union, to the extent that Soviet comrades participated in sessions of the SED. That meant that a Soviet official participated in the Politburo as well.

'Everything from the Soviet Union had to be praised, glorified and imitated. That kind of propaganda was loathsome to me. It was also rubbish, because there were many things that were better in Germany than in the Soviet Union. Soon, it was clear that we weren't living in an anti-fascist Germany but rather in a Soviet province. There were more pictures of Stalin, more references to everything Soviet.'

In 1947 Wolfgang Leonhard had a meeting with Markus 'Mischa' Wolf, who would go on to become East Germany's top spymaster, which reinforced his concerns about who was really calling the shots in the SED. Leonhard had known Wolf since September 1935 when they both at school together in Moscow. 'I used to meet Mischa Wolf often. In 1947 he worked in broadcasting under the name of Michael Storm. Mischa always had a way of explaining to me what was really going on.

'I told him, "Mischa, you don't have to tell me what's going on. I work for the Central Committee of the SED." Mischa said, "There are higher authorities than your Central Committee." He received his special information from higher Soviet circles, not just from the secret services. Within the upper circles of the foreign intelligence service were high officials who certainly knew more than the chief members of the SED's Central Committee. And Mischa smiled and said, "If I were you, I would stop talking about the 'German road to socialism'. It will soon be abandoned."

'I was sceptical at the time but Mischa was right. At times like that, he would show that he was better informed than an official of the Central Committee like me.'

Leonhard also became concerned at the lifestyle of the party elite who enjoyed special restaurants and luxurious villas. Nor was his own lifestyle above criticism, especially during those austere post-war years in Germany. 'I didn't experience an ordinary lifestyle, because I belonged to the privileged class. We used to dine four times a day in beautiful restaurants and received food packets. I never had to endure any material difficulties. But I was critical about whether it was right that huge food packets were sent to chosen circles. I had many concerns, but to refuse wasn't an option.'

By 1948 Leonhard was working at the Party Academy just outside Berlin. By then, he was becoming attracted to Tito's brand of socialism in Yugoslavia which was developing independently from Moscow. Given the rift between Tito and Stalin this was a dangerous view to hold let alone express. Unfortunately, Leonhard had expressed his views and word of this reached the ears of the director of the Party Academy, Rudolph Lindau. 'I was summoned to a meeting. There was Lindau with five party officials. It was very serious. At these sessions when party members were interrogated, they could only answer "yes" or "no".

'They questioned me about things they had found out from others, "Is it true that you have recommended books by Arthur Köestler?" I replied, "Yes, it is. But I distanced myself critically from them." They said, "It's enough that you even recommended them." One question followed the other, each starting with "Is it true that…?"

'Through an informer network within the party school, they knew what I had discussed with others. Lindau told me, "We have everything. It is so serious, Comrade Leonhard, that we won't make any decision right now. The party leadership in Berlin will decide instead. In two or three days the Politburo will communicate its decision about your case."

'When I heard that, I knew that I had to leave the country instantly. From the SED school I went straight to Berlin, then through Dresden to Czechoslovakia. And from there to Yugoslavia. If I had stayed, imprisonment, at least, awaited me. I knew a number of higher officials who were kidnapped and then finished up being killed. So, on 12 March 1949, I began a new life.'

Almost seven months after Leonhard's flight from the party school, the 'Workers' and Peasants' State' of East Germany was born. Like the other communist states of Eastern Europe it was a child of Stalin, despite the fact that the Soviet leader had once remarked that 'communism fits Germany like a saddle fits a cow'.

GÜNTER BAZYLI

GÜNTER BAZYLI JOINED the party because it was the only way to advance through the army ranks. Born in 1937, he has strong memories of fleeing 'a sea of fire and blood' as British planes bombed his home town. The enemy, as he grew up, was the Allied troops advancing into Germany.

His father, a soldier in the German army during the Third Reich, was de-Nazified by the British and was reunited with Bazyli only in 1949, the year the East German state was founded. After being politically active in the Free German Youth (FDJ), Bazyli joined the army (NVA) in 1955. Garrisoned in Potsdam, he was trained to counter airborne attack and infiltration by the West. By 1956 he was a corporal but, to rise up the ranks, he needed to join the SED. 'They were expecting people to be trained as officers but those who weren't in the party couldn't become officers. If I joined the party I could belong to the elite within the army.

'They constantly made it clear that those people who left our country had all been seduced by the enemy. The West had turned them away from socialist ideology and so they were now deserting us. Everyone in the DDR knew that they would close the border and that people would feel as if they were in prison. At stake were the very foundations of socialism. We were terrified that socialism would be taken away from us, and that fear was omnipresent; it ate into our daily lives.

'Imperialism and capitalism always wanted to challenge us because we lived our lives in the spirit of socialism. Over three million people had already escaped. More than 1,500 people had already deserted from the armed forces. Something had to be done. It was said that we were bleeding to death. We were convinced that the Wall had to be built to protect us.'

In 1962 Bazyli joined the border guards in East Berlin on the 'front line' of the war with capitalism. With compulsory military service having been recently introduced, there was concern about the political reliability of young conscripts serving at the border, so the Stasi vetted each one. 'When I was posted at the border, my orders were to arrest border trespassers and, if they didn't freeze upon request, to fire a warning shot. If they still didn't freeze, they would be shot dead.

'And then, when I became a squadron commander in 1974, the Politburo, seeing more desertions and escapes, introduced stricter rules. Commanders and squadron commanders were to be punished if the number of escapes went up.'

Documentary evidence released after East Germany collapsed shows that the guards were under instructions to shoot only as a last resort. However, in 1997 evidence of a 'shoot to kill policy' emerged in a seven-page document found among the Stasi archives in Magdeburg. Dated 1 October 1973, the document makes no mention of shouting or firing a warning shot before shooting at escapers. It states: 'Don't hesitate to use your weapon even when border breaches happen with women and children, which traitors have often exploited in the past.' The order was issued to Stasi agents working at the border who were specially tasked to infiltrate border guard units and prevent defections by the border soldiers. At least 37 border guards were shot dead trying to escape. If the order to Stasi agents was explicit, statements by the communist leadership at the time were hardly calling for restraint from the border guards in dealing with escapers.

In August 1966 East Germany's defence minister, Heinz Hoffman, said, 'Anyone who does not respect our border will feel the bullet'. Eight years later, Erich Honecker stated, 'Firearms are to be ruthlessly used in the event of attempts to break through the border, and the comrades who have successfully used their firearms are to be commended.'

'There was no alternative [to shooting],' explained Bazyli. 'Otherwise they might have shot me. If I refrained from shooting, I might just as well have climbed the fence myself. I didn't want the integrity of me or my soldiers questioned. Soldiers don't have alternatives. We wore a weapon and had sworn an oath of allegiance.'

By the early 1980s, the Wall that Bazyli's troops were patrolling had become a formidable obstacle. First, there was a three-metre high concrete wall, known as the 'hinterland' fence. Then came a two-metre high 'signal fence' of barbed wire and steel mesh strung up between concrete posts. When touched, this fence activated an alarm and, sometimes, a floodlight. Anyone who breached those defences still had to cross ground festooned with anti-personnel devices, such as steel bars placed on the earth and then covered with metal spikes.

By now, escapees could be seen from the observation towers positioned every hundred metres along the Berlin section of the Wall. After this, there was a floodlit access road to cross, followed by an area known as the 'death strip'. This was a six-metre wide, sand-strewn area (on which footprints were easily discernible) where escapees would often be confronted by Stasi-trained dogs. To get that far without being apprehended or shot was an achievement in itself. Finally, there was the 3.6-metre high 'Grenzwall 75', topped by a 30-centimetre diameter sewer pipe to prevent climbers from getting a good grip.

In the early evening of 25 December 1983, 21-year-old Silivio Proksch and his brother Carlo left their parents at their house in Pankow, East Berlin. They were heading home after a drinking session when Silivio said goodbye and parted company with his brother. He made straight for the Wall. Bazyli was then in charge of the border guards in that part of Berlin. Proksch ignored the warning shots and reached the border strip before firing began in earnest. He later died of his wounds in hospital. At the time, the state denied Proksch had been killed. Only after 1989 did his family discover the truth. Later, after the DDR had ceased to exist, Bazyli visited Proksch's mother to apologize.

On 1 December 1984, Michael-Horst Schmidt, aged 20, also attempted to escape across Bazyli's section of the Wall. He was shot in the back and knee by two of Bazyli's soldiers with automatic rifles and bled to death.

By the middle of the 1980s, and especially following a trip to the Soviet Union after Mikhail Gorbachev had come to power, Bazyli started to have doubts about the system that had German guards shooting their fellow countrymen. He was also concerned about the increase in border surveillance measures. Following a dispute, Bazyli was removed from his post but he remained in the army. 'The Germans used to be labelled as the most loyal sons of the Soviet Union. Sometimes we would feel ashamed about that. Then I was discharged from my former position due to "political shortcomings".

'We had to come to terms with our own history. I felt sad when I thought about what I had done with my life. My grandfather was in the First World War, my father was in the Second World War, and

I was in the third war, the Cold War. Generations of people used to do their duty and obey orders. You would always feel you were doing the right thing. But it couldn't have been right.'

On 4 November 1989, Bazyli was at his mother's house in Plauen witnessing a large demonstration against the regime. 'We watched the people marching; they were neatly dressed, sober, they had their children with them and they waved flags. Tears came to our eyes. The following day, when I got back to work, I quit the party. More officers quit the party. Everywhere crowds of people were on the streets.

'On 9 November, I was on duty in the morning and we knew that chapter of our lives was coming to an end and that they would put us on trial – we gave out orders to shoot people at the border. In retrospect, I was happy that they removed me from my position as chief of staff, otherwise I would have been responsible for the deaths of even more people.'

After unification Colonel Günter Bazyli stood trial for the murder of six escapees. He was also tried for his involvement in the development and authorization of formal instructions which stated that lethal force could be used at the border. He was sentenced to two years in prison and placed on probation.

Only one in fifteen escape attempts from East Germany ever succeeded. Best estimates today are that 250 people died at the Berlin Wall. Another 370 died along the border dividing East from West Germany, and 189 died trying to escape across the Baltic. Altogether over 1,000 people were killed trying to escape from East Germany.

Bazyli is no longer a communist and he doesn't miss his life as a border guard commander. 'Our life consisted of combat, of standing on the front line, where on one side your own people were running away and on the other side stood capitalism. That used to be very nerve-racking. I don't miss it.'

WOLF BIERMANN

WOLF BIERMANN HAD a communist background and in 1953 he opted to leave his home in the capitalist West for a life in the East because he believed that East Germany was the 'better Germany'. His final ejection from East Germany, 23 years after he arrived, would prove a watershed in the history of the party and East Germany. As Biermann himself puts it, 'They wanted to get rid of me the quiet way. Instead, they kicked off an avalanche with their fat feet.'

A poet, songwriter and musician, he composed and performed political songs that condemned the 'spoiled old men' who ruled his adopted country and the 'real existing socialism' that they had created. What made his criticism so potent and irritating to the political elite was the fact that he was such a staunch socialist from a family of communists. 'I was born in 1936, during the Nazi period, in Hamburg. My parents met through the Communist Party on the barricades. My father died at Auschwitz. I arrived in the DDR on 15 May 1953. The tears for the great leader Stalin hadn't dried and the blood of 17 June hadn't been shed yet. If I had seen tanks killing demonstrating workers, I would have known that those who let the tanks roll on top of the workers were enemies of the workers, counter-revolutionaries and anti-communists.

'Moving to East Germany at the age of 17 was wonderful. I was protected by my ignorance. I was young and inexperienced. And I was happy. I wasn't sure what to study after my A-levels. But my mother knew exactly. She realized that the economy didn't work in the DDR. For her, it was obvious that I had to study economics in order to put things right in East Germany. So I studied economics at Humboldt University in Berlin.

'In East Berlin I got caught up in the maelstrom of the Berliner Ensemble, Bertolt Brecht's theatre, which used to be the most famous in the world. I was lucky because Helene Weigel, Brecht's wife, employed me as an assistant director. By then, I was a bit older and wiser and began to criticize the conditions in East Germany more and more.

'My disillusionment with communism didn't happen at one particular moment, it was a slow process. You can only be disappointed if you have been deceived. For a long time, I would bravely strive against the idea that communism was a badly designed system. At the beginning, I was sure that it was me who was wrong, not the comrades, because that's what my mother and others had taught me. After two years at the Berliner Ensemble I decided to study again. It was during that period that the Berlin Wall was built.'

At the time Biermann saw the Wall as a regrettable necessity, built to prevent East Germany imploding from the constant exodus of its citizens. He even took part in an 'agitation' group formed to reassure East Germans as to why the Wall had been put up. 'We had to go from house to house to secure the "ideological safeguarding of the building of the Wall". What that meant was that I and a fellow student tried to explain to people that the Wall would only be there for a short time. We were actually convinced of that ourselves. For us, the building of the Wall was like jumping from a car that is speeding towards an abyss. Of course, it was very hard to jump off, but at least we wouldn't end up in that abyss. That's how we saw it then.'

In 1965 the SED Central Committee held its Eleventh Congress. It was to become known as the 'demolition plenum' and it became notorious for its attack on culture. Future party leader Erich Honecker attacked artists who were disseminating 'the insidious immorality of imperialism' and 'a lifestyle alien to socialism'. Wolf Biermann was singled out for allowing the enemy to make him a standard-bearer for 'rebellious youth'; he was labelled a 'rowdy'. The attack on artists seemed to release frustration the party felt, but couldn't express, about problems with East Germany's economic relationship with the Soviet Union. 'The atmosphere was hysterical. They lost their heads and panicked. They took it out on the artists. I was banned. It was a huge mistake that they named me. I became famous because of that even though that hadn't been their intention.'

Biermann was accused of being a 'class traitor' and was prohibited from performing in public. He was also forbidden to publish his work. After he was banned, Biermann went 'underground', wrote political songs in his flat in Chausseestrasse and performed privately. 'I wouldn't use the word "dissident" to describe myself; that's a Western word. I think of my mother Emma, who was a member of the Communist Party in Hamburg. Her comrades would try to force her to criticize me. They wanted her to say, "I am embarrassed by my son. He has betrayed his father's heritage." But my mother wouldn't do that.

'If she really had thought of me as a counter-revolutionary, she would have kicked me in the pants although that would have broken her heart since I was the only thing she had left after the Nazis had killed our whole family. But she would have done it, had it not been that she believed that I was right and that the party comrades were wrong.'

Eventually, one particular poem of Biermann's, published in a satirical magazine, proved too much for the political leadership to tolerate. By this time, Biermann had been banned from performing in public for over ten years. But he was now granted permission to sing abroad and left the country to attend a concert in West Germany. In his absence he was stripped of his East German citizenship and refused re-entry to the DDR. The Politburo had planned for this to happen before Biermann went abroad, although they claimed that their action was in response to his concert in West Germany. They said his attitude there had demonstrated hostility to East Germany.

Biermann's expatriation had a significant impact on the party. An open letter protesting at his enforced exile was sent to the official party newspaper, *Neues Deutschland* (*New Germany*), by 12 artists, many of whom were themselves members of the party. Within days, over a hundred writers and artists had joined the protest. Ordinary East Germans also expressed their concern. Some of the writers and artists who supported Biermann were expelled from the party, some were imprisoned, others left the country or were expatriated themselves. But the party was caught off-guard by the scale of the opposition to Biermann's treatment. Erich Honecker would later admit privately that the exclusion was a mistake. In exile, Biermann finally cut his communist ties.

GÜNTER SCHABOWSKI

IF WOLF BIERMANN was the shining light the Communist Party didn't want, Günter Schabowski was, for most of his career, one of the brightest stars in the SED's firmament. A loyal member of the party for almost 40 years, Schabowski started working for a communist trade union paper after the Second World War and ended up as a member of the country's ruling elite, the Politburo.

But the role he played in the final chapter of the party's existence resulted in his being thrown out of the SED. Since the unification of the two Germanies, he has been highly critical of the party and his own role in it. 'I was only 16 when the war ended. I was in a Nazi camp where they trained 16-year-olds in the use of arms. We had been evacuated from Berlin and we were the last reserves to be trained by the Nazis in using bazookas. I and four or five schoolmates of mine were very much opposed to that. That was in northern Czechoslovakia.

'One morning we were caught off-guard by Soviet tanks. We saw them approaching on a nearby hill. We realized that that was the end. We then left the camp and went through the woods. I went back to Berlin on foot. It took me weeks. Berlin had been completely destroyed but our house had been only slightly damaged. And that was why in the autumn of 1945 I went back to my former school. It was one of the first schools to be reopened. I had benefited from the war in that I took my A-levels when I was only 17 whereas some of my classmates were already aged 20 and 21 because they had served in the army.

'That was in East Berlin, which had been occupied by the Soviets. We saw them as our liberators just like people in the West thought of the Americans and the British as liberators. We were totally against the Nazis because we understood that they were responsible for the catastrophic war.

'After my A-levels I was looking for a job and, by pure chance, I found a job at a trade union newspaper, the *Tribune*. There were absolutely no jobs at that time: the factories had been destroyed. The German journalists working on the newspaper were by and large communists and a couple of social democrats worked there too. They had been in the concentration camps. They explained the world to us. And what they said made sense. Who was really to blame for this war? The Nazis were only what emerged on the surface. Who had backed them? It was the financiers, the capitalists, the Krupps and the like. And the war crimes trials confirmed that.

'For us those trials were the confirmation that the things we were told by the communists were true. We ignored the negative aspects of the Soviet occupation. Those guys from the Soviet Union would steal bicycles and watches; they would rape women during the first days of the occupation. But we didn't talk about that. Their crimes were regarded as legitimate because they had prevailed over the Nazi tyranny.

'What I was told seemed convincing to me and I gave voice to those things through the newspaper. That's how, at a very young age, I started explaining and voicing the people's and the proletarians' "true interests" so to speak.'

In 1952 Schabowski became a member of the SED after two probationary years. Then he received promotion at the *Tribune* in a rather extraordinary way. 'When Stalin died in 1953, all the newspapers in East Germany published pages and pages of obituaries, tributes, the pages were framed in black. There was one exception: Stalin was referred to as the 'Father of War' rather than the 'Father of Peace' in one of our pieces. It had catastrophic consequences for the editorial staff of the newspaper. The following day plain-clothed Stasi officers entered the office to find out who was to blame for this. The Stasi found out that the typesetters were social democrats and the editor on duty that night had been a social democrat in the past and he got the blame. Half of the management were replaced. I wasn't on duty that night. I was among the younger and more promising staff. That's why in 1953 I became vice editor-in-chief at the age of 24.'.

'As a journalist, I used to be a bone-headed advocate of the party line. The media used to adhere to the Leninist maxim: that journalists are collective promoters, propagandists and agitators. That explains why journalists always had to make a selection. Some information would simply be omitted. The people knew about that, of course, because news omitted in the East would get to them through the Western media.'

Shortly after his promotion at the *Tribune*, sections of the East German people rose up against the state on 17 June 1953. The East German papers, his included, reported it as a counter-revolution and

Schabowski's faith in the party's interpretation of events was absolute. 'The rebellion was something enormous, something unprecedented. It started in Berlin among the construction workers and then spread throughout the entire country. It was a revolt against everything connected with the dominant role of the Soviet Union in our country. People also hoped for a reunification with West Germany. It was a huge uprising and the first ever to take place in the Soviet bloc. People took enormous risks. But it was put down pretty quickly. People were arrested; hundreds died.

'At the time I saw it as a counter-revolution. I used to have a Marxist view, a narrow view. I felt the bad living conditions that had partly caused the uprising resulted from crimes committed by the Nazis. My country had inherited a lot of economic difficulties.'

By the time the Berlin Wall was constructed nine years later, in 1961, Schabowski's faith in the system had actually increased. 'My attitude never changed. On the contrary, my belief grew firmer. The people's material well-being improved over the years. The building of the "anti-fascist protective Wall" was totally justified in the eyes of communists like me to prevent people being seduced by Western propaganda.'

Schabowski remained at the *Tribune* until 1968 but, as a promising and ambitious activist in the party, he was destined for higher office. After a spell in Moscow, he became the chief editor of *Neues Deutschland*. In his office sat a red telephone that linked the paper directly to the Politburo member responsible for agitation and propaganda. The paper's running order was decided at regular meetings with party officials like Erich Honecker, who would also sometimes be involved in the layout. One edition of the paper featured over 40 pictures of the party leader.

For party members like Schabowski, the journalist's role was an ideological one. 'The journalists' job was not to write about reality, we were interpreters of reality. In contrast to the 'simple citizens' we knew exactly what was necessary for the building of a better society. We always used to think that. We tried to reach the masses, those who had been influenced by the Western media and the many who were still blinded by the Nazi past. And that's why we needed to constantly remind the people that we were in the process of constructing a better society and that the class enemy was to blame for our present condition and for putting obstacles in our way. We needed to do that because people didn't give a damn about Marxism when they lacked gloves or warm jumpers in the winter and fashionable bathing suits in the summer.'

In 1983, at Erich Honecker's invitation, Schabowski joined the Politburo. Before long, he became aware of an increasing gap between the people's concerns in everyday life and the Politburo's preoccupations. 'The party was like a network of power which expanded over the whole of society. And the Politburo was the highest congregation of the faithful. It had the last word on all decisions, on how to behave, on what measures were necessary. But it was grotesque. If you take a look at the decisions made during the last year, for example, we were constantly concerned with minor matters. We never dealt with the reasons that caused the unrest in the spring and summer of 1989, which led so many to escape from the country. We would deal with matters like memorial days, for example, and things like that. It was absurd.

'We neglected the spirit of our society because we didn't want the people to feel the way they did. We didn't want our class enemy to dictate the agenda of our Politburo meetings in relation to what was happening. That was how we used to think.'

However, the Politburo could not ignore events outside East Germany. On 2 May 1989, Hungary started to dismantle its border fence with Austria. This gap in the Iron Curtain was a threat to East Germany's survival. 'That was a very important date for the end of the DDR and of the Wall. That day the Hungarians cut open the barbed wires at our borders. The Politburo didn't discuss it immediately. We would know about all these alarming situations, but we would never discuss them.

'However, Honecker sent the foreign minister to Moscow because the Hungarians needed to be rebuked and the barbed wire needed to be restored. The minister returned from Moscow with bad news. The Soviets had said that we shouldn't take it too seriously.

'Their attempts to reassure us made us realize that the very existence of East Germany was now in doubt, as it appeared Moscow would no longer guarantee our survival as a separate nation. And that was the decisive factor. That was what we, the younger ones in the Politburo, were thinking. So we realized we had to save ourselves. The means for salvation would be the complete opening of the borders. Of course, it would take us months to come to such a conclusion. All we were concerned about was to find an answer to the question, "What needs to be done to save the system?"

'It's not that the Politburo didn't know about what was happening. But we felt devoted to our mission. Despite the protests, which put us in a more and more difficult situation, our ideology remained unshaken, otherwise we would have been labelled as weak Marxists or weak Leninists.'

Schabowski and others calculated that once people had the freedom to travel they might opt to remain in the DDR in the long term. He thought such an approach might cast younger Politburo members like himself in a reforming light. And he calculated that some countries in the West, like the United Kingdom and France, would not be keen on a reunited Germany.

The other part of the plan was to remove the party leader, Erich Honecker. 'It came down to a plot. It's interesting how political leaders in this absolutist structure are only ever overthrown by plots. So the three of us [Schabowski, Egon Krenz and Siegfried Lorenz] decided to depose Honecker. It was clear that we would have to do that within the Politburo. And that's what happened during a Politburo meeting in mid-October. We arranged it with eight of the older and most influential Politburo members. We knew that if they would agree, the others would go along with it. The eight were convinced that the crisis in the GDR needed to be solved urgently, and that the best thing to do was to get rid of Honecker. They agreed to back us, probably because they hoped to stay where they were in doing so.

'Eventually, the topic was debated during one Politburo meeting and everyone voted for Honecker's removal. The bizarre thing was that Honecker himself voted for his own removal. The grotesque thing was that in doing so he reserved the right to remain part of the political leadership. That was typical of the communist system.

'The Politburo was subject to immense pressure because of

what was happening on the streets. And also because Gorbachev had adopted a different course so to speak, and we had to try to adapt to it.'

In an attempt to stave off disaster, the Politburo now started to make concessions over East Germans' freedom to travel outside the country. 'The true reason behind the reforms was not to give more rights to the people, to render their lives more humane, but to maintain the system; to save it from its impending downfall.'

On 4 November 1989, an enormous crowd gathered on the Alexanderplatz in East Berlin. It was a demonstration coordinated by Church activists and artists. Keen to defend themselves, leading figures from the party, including Stasi leader Erich Mielke and Günter Schabowski, addressed the gathering but both were booed, indicating the steps they had taken towards reform were insufficient.

Schabowski played a key part in the opening of the Wall on 9 November; in fact, his role in the event led him and others in the party hierarchy to be denounced by sections of the party. 'We resigned in December in order to give way to other, more credible colleagues. We resigned because we respected the party and hoped that we would be allowed to remain members in doing so. But, in January 1990, we would be dismissed from the party, because it needed to save itself. The party Control Committee summoned us. All old members like us were kicked out.

'They accused me of treason. That was the first time that the term was used in relation to the opening of the border. I was scandalized and furious about that and left, never to be seen there again. I felt like I had a lump in my throat because the party had rejected me. I was embittered about how the party had treated me. Two years later I had recovered and thought that I must write a letter of thanks to them for firing me because that had helped me to clear my mind of all that Marxist-Leninist rubbish.

'The real confrontation with my infatuation with the ideology of communism took place only from 1990 onwards, when I started writing my book. I reread Marx and found many things in his writings that would appeal to anyone. But his main concern was disempowerment, and such disempowerment cannot take place without using force. Therefore, the Stasi was a necessary product of that ideology. Marxism is not possible without violence. I came to the conclusion that in the last instance ideology is closely linked to psychology.'

In 1997 Günter Schabowski, as a leading member of party and government, was tried in connection with the border guard incidents where escapees were shot and killed. He was convicted and sentenced to three years in prison. He was released following a pardon after serving only a year of his sentence. Today, he remains highly critical of the party and his role within it. 'What kept East Germany together was the party. The reason why those blockheads called me a traitor was that opening the border meant the end of the party and the end of the GDR.'

2

GHETTOES OF THE GODS

We live in a land of legends
In the epoch of great deeds
The epoch that bears
The lofty name
Of the most brave conducator.

Comrade Nicolae Ceauşescu is
The loving father of all children,
He shows us the road
Towards communism

'Our Ardent Love for the President of the Country', from a collection of children's poetry, 1988

THE PERSONALITY CULTS of Ceauşescu and his wife Elena had some of the traits of a religion. Nicolae was variously described by his worshippers as 'a secular god', the 'genius of the Carpathians' and 'a torchbearer amongst torchbearers' who was 'as unique as a mountain peak'. His courtiers compared him favourably to Julius Caesar, Alexander the Great and Abraham Lincoln. He proclaimed himself a lay god who was founding the first communist dynasty. He became *conducator*, a Romanian term meaning 'leader'.

The joke was that while the Soviet Union may have achieved 'socialism in one country' under Stalin, Romania achieved 'socialism in one family' under Nicolae Ceauşescu. By 1989, 27 members of the Ceauşescu family held top positions in party and state and Romania was a personal playground for the 'Mother and Father of the Nation'.

ION MIHAI PACEPA, ŞTEFAN ANDREI, DIMITRU BURLAN AND NICOLAE MELINESCU

IN 1972 Ion Mihai Pacepa, a former two-star general, became Ceauşescu's adviser for national security and technological development, state secretary of the Ministry of Interior and first deputy of Romania's foreign intelligence service (*Departamentul de Informatii Externe* – the DIE). In the spring of 1978 he was also made chief of Ceauşescu's Presidential House, a role Pacepa describes as 'like being the White House chief of staff, national security adviser and the head of the Department for Homeland Security at the same time'.

He helped prepare Ceauşescu's visit to London in June 1978 during which his leader was knighted at Buckingham Palace by Elizabeth II. In April the same year he had accompanied the

Romanian leader on a visit to the United States to meet President Jimmy Carter.

In July 1978 he defected to the West. Over 30 years later he remains the highest-ranking intelligence officer ever to have defected from the former Eastern bloc. When Pacepa arrived in the United States the Americans spent three years debriefing him. Meanwhile, Ceauşescu tore apart the Romanian secret service and the upper echelons of his government looking for other 'traitors'.

Today 'Mike' Pacepa is an American citizen living at an undisclosed location, but his memories of working closely with Ceauşescu 30 years ago remain vivid. 'Ceauşescu exulted in a Stalinist cult of personality. He wanted to detract from his humble and colourless past. As president he spent his time living in 21 lavishly furnished palaces, 41 luxurious villas and 20 hunting lodges. Ceauşescu had a Western idol. He dreamed of becoming a communist Napoleon – who was also five foot three – and, like Napoleon, he built his country into a monument to himself.

'He had belonged to what Marx called the "lumpenproletariat," a shoemaker's apprentice who never practised his humble craft and had earned his living by political craftiness. He was indoctrinated in Moscow at the peak of Stalin's cult of personality. He did not care a rap about the party.

'Ceauşescu fashioned a ludicrous mixture of Marxism, Leninism, Stalinism, nationalism, Roman arrogance and Byzantine fawning. His "ceauşism" was so slippery, undefined and ever changing that he filled 34 volumes of his collected works without ever being able to describe it.'

It hadn't always been like this. Shortly after coming to power in the 1960s, Ceauşescu had been a popular communist and nationalist who opposed the Soviet-led invasion of Czechoslovakia in 1968.

Ştefan Andrei worked for Nicolae Ceauşescu for 24 years in various high-ranking capacities, including that of foreign minister. 'There wasn't just one Ceauşescu. In the beginning he made a series of positive proposals about raising the population's living conditions. He emphasized Romania's independence from the Soviet Union. And in those days he listened to other people's opinions.

'Nicolae Ceauşescu was very demanding, tough, severe and precise. He got angry very quickly. He was hard-working, punctual and naturally intelligent. He was educated in the spirit of Leninism and Stalinism, not Marxism. He had been influenced by the fact that he went to prison at a very young age, before he was 18. He was painfully aware that he was short, that he stuttered, that he was ugly. He didn't have any friends. And generally he was always on the defensive in a conversation.

'The so-called "barons" of the party played an important role in creating the personality cult. They wanted the Soviets to know that, in the event of an invasion similar to what happened in Czechoslovakia, we had a leader who was listened to and followed by the whole nation. That was why they decided to underline Ceauşescu's personality, first in the press, radio and TV. And later, when he made visits abroad, they organized mass meetings where his name was shouted out by everyone.'

During the 1970s Ceauşescu began to believe the myth he and the RCP (Romanian Communist Party) had created. He then began to rule the country as a personal dictatorship.

Dimitru Burlan was an officer in the Securitate, Romania's secret police. He worked for its Fifth Department, which was in charge of the security of all dignitaries. His main duty was to select and recruit staff to work with Nicolae Ceauşescu and his family. 'I travelled across Romania to find staff for the Ceauşescu's household because there were very strict criteria. They could not be taller than Nicolae and Elena Ceauşescu. It was forbidden to recruit "dark haired or dark skinned" people. Staff had to look pleasant. It was forbidden to have any kind of marks like moles, or scars on the face.'

If Ceauşescu's staff had to be unblemished, then his own public image had also to be entirely without imperfection. This meant a lot of work for people like Nicolae Melinescu, a producer with Romanian state television. Part of his job was to ensure that the rules about how the Ceauşescus could be portrayed in the Romanian media were observed. And with President of the Republic Nicolae Ceauşescu and his wife, Comrade Academician Doctor Engineer Elena Ceauşescu, leading the news bulletins every evening, this meant a lot of work. 'There was a long list of shots which were forbidden. And that included all natural gestures like blinking, or stuttering. He'd speak for hours on end and he hated air conditioning. He wouldn't be shown wiping his forehead or his chin, either with a hand or with a handkerchief, or scratching his nose or his ear. He was never shown chewing food or drinking from a glass or a cup of water, never.

'He had problems with the Romanian language although it was his mother tongue, and he stuttered a lot. This was why he did not allow live coverage of his speeches. They were recorded in the morning and we would all go crazy editing the whole afternoon because at 7 o'clock there was the main news programme, which opened with his speeches. And we had several people who had to hammer out all these shortcomings in his speeches. This was part of the propaganda, to build an oversized picture of the leader.

'On one occasion there was a picture that was two seconds long in which Ceauşescu did everything wrong. He scratched his nose, blinked, stuttered and it was all left in. When it came on screen all hell broke loose. I was blamed for that mistake and I accepted it; it was my job to watch what was being shown. As a result I was banned from everything, my salary was cut for three months. It was very bad, one of the worst things that could happen.'

The list of proscribed images relating to Elena Ceauşescu was also long and detailed. 'Elena Ceauşescu was very careful about her image. She wanted to be the Mother of the Nation. She never kept in the background and therefore there was a huge list of dos and don'ts when recording her pictures. First and foremost, she was never supposed to be shown in profile because she had a huge nose and she wasn't a beautiful woman anyway.

'She wasn't supposed to be shown peering. Both she and her husband didn't want to wear glasses. But their eyesight was not good; it was natural, as they were getting old. She didn't like to be seen having common gestures. She didn't even want to be shown moving her handbag from one hand to another because she thought that would show she was nervous or impatient. And the list went on and on and on.

'She had problems with her legs. She wouldn't be shown for instance in a full shot, walking like a normal human being. She had a very undignified way of walking. And therefore when she walked with her husband on state visits, either abroad or in the country, they were both only shown from the waist upwards. Nothing was allowed to destroy the ideal image of the family leading a nation.'

Predictably, behind this 'God building' lay a deep insecurity. Ceauşescu called the intelligence service run by Mike Pacepa his 'magic wand' and used it at every opportunity to identify enemies, whether real or imagined. 'He was a paranoiac who saw enemies everywhere. Ceauşescu's distrust of everyone around him generated a huge ultra-secret monitoring centre. When Ceauşescu made me his national security adviser, he also gave me the task of managing this bugging centre, which was concealed inside the headquarters of the Central Committee of the Romanian Communist Party.'

To give this unit even better cover, Ceauşescu lent it his own name, assigning it the designation of 'Presidential Archive', a supposedly private collection that no one but Ceauşescu himself and his 'archivists' were allowed to poke their noses into. Among those bugged were the country's vice-president, the prime minister and his deputies, the secretaries of the Communist Party and the most important members of the cabinet, such as the ministers of defence, foreign affairs and foreign trade. Eventually, Ceauşescu went so far as to have the centre monitor his own children and all the members of his and his wife's families.

Ceauşescu also used his intelligence and security services to deal with political rivals, and sometimes manufactured incriminating intelligence himself, as Pacepa recalls. 'When he was afraid that someone could become more popular than him, Ceauşescu either insinuated that his target was guilty of bourgeois behaviour, framed him for stealing, mismanaging state secrets, or other common crimes, or banished him.

'In 1965, when Ceauşescu was plotting to assume the title of Romanian president, he installed concealed microphones in the house of the then president, Chivu Stoica, learned that he was having an affair with a young niece, and persuaded him to resign on the promise that he would be kept on as an honorary figure for the rest of his life. Soon after that Ceauşescu made himself head of state and ordered that Stoica be demoted from all his positions. On 18 February 1975 Stoica committed suicide.'

Ceauşescu's insecurities also extended to fears about his health. Originally, he did have a genuine health problem, which close colleagues like Ştefan Andrei knew about. 'Ceauşescu had problems with his throat. In fact, up until his 20s he could barely speak. Doctors treated him for months – he had to exercise by shouting – in order to learn how to pronounce properly. He had a sensitive throat and he caught colds very quickly. That's why he couldn't stand air conditioning. For me, as foreign minister, it was a nightmare to accompany him on trips to African countries that had to be air conditioning free.'

Over time, however, what may have started as a medical problem developed into hypochondria, which staff like Securitate officer Dimitru Burlan had to deal with. 'NC was especially afraid of illness. He couldn't stand a draught for example. In the conference rooms all windows had to be closed once he entered and nobody would be allowed to walk in or out. Even at a Great National Assembly session

I did not allow a member of the Politburo to enter the hall after Nicolae Ceauşescu was in because of his fear of draughts.

'During all visits, at home or abroad, or even in his office every morning the staff from the food safety agency would disinfect things like the doorknob with alcohol. If he had to shake hands with a foreigner there was always in his entourage either an officer or somebody from the food safety agency who had a medical kit containing tissues dipped in alcohol and he'd be given one of them to wipe his hands.

'If he'd visit a factory or a school they'd prepare the toilets. He had problems with his prostate and had to use the toilet often. Everything was disinfected. The toilet was wrapped in tissue. It was disinfected with alcohol. There was fresh toilet paper. All the toilet area was disinfected and in front there was placed an officer who'd allow nobody to go in except the Ceauşescus.'

Mike Pacepa witnessed similar obsessive behaviour. 'He would wash his hands with alcohol every time he shook someone's hand (even President Carter's) and eat only the food that someone else had already tasted for poison.

'Over the years, Ceauşescu's hypochondria grew exponentially. On 12 April 1978, during his last visit to Washington, I was in the car with him driving away from an official ceremony at the White House. He took a bottle of alcohol and splashed it all over his face, after having been affectionately kissed by President Carter in the Oval Office. "Peanut-head," Ceauşescu whispered disgustedly into my ear.'

Of equal concern to Ceauşescu was that the poor state of his health in his later years should remain a secret, especially from the prying eyes of Western intelligence agencies. Accordingly, his foreign minister, Ştefan Andrei, recalls that he took a chemist with him on visits abroad for a very specific purpose. 'As a rule he didn't eat at official dinners on foreign trips. He had his meal at the residency – cooked by his cook. He was accompanied by a chemist who was in charge – among other things – of destroying his excrement so that nobody could test his faeces to check the state of his health. On two occasions – in the Soviet Union and in the former West Germany – the chemist couldn't be present and the Germans and Soviets broke the news – publicly – that Ceauşescu was very ill. Apparently his kidneys were failing because of diabetes.'

But topping the list of Ceauşescu's fears was that of assassination, which took on a new dimension after he visited Cuba in 1972, accompanied by Mike Pacepa. 'That obsession took on gargantuan dimensions after his visit to Cuba. Fidel Castro told him he had just uncovered a CIA plot to smear the insides of his shoes with a poison that would make his hair fall out – and Castro without his beard was no longer Castro. When he returned from that trip, Ceauşescu decided he would never wear any of his clothes twice and he demanded that all his clothes be destroyed once they had been used.

'As all Ceauşescu's living expenses were paid for by the government – as were mine – he could certainly afford this extravagance without even blinking an eye. All Ceauşescu's new clothes were packaged in sealed, transparent plastic bags and deposited in a climate-controlled warehouse. The rule was to keep a year's supply in stock: 365 suits, 365 pairs of shoes, and so forth.'

One of Securitate officer Dimitru Burlan's claims to fame is that he was Ceauşescu's double for ten days, a period when there seemed a genuinely credible threat to his leader's life. 'In 1972 I was a member of Nicolae Ceauşescu's escort. The Romanian secret service had received information that our leader might be the target of an assassination plot organized by the Russian secret service. This was possible because at the time Nicolae Ceauşescu was held in high regard by all Western countries. The Romanian Communist Party and the Socialist Republic of Romania were opening up towards the West. Romania was the only socialist country that had diplomatic connections with the Federal Republic of Germany, with Israel, with China. That's why the Russians didn't like Ceauşescu's politics, and that's why there was information about a possible plot against him.

'Nicolae Ceauşescu approved a request from my bosses in the Fifth Department for a Securitate officer to replace him for a while in the presidential car, in order to fool the Russian secret service. There were two officers in the escort who looked a little bit like Nicolae Ceauşescu – a colleague, Vasilescu Constantin, and me. But because my colleague was taller than Ceauşescu by about 15 centimetres, they decided that I should take Nicolae Ceauşescu's place in the car.

'It happened in November 1972. At approximately 7.30 a.m. I would leave the Ceauşescus' residence accompanied by all the official cars – police cars, escort cars, ambulance, anti-terrorist unit cars. Along the way there were the same security measures in place as if Ceauşescu himself was in the car. I was dressed like Ceauşescu in a dark trench coat and wearing a hat. Once we got to the Central Committee headquarters I'd step down from the presidential car, climb the stairs and enter the building. From that point on I'd go about my own business. I'd return to the Central Committee building about 30 minutes before Ceauşescu was ready to return home. I'd again get into the presidential car. He used to sit next to the driver – he never sat in the back. We'd leave together with all the Securitate officers from the escort and their cars, and we'd go back home.'

Ceauşescu's paranoia was serious enough for him to be prepared to order the assassination of those he perceived to be enemies. As he sought to involve Mike Pacepa in this activity, so the latter resolved on a new life. 'My last meeting with Ceauşescu took place on 22 July 1978. It was a Saturday. Ceauşescu and I were pacing along the restricted, presidential shore of Lake Techirghiol, near his summer residence at the Black Sea. "Who slept with whom last week?" Ceauşescu asked me with a wink. I filled him in on the latest juicy gossip, and then he said, "Now let's take the hydrofoil out and look over some of the pelican colonies".

'Ceauşescu had long been fascinated by the structured society of the white pelicans in the Danube delta. The old birds – the grandparents – always lay up on the front part of the beach, close to the water and food supply. Their respectful children lined up behind them in orderly rows, while the grandchildren spent their time horsing around in the background. I had often heard Ceauşescu say he wished Romania had the same rigid social structure. "Put an Uzi in the hydrofoil too," he said – the small Israeli sub-machine gun was his favourite. Ceauşescu was as passionate a hunter as he was a bird watcher, and, after happily observing a pelican colony for a while, he would always reach for his Uzi.

'Only when we were inside the hide specially built for Ceauşescu in a remote corner of the delta and he was sure that not even a passing bird could overhear us, only then did Ceauşescu finally let me know the real reason he had summoned me to his summer residence at the Black Sea. "I w-want Noel k-k-killed," he whispered into my ear. He stammered both when he was nervous and when he was excited. Noel Bernard was at that time the director of Radio Free Europe's Romanian programme and for years he had been blackening Ceauşescu's carefully crafted image with his nasty commentaries. "Did you h-hear what I said?" "Yes, comrade," I murmured. "And a few days later, blow up that w-whole wasp's nest." The "wasp's nest" was the Munich headquarters of Radio Free Europe.

'The end of Ceauşescu's sentence was masked by the methodical rat-a-tat of his Uzi. He aimed with ritual precision, first at the front line of pelicans, then at the middle distance, and finally at the grandchildren in the back.

'For 27 years I had been living with the nightmare that, sooner or later, such orders to have someone killed would land on my plate. In 1951, when I became an intelligence officer, I swore to myself that I would avoid involvement in any operations that could lead to loss of life. I did a lot of reprehensible things during all those years, but I had kept that resolution. Up until that moment at the lake I had been safe, since the long-time DIE chief, General Nicolae Doicaru, had been in charge of all the DIE's "wet operations", as our intelligence jargon termed the killing of political opponents abroad. The previous March, however, Ceauşescu had appointed me head of his Presidential House, and there was no way for me to avoid further involvement in political assassinations, which had grown into a main instrument of foreign policy throughout the Soviet bloc.'

The next day, 23 July 1978, Mike Pacepa left Romania, never to return. One of those he was glad never to see again was, as he describes her, that 'nasty greedy peasant' Elena Ceauşescu. By the 1970s Elena was a virtual co-ruler of the country with her husband. She was the first deputy prime minister and accredited with numerous bogus scientific qualifications. She too had her cult following and is often compared to Mao Tse-tung's wife, Jiang Qing, whose political role was similarly resented by Mao's communist colleagues. Ceauşescu's foreign minister, Ştefan Andrei, recalls: 'First of all, when someone was due to be named as a minister, she'd say "I don't agree!" and her opinion was final. She decided on nominations – because she was the head of the Central Committee's commission in charge of nominations. There were many instances when I talked to Ceauşescu and he would tell me, "Make sure nobody knows!" meaning she shouldn't know. Of course, I had very serious problems. For instance, she couldn't stand Colonel Gaddafi of Libya because he didn't pay any attention to her. So, she didn't agree to my proposition to organize a visit there. And when we got there, Gaddafi wasn't present at the airport. Then Elena started to nag Ceauşescu. "You follow Andrei's advice! Look how stupid it is. This man Gaddafi is mocking us – he couldn't even be bothered to welcome us at the airport."'

Those working for Elena remember her not only as intimidating but also as grasping. Mike Pacepa recalls that before the Ceauşescus visit to the United States she demanded a full-length mink coat from their hosts. The Americans were, by all accounts, astonished by the demands made of them by a Romanian advance party. As a couple, Elena and Nicolae struck Pacepa as an incongruous pair. 'They looked like they were born for each other, but they were as different as people could be. Nicolae was a puritan peasant. In the early 1970s I went with him to Italy, where the leadership of the Italian Communist Party took him to a nightclub. When one of the dancers started stripping, Ceauşescu got up and left. But Elena was frivolous. She was as ugly as hell and as cold as a cucumber, but after becoming first lady she had her biography embellished to state that she had once been a beauty queen.'

As Ceauşescu aged, Ştefan Andrei noticed significant changes in their leader. 'Ceauşescu aged very fast. He suffered from hereditary diabetes, which he never had properly treated. He only accepted insulin treatment in the last two years of his life. He had problems with his prostate. Doctors were afraid to perform surgery on him for fear of finding prostate cancer. He had liver problems as well, high blood pressure, too. All these became worse. His face was full of age spots. He was weak and his cheek was as thin as paper – one had the impression that one could cut his skin with one's nail.

'As his health got worse he became even more nervous. He wouldn't accept any conversation. He wouldn't accept others' opinions. He threatened people – right and left.'

As Nicolae's health deteriorated, Elena's power and influence grew. On one occasion she ordered Dimitru Burlan's Fifth Department of the Securitate to bug her own husband. But it was perhaps her children, sons Valentin and Nicu and daughter Zoia, who were most frequently on the receiving end of their mother's use of the Securitate for domestic purposes. Zoia in particular was a rebel and Elena didn't approve of most of her boyfriends. Once Elena asked Burlan to take her to Herastrau Park in Bucharest where her daughter was taking a stroll with her boyfriend of the time, the future post-communist prime minister, Petre Roman.

'She wanted to see for herself what Zoia and Petre were doing in the park. She didn't want Petre Roman as Zoia's boyfriend. She called Petre's father, Walter Roman, for a chat and told him that one Jew in the family was enough and she didn't want a second one – she was referring to her brother's wife who was Jewish. Then Elena C and Walter Roman decided to send Petre to Toulouse to study.'

Dimitru Burlan recounts how Elena arranged a marriage for her son Nicu to Poliana Cristescu, a woman of whom she approved. It was not a union that Nicu had sought. 'Nicu's father had a rule that everybody who held a position at the top of the party had to be married, so when Nicu became a member of the Politburo, he had to get married.

'In the mid-1980s Elena had bought her children their own villas. When Nicu's wedding to Poliana was due, Elena organized the ceremony at his new villa. All the staff were selected, checked and recruited by me. I think that the wedding took place on a Thursday – in the presence of the Bucharest general mayor, Elena C, Nicu, Poliana, Zoia and a few others. After the ceremony, having signed the marriage certificate, Nicu said to Poliana, "Now go live with my mother. She should fuck you because she chose you."'

Of course, the behaviour of the Ceauşescu children, or at least of Nicu, would make any parent want to have them closely watched. Mike Pacepa has vivid memories of Nicu's partying. 'In 1972, when

I became Ceauşescu's national security adviser, Nicu, then 21, was already a drunk and a lecher. Nicu was Ceauşescu's favourite son and the tyrant was grooming him as successor at Romania's helm. Under Soviet-style communism, where the rulers had unchecked power and were supposed to keep their thrones for life, most first children were exceedingly pampered and became worthless human beings. Nicu became a rotten, spoiled brat.

'He disliked school and became famous for never reading a book – unlike his stepbrother Valentin, who became a scientist. Nicu's main speciality was to stage wild orgies. He raped countless women, was involved in innumerable car accidents and spent a good chunk of Romania's wealth at gambling tables around the world.'

At this communist court of paranoia and excess, one constant factor in the relationships of the first family seems to have been Nicolae's genuine affection for Elena, which is borne out by electronic eavesdropping according to Dimitru Burlan. 'I think – judging by what I heard, including from our bugging devices – that Nicolae Ceauşescu really loved Elena. Nicolae Ceauşescu never had an affair. In her case there was gossip – but I never had proof.'

While Elena seems to have inspired universal loathing from those outside the family, a number of those who served Ceauşescu, including Burlan, regret his passing.

VERA OELSCHLEGEL

LIKE THE CEAUŞESCU family, East Germany's political elite enjoyed special treatment. From 1960 the leadership, their families and staff all lived together in a secluded and well-guarded compound in a forest enclave north of Berlin. This elite residential settlement, the Waldsiedlung Wandlitz, about two kilometres from the town of Wandlitz, was surrounded by a wall eight kilometres long and two metres high with guard towers placed at intervals. Trees and giant rhododendrons were planted to screen the settlement from passers-by.

Wandlitz was variously called 'Volvograd', because of the chauffeur-driven Volvos used to ferry East Germany's select few back and forth, the 'Ghetto of the Gods' or just 'the Ghetto'. It consisted of an inner ring, where at one time 39 members of East Germany's top leadership lived, and an outer ring for officials and staff such as cooks, housekeepers, gardeners and bodyguards.

Staff reported to the Stasi's Main Department for Personal Protection and their pay was related to the Stasi rank they were given. Wandlitz had its own social club, the F Club or Functionaries Club, a restaurant, swimming pool and a cinema. The cinema had fixed screening times. Like in normal cinemas, the programming was advertised. From time to time films were imported from West Berlin or foreign countries explicitly for Erich Honecker. There were shops with Western goods, a kindergarten, a petrol station with free petrol, a laundry and a veterinary practice for family pets. Nearby was a private clinic and bunkers in case of war. A private road led to a lake with bathing huts and boathouses. Members of the Politburo and their families lived in three-storey houses of beige stucco in streets without names.

Although they lived a privileged existence by comparison with the rest of East Germany, by Western standards it was a society of drab, petit bourgeois conformity. A sense of isolation inside 'the ghetto' was aggravated by the lack of socializing among the elite. Vera Oelschlegel was a distinguished actress and theatre director who married a senior SED politician, Konrad Naumann. From 1976 to 1985 Naumann was a member of the Politburo. Wandlitz was, she says, a disintegrating society with no charm. 'All of a sudden I was forced into this elite circle. The security was completely over the top, and we had to live surrounded by bodyguards and surveillance. It was disgusting. And obviously it was in stark contrast to my life in the theatre.

'I didn't fit in that Wandlitz circle. I was a kind of black sheep. They would tolerate me and perhaps even thought for a while that it would be interesting for them to have an actress there. But living in Wandlitz was terribly lonely. There wasn't a good relationship among neighbours. Sometimes I would hear Schabowski shouting at his children or Mielke whistling after his dachshund. But that would be it. Or, I would meet them in the shops. However, we would only say hello to one another. Basically, it was a very sad ghetto. The lifestyle there was a very well-behaved lower-middle-class one with a doilly on the Vertico TV and watering the pot plants in the garden. In general, it was fusty and cheerless.

'And I'm sure that the whole house was bugged and that they were keeping close track of who my husband contacted or who came and went. There would be arguments between my husband and I, and on certain occasions other people would repeat some of the things we had said and I would think, "How does he know about that? Has Konrad told him or what?" After that I got a very small apartment in

Berlin so that between my work as theatre director and the evening show as an actress I could relax for an hour or so in complete privacy.'

From her privileged position Vera witnessed Honecker and other members of the elite tentatively indulging in the excesses available to them. Although tame by present Western standards, the facilities open to the East German leadership were beyond the wildest dreams of ordinary citizens. 'Honecker would go on holiday to the Crimea and so would we. He would invite us to his majestic villa and show his true colours. We would eat a lot – the tables were overloaded with food – then we would lounge around the villa. And there was another villa on the beach. If the sea was too rough, you could go swimming in a pool filled with seawater. On holiday Honecker would sometimes act the fool. My impression has always been that he was a very inhibited and humourless person. I think he felt under huge pressure, which came both from outside and from his inner self, and that eventually he might have felt out of his depth.'

Honecker was a moderate drinker, but the higher echelons of politics were influenced by a drinking culture that emanated from the Soviet Union and Vera quickly discovered that she was married to an alcoholic. 'It goes without saying that alcoholism is a catastrophe whatever the profession. To imagine that somebody with such political power had an alcohol problem is very scary. I was embarrassed for him more than once.

'I have a terrible memory of a boozy session with members of the French Communist Party. I was in Paris with Konrad Naumann and it was a merry-go-round of booze. They rode that merry-go-round non-stop. Our glasses would never be empty. They would always drink schnapps, never wine; always top-class schnapps. That night I woke up in our hotel suite. All the lights were switched on. I was very scared and got out of bed. My husband wasn't lying next to me in bed. I checked all the rooms and found the door to the hallway was open wide. I found my husband in the hotel lift, which he had mistaken for the loo. At that moment I thought that if I had called the press his Politburo career would be over, and my destiny would have changed. But I let it be.

'People behaved differently after drinking: some would sing, others would rail or go out and throw up. It depended on the person. After Gorbachev had banned drinking at official functions, they didn't know what to say to each other any more. To stand up and propose a toast was something that suddenly was missing.

'My marriage to Konrad Naumann was a mistake. I wanted a divorce but it was pretty clear to me that if I ended my marriage my career in the theatre would be over too. Erich Honecker summoned me to his house in Wandlitz, and said to me in no uncertain terms that it wasn't going to happen, that no court in the DDR would carry out this divorce. He pretty much gave me the party order to stay with this man, full stop.

'I was very surprised when, coming back from a tour, Konrad told me that he was going to be kicked out of the Politburo. He told me in secrecy because he knew that our house had been completely wiretapped. He drew me into the bathroom and turned on all the taps and switched on the radio, and in a low voice whispered into my ear that he was being dismissed.

'After that he was shunned by everyone in the Politburo. Almost immediately he lost his special privileges and they did everything to make sure he was out of Wandlitz very quickly. We were given a house in Karlshorst, and Konrad was ordered to work in the state archives in Potsdam. A staff car came for him every morning. I never went there but they had him working behind locked doors, sorting files or whatever and then at the end of the day the car would drive him back again.'

According to Vera, the insularity of life in the Wandlitz 'ghetto' was a factor in the leadership's misjudgement of the situation in the final period leading up to the collapse of East Germany. 'They didn't want to know what was going on outside. Of course, they could have known – lots of them had children who lived elsewhere – but they were simply afraid. The Stasi gave the Politburo very precise reports on the state of affairs – they didn't sugar-coat anything, that would have been foolish of them. They said, there's a lot of unrest, there's a lot of dissatisfaction, people are gathering, protesting. The Politburo didn't take it on board; they didn't want to take it on board. It was, "Let's give them bananas, then maybe there'll be a bit of peace." They didn't examine the causes: what are the roots of this, why is it happening, what needs to happen now?

They went to work in town, with flashing lights in front and in their fast cars, they had staff who lived very normal lives – secretaries, drivers, porters or whatever – but they still built up this world of illusion, and the worse things became, the more the world of illusion became cemented, because things couldn't be what they weren't allowed to be.

'They did exercises to deal with the outbreak of a third world war, but they were not prepared for what would happen if the DDR collapsed.'

Towards the end of East Germany, Vera took part in some of the street demonstrations in Berlin. 'Instead of orders being given to open the Wall, orders might have been given to shoot at DDR citizens. This fear persisted. That was one thing. The other thing was that we didn't demonstrate for reunification, but rather for a better DDR, for an open DDR, for a DDR that exercised a human socialism. We stood in that square for eight hours and we were full of hope.

'Today you can hardly imagine that the East German state, which had been so lethargic, which had stagnated for so long, would collapse so quickly.'

BERND BRÜCKNER

THE SCHORFHEIDE IS an area of low-lying forest and lakes north of Berlin. It was once a popular hunting resort for the German elite. Kaiser Wilhelm II and Hermann Göring used to hunt for deer and wild boar amid the oak, pine and beech forest. It was here that East Germany's communist leadership established their holiday homes and hunting lodges.

On 16 May 1962, some 20,000 hectares of the National Hunting Resort of the People's Army was opened. That same day the first national hunt took place and 15 huntsmen in traditional green leather jackets shot 17 deer and three sows. This was followed by a buffet of roasted pig, caviar, vodka and cognac. It was the revival of a tradition that lasted until the very end of the socialist state. On the day the Berlin Wall came down, Erich Honecker was there, hunting red deer.

During communist rule, much important business was done during these hunts by a small cabal of Politburo members centred around Honecker and Dr Günter Mittag. Foreign leaders like Leonid Brezhnev and Fidel Castro also enjoyed extravagant hunting parties.

Bernd Brückner, once Honecker's personal bodyguard, went on many such hunts with his former employer. 'The forest contained red and fallow deer, wild boar, rabbits of course, and 30 Siberian elk, which had been a gift from the Soviet Union. Most of the visitors were lousy shots but not Erich Honecker, he was very good. He had been hunting since the 1950s. He was determined; it might have rained cats and dogs or even snowed, but he still wanted to go hunting. We usually went hunting on Tuesdays after the Politburo meeting. But we also went on Fridays and Saturdays so, on average, Honecker went hunting three times a week. In fact, as the years went by his passion for hunting increased.

'When the minister for state security went on a hunt with us, the security contingent was greater than when we went out with the prime minister. Mr Mielke feared for his security more than Honecker. Mielke had specific ideas about hunting but he wasn't a very accurate shot. The forester who accompanied him would "interfere" in order to make him look successful at least once during every hunt.'

So many animals were shot that fresh stocks of deer had to be imported. At times, the slaughter was extreme. From the 1970s the communist elite accounted for at least 1,000 red deer and 1,500 fallow deer each year. Large numbers of wild boar and vast numbers of rabbits were also killed.

Sometimes Bernd Bruckner was concerned about the excessive nature of the killing. 'When Honecker went hunting with his best friend, Dr Günter Mittag, they overdid it. They didn't respect hunting restrictions on certain game, they shot everything. That was too much.'

Bruckner also witnessed Honecker's liking for Western soft-porn films. 'From time to time certain VHS cassettes appeared. They weren't screened publicly, but certain persons took them home. Erich Honecker possessed some. We discovered this once when we saw he had more cassettes than usual in his holiday home. The films had female names as titles and we thought: Ah! Something is going on here. Titles like *Emanuelle* made it clear that the content was other than party material.'

JÜRGEN KRAUSE

LIKE VERA OELSCHLEGEL, Jürgen Krause lived for a time at Wandlitz. He was party leader Erich Honecker's cook. He was struck by the chilly atmosphere of the place. Nonetheless, despite its idiosyncratic nature, he remained proud to work there. 'I was qualified, not just professionally but politically. I got a distinction in my party education classes and it was a great honour to cook for the government. I didn't care if my telephone was being tapped or not, today everybody gets upset about that, but for me it was clear when I moved into Wandlitz that, of course, my telephone calls would be listened to. That didn't bother me; I didn't have anything to hide. I was a communist, and still am today, and I'm of the opinion that communism is a good thing when it's done right. And at my age that's OK, and no one can convince me otherwise.

'I was brought up as a communist, as a servant of the government, and of their families and relations and acquaintances and guests, which was my main job, and I put my whole professional specialist effort into that, and it actually made me very proud.'

Krause would often prepare the food for after the hunts attended by the communist leadership. He remembers how the numbers of animals killed, although large, would on occasion be artificially inflated still further. 'There used to be a big rabbit hunt every year for the foreign diplomats. After the shooting they would lay the dead animals out on display so that the diplomats would feel they'd shot more than a thousand rabbits in a day; it was a really big deal. But the hunters didn't shoot all the rabbits. They received a little help. They did shoot a lot of rabbits, that's a fact. But there weren't always enough to make a really impressive display, and so before the guests arrived we'd go along and if you kicked some of the rabbits by accident you'd think, my god, that thing's frozen. That's because they used to have rabbits on ice and they'd add these frozen rabbits from the fridge, so that they could say, yes, look, we've bagged all these rabbits; it's a tremendous success, and they could make a big statement with this.'

Krause also had bodyguard as well as culinary duties. 'We had firearms training, more intensive than in the army. I had pistol training. There were certain circumstances where if a top functionary was shot at then you would have to protect him with your whole body. If Honecker was shot at I was to jump on top of him to protect him.'

As Erich Honecker's personal cook, Krause sometimes was allowed to join members of the Politburo at private screenings of Western movies. 'I sometimes had the pleasure to sit next to the projectionist, who was also a bodyguard, and watch the film the Honeckers were watching. This meant that I'd seen all the James Bond films. Honecker really liked to watch them too. If we're talking about sex films, films of an erotic nature, if I can put it like that, of course some people watched them now and then, Honecker too. He used to watch them privately with his wife for example, on cassette, so they didn't need a projectionist or anything. They were definitely erotic films.'

Krause remembers the shops in the outer ring at Wandlitz as being well stocked, on a par with those of Berlin. In addition, they sometimes sold special items like bananas that were largely unobtainable. One year he got grapes for his family at Christmas. He also had access to toys for his children, like Matchbox cars which were almost impossible to find in East Germany. He has particular memories of Wandlitz at the end of the communist era in 1989. 'The mood in Wandlitz in general was pretty lousy, very tense – particularly right at the end. I was there right until the last day. In the end we were pretty relieved it was over. I moved out afterwards because I couldn't take the stress of being on view there, like an ape in a cage. People were throwing our apartment door open and coming in to see what kind of luxury we lived in; it was too much for me, and I left.'

3
TRIALS & PUNISHMENT

'Our highest revolutionary staff is Moscow and we do go to Moscow to learn. And do you know what? We to to Moscow to learn from the Russian Bolsheviks how to break your necks.'

Klement Gottwald, first communist leader of Czechoslovakia in a speech to the Czechoslovak parliament, 21 December 1929

ONCE COMMUNISTS WERE in control of the Europe's Eastern bloc they began to systematically punish those they perceived as enemies. In the Soviet occupation zone of eastern Germany, a system of 11 internment camps was established modelled on the Gulag archipelago. These permanent camps were set up at places like Sachsenhausen, Bautzen, Berlin Hohenschönhausen (which was later handed over to the Stasi as a detention and interrogation centre), Buchenwald, Torgau and Mühlberg, some of which had been concentration camps under the Nazi regime.

The Soviets claimed that the camps would be used to intern terrorists, leaders of fascist youth organizations, members of the Gestapo and other agencies associated with the Third Reich. In reality, the remit went far beyond de-Nazification. Camps were used to house opponents of the SED (Socialist Unity Party) as well as members of the intelligentsia, the bourgeoisie, aristocrats, capitalists, social democrats and communists who didn't meet with official approval. Prisoners could include children as young as 14. Breaking the law was not a prerequisite for ending up in the gulags of eastern Germany.

Terror was the main tool used by the Stalinist system. Forced confessions were obtained through physical and psychological torture. There was extensive use of beatings, sleep deprivation and threats to deport prisoners to Siberian labour camps. Justice was swift and arbitrary. Many trials were conducted in front of Soviet military tribunals in Russian. There were no witnesses and no right of defence.

Living conditions in the camps were appalling and conditions worsened when food rations were reduced in November 1946. Malnutrition and diseases like dysentery, typhus, pneumonia and especially tuberculosis were rife. Medical care was primitive and wholly insufficient. Anyone with inadequate clothing was vulnerable in cold, damp living conditions. Camps were overcrowded and insanitary, lacking even basic toilet facilities. Rape and torture by sadistic guards was commonplace. Unsurprisingly, the death rate of internees was high, especially in the early years, the bodies often buried in mass graves.

About 154,000 Germans were interned in special camps and

some 43,000 died there. Another 35,000 non-Germans were also interned. Several camps were closed due to the high death rate and, by 1950, all the camps were shut down. While many prisoners were released some were sentenced again in East German courts.

ERIKA RIEMANN

AS A TEENAGER, Erika Riemann spent 18 months at Sachsenhausen as part of a ten-year sentence as a political prisoner. She was also in Bautzen, Torgau, Hohenschönhausen and Hoheneck. She was released in January 1954, as part of a general amnesty for political prisoners, and fled to West Germany. Her crime amounted to little more than child's play. Now in her late 70s, it took nearly half a century before Erika could talk publicly about her story.

As a schoolgirl living in Mühlhausen, Thuringia, in 1945, high-spirited Erika visited her newly renovated classroom with friends. What happened next would affect Erika for the rest of her life. 'We saw that Adolf Hitler's portrait had been replaced with Stalin's. I had stolen a lipstick from one of the refugee girls but I didn't dare to put it on because everyone would have realized that it was me who had taken it. But I wanted to make use of it somehow. So I drew a bow on Stalin's moustache.

'It wasn't a good move. I never wanted to be an artist again in my whole life. Because of that trick the Soviet military court sentenced me to ten years of forced labour in Siberia. I served that sentence for eight years and 16 days, but not in Russia.'

Following her arrest she was kept in a castle dungeon at

Ludwigslust for questioning. Despite her adolescence her interrogators did not spare her. 'For a long time it all didn't make sense to me. The interrogations always took place at night. They lasted for hours and I didn't understand what it was all about. I had to sit on a chair; I wasn't allowed to speak or to move. Whenever I moved my head to the side, I was slapped in the face or hit on the back. They always asked exactly the same questions. If you don't get anything to eat or to drink for hours, you get very tired and get to the point of falling asleep, but you have to continue to sit upright.

'All that brings you near the point of breakdown. In the end I confessed to everything even though I had done nothing. I even had to confess that I was part of the Nazi resistance movement. You just confess to everything they want to hear, because all you want is to get back to your cell and get some sleep.

'Now that I've grown old, I don't understand how I was able to stand all that. Probably I was able to take it because I was young. I didn't take them seriously; I thought that they were putting on an act. It was only after I had been sentenced, when I was with the other prisoners, that I realized that it was for real.'

Court proceedings were in Russian as was the documentation relating to her case. Although she signed papers just once, her signature appears all over the records that she's seen since.

Erika was taken to Bautzen prison near Dresden, where inmates were locked in cages inside the cells and forced to share a single narrow bed with another prisoner. 'My quarters were full of bugs. I hadn't seen bugs like these before. There was no toilet, or anything.

The next morning I was covered with pustules and I thought that I was sick. I told the guard that I wanted to see a doctor. When I got there and had taken off my clothes, they just laughed themselves silly. I had been bitten all over by the bugs and the Russians laughed themselves silly about it.

'I wasn't able to defecate so I had to see a doctor. I had never had a gynaecological examination before. They found out that I hadn't had sexual intercourse and that's how I got the nickname "*tzelitska*" [Russian for virgin]. That name accompanied me for all the time of my detention, it was even written in my files.'

Later in her time at Bautzen, a young Russian soldier professed his love to Erika. When she resisted his attentions he struck her in the mouth with a bunch of keys and she lost her two front teeth. The soldier was later sentenced to three years for the incident.

She also had a spell in the prison fortress of Torgau, where many women were raped. 'I hadn't been raped yet but the decision had been made that I would be the next one to be raped. There was a Russian doctor there, imprisoned because he had had an affair with a German woman, so his German was very good. One evening I was taken out of my cell by two Russian guards and by pure chance the doctor passed by. The two guards talked together in Russian. The doctor told them to leave me alone because I had syphilis. One of the Russian guards got very angry and kicked me. The doctor took me to the infirmary. It was there that he explained why he had said that... to stop them raping me.'

To stay in the infirmary and sidestep deportation to Russia Erika agreed to help the doctor care for the patients. Typically, they were skeletal men with high temperatures, swollen faces and diarrhoea. 'All I could do was to wet their lips and try to clean them up. What I saw and felt there caused me lifelong shock. But it saved me from deportation to Russia.'

Later, at Torgau, she faced humiliation when she was forced to strip. 'All the men were baying and howling at me and I was naked among them. I cannot talk about it. I have felt the repercussions of that all of my life. I felt ashamed and dirty. I'm a mother and a grandmother, but still, after all these years, I still feel dirty and debased.' Erika was subjected to repeated physical and sexual abuse during her incarceration.

Erika was then moved to the former Nazi concentration camp at Sachsenhausen just outside Berlin, which was run by the German police. 'I talked with other inmates about our cases; it was clear that none of us were criminals. Some were imprisoned because they laughed at a joke about Stalin, asking, "Have you ever tasted Stalin bacon? It's impossible because that pig is still alive." Twenty-five of them were arrested... for laughing. Other inmates were mothers who had illegally tried to cross the border or had foraged food.

'We had been very happy when we were committed to the Germans because we thought that they would review our cases, realize that we were innocent and eventually send us home. That was a big mistake. The Russian officer said, "Put the Germans under German control and they will be sufficiently punished." That was very true. What we had to endure under the Germans was worse than everything we had experienced under the Russians. There were some very hostile people in Sachsenhausen.'

Every two weeks the inmates were taken to a shower block where they left their clothes to be deloused while they bathed. 'They told us that they would do the same things they had done with the Jews, that there wouldn't be water coming out of the showers but gas. That was a terrible situation. The adults among us knew that people had been murdered in the concentration camps, but I didn't know anything about it. I only got to know about it later. The threat caused great panic and then we felt very relieved when only warm water came out.

'It had a long-lasting effect on me. Some people knew what the Nazi's had done in the Sachsenhausen concentration camp in the war. I couldn't believe it. I just knew about it from hearsay. I wasn't aware of anything like that when I was a little child back in my home town, and neither were my parents. They never talked about such things.'

Erika fell ill with appendicitis while she was at Sachsenhausen. When she finally consulted a doctor he told her she faced an operation without anaesthetic as the Russians had commandeered all the drugs to make liquor. 'They strapped me down, put a cloth in my mouth and started operating on me. I can't say if I felt anything because I really don't remember. I fainted and eventually I came to. I had survived.

'I was put back in the barrack with a number of other sick women. We got hard toast to eat. The women chewed the bread and then gave it to me to eat. It was the first food I ate after my operation. Years later, I searched for the doctor who had operated on me. He had survived and lived in Cologne. He remembered that he couldn't believe that I had survived the operation.'

Taught to dance by an incarcerated Russian ballerina, Erika was picked to work in the camp's theatre. 'Our programmes had to be approved by the commandants. Once we had planned to start with a piece by Mozart. But one officer considered Mozart a fascist and the piece was removed from the programme. So we changed Mozart's name to Mozar and put his piece at the bottom of the programme, and they approved it.

'Everyone was very excited about the concert and curious to know what would happen during the performance of the "fascist's" music as the officer who did not want us to perform it sat in the front row. But he was the first to stand up and clap his hands and proudly exclaim, "A Russian composer! A Russian composer!" We all stayed silent before starting to applaud. The whole camp was very happy about the prank we had played on the officer.'

The youngest inmate at Sachsenhausen, where her personal memorabilia is now exhibited, Erika struck up friendships that have endured. But today she also remembers those who didn't make it and were buried in the precincts of various camps. 'My insides still ache when I come here to Sachsenhausen. But it's not so bad any more; I don't have to run to the toilet straight away. We should have a memorial here at the camp and be able to pay a tribute to those who died here under communist rule. I always think that because I was and am still, of course, the youngest inmate, I need to do something for those people.

'After Sachsenhausen, I was sent to Hoheneck prison, where we were committed to the People's Police. I had to endure terrible things there. Hoheneck could accommodate 600 women, but we were 1,200. There were no beds, no food, no anything. There were no toilets; all we had were buckets, which served as toilets. The smell was awful. In the morning we hung the buckets on sticks and four people had to carry them away to the dunghill. The conditions we were living in were unthinkable even in 1950; all that dirt, the famine and the misery that reigned, and we then were exposed to harassments from the wardens.

'We didn't get anything to read and there was very little work. One day we got a newspaper, it was around the time of Stalin's death. The women read in the papers that in Russia prisoners of war had been released. But nothing had happened here. So we wanted a commission to review our cases. But as no one listened to our request, we went on hunger strike.

'It worked very well at first. We gathered bread and water for the sick, who couldn't have survived without food. When they served dinner, we said that we weren't hungry. The first time the wardens didn't take us seriously and just took the food away. But by the next meal they were getting worried. I remember that people from outside the prison demonstrated on our behalf. We shouted out of the windows in order to make people aware of our existence. Then the wardens came in with their rubber truncheons and everything happened very quickly. We rushed towards them and I fell and got hurt. I was hit on the head. They took everything they could find from us, including the bread and the water we were hoarding for the sick. It was impossible to continue with the hunger strike, because somebody would have died, but the elderly women said that they'd rather die than surrender. I don't recollect exactly how things went, but eventually we stopped the hunger strike.

'I ended up in hospital because of the blow on my head. I lost my sense of taste and smell. Also, I couldn't see any more. I was blind. I was put in solitary confinement. Though after a while I was able to see again, I could neither taste nor smell. Then I just gave up. I didn't want to struggle anymore. My closest friend had been transferred to Waldheim, so I felt very lonely because I couldn't talk to anyone and also because I was in solitary confinement. I didn't see any sense in living; I didn't want to continue.'

Erika tried to hang herself in December 1953 while in solitary confinement, but she was rescued, hospitalized and then sent back to a single cell. She was finally released on 18 January 1954, aged 22. 'Each one of us got a scarf and we were very happy about receiving something brand new to wear. We only realized later that the scarves were given to us for identification purposes: all the women with yellow scarves were sent to Leipzig, those with red ones to Berlin and those with blue ones to Thuringia. Everywhere we went people were able to recognize us from our scarves. But we didn't know that at the time.'

While Erika was in prison, her mother had fled from East to West Germany. 'I was sent to my grandparents, who still lived in Mühlhausen; no one was allowed to go to West Germany. Although the telephone lines worked badly in those days, I got in touch with my mother in West Germany. My friends from school and those who knew about my release had arranged a welcome-home party for me. Before we left Hoheneck we had to sign a document stating that we wouldn't talk about our arrest and say only that we were treated well.

'During the party I drank alcohol, which affected me and I told people that I wanted to join my mother in West Germany. And only two days after that party, my uncle, who worked for the police, told me that I had to leave if I didn't want to be arrested because it was known I was planning to "flee the country". That night, my uncle accompanied me to the border and helped me to escape. That's how I got to West Germany.

'I first went to Friedland with a number of demobbed soldiers. In Friedland I was given some money and told that my mother would be informed I needed picking up at the train station in Hamburg. But when I arrived in Hamburg my mother wasn't there. I stood there with my little wooden suitcase; I didn't know what to do, so I started to cry. A Red Cross employee saw me and helped me into a taxi, which drove me to my mother's place. I stood at the front door for a very long time before I realized that I had to push the handle down to open the door. I was used to people opening doors and locking them behind me. I must have waited at the door for an hour. Then someone came and opened the door and I felt very bewildered. I went up the staircase and there was my mother and my two brothers.

'I can't forget my past. I think that I'm not able to keep a relationship going. I have been married three times. I had a very hard time with my partners. I had to leave them after a while because I couldn't bear to stay in a relationship. I have never forgotten about my past, it is still with me. Nowadays I'm able to cope with it. But I have never forgotten about it.'

JANA HORÁKOVÁ-KANSKY

AN INTEGRAL PART of the Stalinization of Eastern Europe and the paranoid pursuit of 'enemies of the people' was the show trial, based on those orchestrated by Stalin in the Soviet Union during the 1930s. The largest show trials in Eastern Europe were held in Czechoslovakia. The trials were spread over six years and led to 178 executions plus the deaths of another 244 people shot while 'attempting to escape'. Caught in the cross-hairs of the hard-line regime were army generals, opposition politicians, Catholics, Jews, and specific members of the communist leadership. The verdicts were a foregone conclusion and the accused had to rehearse their courtroom testimony in advance of their trials.

Only one woman was ever executed during the Czechoslovakian show trials. Milada Horáková (1901–50), a law graduate from Charles University in Prague, democratic Member of Parliament and wartime resistance hero, is one of Czechoslovakia's best-known victims of communist oppression. Jana, Milada Horáková's only child, was just 16 when her mother was executed on trumped-up conspiracy charges. Her father – who was also targeted by the communist regime – had already made a daring escape from Czechoslovakia, leaving Jana in the care of relatives. But Horáková's story still makes her daughter proud.

After Hitler's occupation of Czechoslovakia in 1939, Horáková had joined the resistance but was arrested by the Gestapo in 1940. She was sentenced to life imprisonment and sent to the concentration camp at Terezin. After the war, she was elected a Member of

Parliament. When the communists seized power in February 1948 she resigned in protest but, despite the obvious risks, stayed in the country and remained politically active. On 27 September 1949, Horáková was arrested again and accused of leading a plot to overthrow the communist regime. Like others in the dock she was tortured while awaiting trial.

Her trial and that of 12 others began on 31 May 1950, with proceedings supervised by Soviet advisers. The trial was broadcast on radio and sections of it were filmed, although uncensored recordings of some of the proceedings were only discovered in 2005.

Horáková was sentenced to death along with three of her co-defendants on 8 June. There was widespread international condemnation of the sentence. Among those petitioning for clemency were Albert Einstein, Winston Churchill and Eleanor Roosevelt. In response, the communists brought the date of the execution forward and it was carried out in the grounds of Pankrác prison in Prague at dawn on 27 June. Death was caused by strangulation through hanging. It would have taken about 15 minutes to die.

Her daughter recalls some of the details of that painful time: 'When the trial was on, we were not allowed to be present in court. And I remember the desperate situation at home since we felt completely helpless. We heard everything on the radio because it was a public trial. It was all calculated to create a sense of terror and fear. It was brutal. My mother was very unwavering. And in her last speech, she said her conscience was utterly clear and she had not betrayed anything. Then we wrote a petition appealing for clemency.'

Horáková's family were allowed to visit her on the eve of her execution. It was the first time Jana had seen her mother since the start of the trial. Jana recalls, 'During that final visit she was absolutely calm, composed. We were not allowed even to kiss each other. There were armed guards standing around us. She did not stop speaking. The visit was supposed to last about 20 minutes. She informed us that she had written letters to all her friends and the whole family that she hoped would be delivered. They were not. They remained in the archives until we received them in 1990. And suddenly she ended the visit herself. It was horrendous. I was there with my aunt and uncle only. Grandfather excused himself. He did not come.

'My grandfather was a very old man at the time. He behaved absolutely fantastically because he did not speak about it at all. And after 27 June when the execution took place he never left home without a black armband and a black tie. That was the third child he had lost in his life. Two of his children died of scarlet fever during the First World War. And then his adult daughter had also gone in his lifetime, which must have been very hard for him. The best memory I have of my mother is the last letter she wrote to me:

> *My dearest child, you must not be filled with dread nor be sad at the thought that I shan't be back. Learn my child to look from an early age at life as a serious thing. Life is hard, it doesn't pamper you, for one caress there are ten blows. Best get used to it immediately and don't give in to it. Decide to fight it. Have courage and clear objectives and you will triumph over life...*

And my only daughter, my girl Jana, my life, my hope, my future projection, live, grasp life with both of your hands, to your last breath, I shall pray for your happiness, my dear child. I kiss your hair, eyes and mouth. I caress you and hold you in my arms. You, whom I have held so little, I shall always be with you and by you.

Jana's subsequent refusal to renounce her mother blighted her own academic career. 'Five times I attempted to enrol at the Faculty of Medicine where I was flatly rejected. Although I had several interviews I was never accepted. And it always came down to the same question, "How do you view the trial of your mother?" And when I said I did not want to talk about it that was the end of my studies.

'I worked – and it was my great luck – at the Second Dental Clinic where I was accepted. They took me on as an apprentice dental nurse. I met many marvellous people there and they kept me on.

'In 1963 I was accepted for a part-time course for dental technicians. I finished the course while working. Again, they gave me a job at the clinic in the dental laboratory. But then in 1966 I began to dare to hope that all this might come to an end. At that time they allowed me visit my father in the United States – under the threat that if I did not come back my aunt's entire family would suffer.'

Jana was reunited with her father at a New York airport and they embarked on a coast-to-coast trip that lasted six weeks. She had to return to her homeland, promising to apply for emigration papers immediately. She finally left Czechoslovakia in April 1968 aged 34 with the permission of Alexander Dubček's regime.

'I think the legacy of my mother for all the people of this nation should be honesty, truthfulness and the maintenance of a clear conscience. If every person maintained these three things then the recovery of the Czech national soul after 40 years of communism would come about much faster.'

When the communist regime was toppled in 1990, 40 years after her execution, Horáková was posthumously rehabilitated. Today, a street in Prague is named after her.

URSULA RUMIN

IN EAST GERMANY in the early 1950s communist paranoia about 'class enemies' and 'agents of Western imperialism' was so endemic that no one was safe. And nowhere was more dangerous than East Berlin, situated on the front line of the Cold War. At that time Berlin was the spy capital of the world.

Ursula Rumin came to the city in 1949 and, like many, lived in West Berlin and worked in East Berlin – as a screenwriter for the DEFA (*Deutsche Film-Aktiengesellscaft*), the state film monopoly of East Germany. Founded in 1946 in the Soviet Zone, it became an important tool for the communists in the re-education of East Germans. From 1947 it was controlled by the SED (Socialist Unity Party), producing newsreels, educational films and movies. Subjects thought worthy of screenplays included 'land redistribution' and the 'two-year plan'. Some DEFA films produced at this time were, despite all these ideological strictures, surprisingly good. Ursula worked on the screenplay for an award-winning DEFA film called *The Destinies of Women*, released in 1952, contrasting the (intellectually and morally superior) lives of women in East Berlin to the (empty) lives of women in West Berlin.

On 21 October 1952, aged 28, Ursula was kidnapped on her way to a meeting and taken to the Soviet headquarters at Karlshorst in East Berlin's Lichtenberg district. Her sudden and dramatic disappearance was a mystery to friends and family. They had no idea what had happened to her. After a summary trial before a Soviet military tribunal she was transported to a labour camp in Workuta, Siberia. She was one of a large number of people sent from the eastern part of Germany to Siberia after the war, many of them never to return.

Ursula recalls, 'During my time at DEFA they [the authorities] had tried to win me over to communism. They wanted me to live in East Berlin. They had offered me a flat and a permanent job. A permanent job meant a permanent salary, which was very important at that time. They also wanted me to take my son, who used to live with my parents, with me.

'I just put them off by saying that it took time to find a flat. Then they asked me to write the script of a highly political film. You couldn't say no, you weren't allowed to. So my excuse was that I felt that the task was over my head, that I wasn't up to making a highly political film, because I wasn't a political person. But they probably did that to test me.

'A colleague, film director Slatan Dudow, always tried to drag me into political conversations and one day he said, "If you don't show an interest in politics, one day politics will show an interest in you!" I didn't take that very seriously. In retrospect, I think he had either wanted to warn me or was involved with my arrest.'

Although she had no interest in politics Ursula was certain that she wasn't a communist. 'I had known what dictatorship meant during the Second World War. I knew what freedom meant. And I wanted to remain free. Anyway, one day DEFA invited me to a meeting. I assumed it would have been about the assignment of a new script. We arranged a time to meet the following day. I went by metro to the Friedrichstrasse where two gentlemen approached me, calling me by name and telling me that they would take me to work.

'I was amazed that my employer cared so much about me that they had sent someone to pick me up at the metro station, but I got into their car. We drove very fast for quite a while. I was a bit surprised about that because DEFA wasn't far away. We then stopped in Berlin-Karlshorst in front of a big iron gate, which was opened by two Russian soldiers. I knew straight away that the building had nothing to do with DEFA. The windows had wooden blinds. I knew that prisons used to have wooden blinds. This building was occupied by the Russians and was part of the territory belonging to the "Berlin Kremlin".'

Mechanically Ursula followed instructions to hand over her stockings and suspender belt and personal items including jewellery. Then she was deposited in a basement cell. 'I was left to myself; they wouldn't give any explanation. It was as though the world had suddenly stopped turning for me. During the whole episode there was no dialogue. The Russians would speak in Russian to one another; no one spoke German. They wouldn't answer my questions and I wasn't able to speak to them in Russian.

'The cell had a wooden plank bed, which reached from wall to wall. The room must have been something like three metres by three metres. A tin bucket for nature's call… that was all there was – no table, no chair, no lavatory and no window. Above the door was a light bulb, which would never be switched off. It was turned on day and night. It was very disturbing later on.

'The next day I had my first interrogation. Several Russian officials were present in that room and I was asked many questions: where I was from, my name, my date of birth, my address – actually all those personal things which they already knew, but which I had to answer. Of course I asked why I had been brought there. They wouldn't say anything, but merely asked questions, which an interpreter translated. Eventually, I realized what the interrogations were aiming at – they wanted to know about my relationships with American, English and French occupying forces in West Berlin.

'I was in Karlshorst for approximately three months. I must say that the interrogations were a kind of physical and mental torture. They would wake you up at 6 o'clock in the morning and you had to get up. During the day you weren't allowed to lie down, you could only sit at the edge of the plank bed. Nothing happened apart from the fact that they would give you black tea and 300 grams of bread in the morning. But in the evening, when it was time to sleep, they would take you to the interrogation. They would do that with me for three or four nights in a row. I wasn't able to sleep at all during that time. It was so bad that I fell asleep during the interrogations. My head simply fell forward and I was gone.

'That sleep deprivation was really abominable, it was almost worse than the hunger.'

A relative who used to have breakfast with Ursula once a week was the first to realize that she was missing and contacted her mother who came to Berlin and broke into her flat. Inside they found the breakfast dishes just as Ursula had left them. They asked the German, American and English police forces, and her office, whether they had any information about her, but no one knew where she was.

'The worst thing was that I wasn't able to contact anyone. They wouldn't show the slightest reaction when I said I wanted to send a message to my family. That was a huge burden for me while in prison. It would have been bad enough for my family to know that I was in prison but not knowing anything at all was much worse.

'They accused me of being in contact with the English and the Americans and said I had to confess and that I had to tell the truth. It was a military court. They were common back then. The People's Police already existed but it was the Russians who were in control.

'I was charged with espionage but they couldn't prove anything. During the hearing I wished to have a defence lawyer, but they said, "What you have to say in your defence, you can say it yourself. We will take it into account during your conviction".

'The trial took place in Lichtenberg, in a women's prison, which the Russians had occupied. There was a big room on the second or third floor, with a big table and a red tablecloth. Four or five Russian officials would sit there. They would talk about your offence and pretend that they had all the necessary proof. They would communicate your sentence. In my case it was 15 years, which was lenient. Generally, the standard sentence was 25 years. It sounds ridiculous nowadays. No German woman, and probably no man, would have been able to endure 25 years in a labour camp.'

Ursula was duly sent to a Siberian camp in Workuta, north of the Arctic Circle. The convicted prisoners travelled by train from Moscow in a long goods wagon fitted with cells. There were 24 women to a cell. 'We sat in a very constricted way or would sit on our companions' knees. The worst thing was not so much fear for my life but rather the hopelessness and not knowing what would happen to me, if I really would have to serve 15 years or if I would be released earlier. But on the other hand there was hope; I wanted to endure it. I wanted to see my family again and let them know where I had been, what I'd had to endure. I felt a mixture of hope and hopelessness.

From Moscow they were transported in a cattle wagon to Workuta, Siberia. 'We could see out of the train. After a while we saw nothing but trees. Then the forest ended and the tundra started. Everything was covered in snow, a lot of snow. The train stopped somewhere in the middle of a snowy landscape. We were told to get off and we jumped into the snow, which was some metres deep, still wearing our summer clothes. I wore summer shoes also. Guards received us with barking Alsatians. They led us through the snow for maybe one hour before we reached a camp.

'We were assigned to brigades which worked on railway construction in the tundra. Tree trunks from the Urals were delivered to the lumberyard. We had to then remove the bark from the trunks and saw them into sections, for building houses. I also worked in a brickyard, where bricks were baked. We had to collect brick-earth in the tundra. To bake bricks was a brutish job, with so many degrees of heat.'

Inmates could only work outside when the temperatures were higher than minus 46°C. If the ice-laden winter wind, known as the *Purga*, was blowing they were kept inside until the temperature was higher than minus 36°C. The summer was almost worse than the winter as surrounding marshlands swarmed with mosquitoes and temperatures reached 45°C or more. There was, she says, no physical abuse within the camp from its female guards. 'There was no rape either. Many women would do it voluntarily. They would disappear behind a barrack with a guard and they started little friendships which gave them little extra privileges, a little bit more to eat or an extra blanket. Friendships were fostered.'

Ursula was released from imprisonment in 1954 in a general amnesty. From her kidnapping onwards she always denied any involvement with espionage. Years later, however, she revealed that she had worked for British intelligence from before her arrival in Berlin. 'I was adventurous and wanted to go to Berlin. I would do errands for the English. One of them would visit me in Berlin. He instructed me and told me what to do. I found that very harmless. I thought, "Why shouldn't I deliver a letter to East Berlin or collect one from there?" I worked as a courier.

'They would pay for my flat and give me a small amount of money – 100 or 200 marks. They ordered me to apply for a job in a bar. I wasn't even afraid. I found it harmless. In retrospect I don't understand how I could have been that stupid. But I wanted to start something new, I wanted to be in Berlin, I wanted to have a new job, I wanted to dance. And doing that work for the English helped me to fulfil those ambitions.

'I never admitted to it. That was my little secret. The communists had their own secrets, and keeping that to myself was my inner triumph. I was waiting for them to tell me, "This and that is what happened. You have done that and that." But that never happened. They didn't know about it. They only groped about and tried to find out something, to make me confirm what they were suspecting. But I never obliged them.'

4

HERO WORKERS

'We will exceed the plan'
'We will catch up and surpass America'
'With work we strengthen peace'
'Shit quickly and you strengthen peace'

Czechoslovakian worker slogans

COMMUNISTS BELIEVED THAT the only source of wealth was human labour. The 'means of production' – primarily farms and factories – were to be taken into public ownership through collectivization and industrialization. This would result in swift technological and economic progress in a working-class society.

Workers were awarded mythical status through official iconography. In statues, paintings and children's books the worker was displayed as hero. The stories of workers' struggles against fascism and capitalism, like that of East German communist Ernst Thälmann who died in Buchenwald concentration camp, became part of every child's upbringing. The image of the heroic worker was an essential element in the narrative of building socialism: the bricklayers of Stalinallee, the miners of Ostrava, the blast furnacemen of Eisenhüttenstadt were all deployed by party propagandists.

Attempts were also made to create closer links between workers and other sections of society, like artists and intellectuals. One idea was that artists would spend time in factories and on farms in order to bond with workingmen and women.

Above all, to be working class under communism was to be on the winning side, defeating the enemies of the past and building the socialism of the future. Unsurprisingly, in these circumstances, everyone wanted to lay claim to working-class roots. To come from the middle class, or, worse still, the aristocracy, was a significant and sometimes insuperable obstacle to career and life chances. Sometimes, class background was sufficient evidence on its own to put a person behind bars.

Being working class was also a requirement for 'getting on'. If you were working class and committed to socialism that counted for a lot more than educational qualifications or vocational skills. In East Germany in the 1950s two-thirds of apparatchiks claimed to be from working-class families when the real figure was much nearer one-fifth.

The act of labour itself was venerated by the state to help boost productivity. In East Germany there was the Hennecke movement, based on the heroic efforts of miner Adolf Hennecke who consistently overproduced, breaking all previous productivity records. It was claimed that in one day he produced 387 per cent of the output of an ordinary worker. He was promoted by the communists as a role model for the nation and rewarded with a place on the SED's (Socialist Unity Party of Germany) Central Committee. However, no truly independent evidence exists to corroborate these claims and, ultimately, the true motivation for breaking productivity 'norms' was usually financial reward rather than any deep ideological satisfaction.

RUDOLF VASILČO

MINERS WERE AN elite workforce. They received better pensions, accommodation and pay than workers in other industries. But they often worked in dreadful conditions. Many of these socialist heroes have since died of occupational diseases while others succumbed to alcoholism. One of the surviving heroes is Rudolf Vasilčo.

Vasilčo was born in 1938 in eastern Slovakia. At the age of 22 he went to work down Ostrava's coalmines. He became a senior foreman at Stárič Mine in OKD (Ostrava-Karvina Mines), held several national records in coalmining and in 1981 was awarded the highest civic order in Czechoslovakia – Hero of Socialist Labour. The gold star that comes with the award is his most prized possession.

Now retired, Vasilčo lives in some comfort at his family house on the edge of Frýdek-Místek, 32 kilometres from Ostrava. He has two garages, a sauna, a swimming pool and a living room awash with marble and onyx. On the first floor of his house there is a worker's shrine filled with mining memorabilia: flags, miner's lamps, miner's hammers and medals. The golden star is kept in a safe.

Vasilčo received the prestigious award in a ceremony at Prague castle hosted by Czechoslovakian president and fellow Slovak Gustáv Husák. 'Husák was an incredibly pleasant man,' remembers Vasilčo. 'When he saw me at a distance, he was already smiling. I met him about six or seven times and he was always very friendly. After the award ceremony, we all were on the main stand during the May Day parade. Today, of course, people have a different opinion about it – everyone sees it in a different way – but at that time, it was something unforgettable. It was a reward for my lifelong work. I felt very proud when I received it and I feel like a Hero of Socialist Labour still today.'

The regime saw great propaganda value in these 'hero' workers and this caused a good deal of resentment, particularly during 'Normalization' (*Normalizace* was the communist term for the restoration of 'order' after the Warsaw Pact invasion; in reality, it meant the repression of society and the imposition of a hard-line communist rule). Some people felt that money rather than idealism was the workers' motivating factor. Critics of the regime saw them as communist stooges. Others just didn't like the fact that some workers seemed more equal than others. Vasilčo dismisses much of the carping. 'Some people were envious of me because they thought I got an enormous amount of money for it but it is not true. As a Hero of Socialist Labour, I have never had any extraordinary advantages and I have never pursued them. I received no financial reward but we were sent to the Soviet Union for a month for free. When I returned the managing director said, "We want to reward you in some way, we will not take the time you have just spent in the Soviet Union off your annual leave." That's all I was given for it. I was paid for that month as if I had been working; nothing more, nothing less.

'Every good worker was rewarded by a holiday abroad, even though it was not somewhere in the West. It was in Bulgaria, Romania, the Soviet Union or Yugoslavia. There were a lot of opportunities for holidays in our country, various chalets, centres, spas, for the miners they were all mostly free or cost virtually nothing.

'The team I led established four Czechoslovak records. If a company did not achieve the planned output it meant catastrophe for the managing director and all employees. So if they fell short by three or four million units, the shortfall could be made up by breaking records. We were trying to meet targets to achieve economic results so the employees would get their bonus.

'Whether you like it or not, your living standards are measured only by money. It was, it still is and it always will be. At that time there was no other opportunity or place to make more money, only in mining. The top-level mining, of course, was also rewarded with the most money. In comparison with a normal salary in a factory, it was three, four even five times more.

'Of course, when I was starting off with my team, I wanted to win recognition and we wanted to make good money, so I sometimes spent 20 hours in the mine. I am not saying I did it all the time but there were days when it was necessary.

'Every student at school wants to have good results, every sportsman wants to achieve the highest performance, nobody wants to be last, and it is the same in mining. If we ignore the fact that we wanted to make good money, we wanted to be recognized and do something extra.'

Given Vasilčo's success at work, it was felt that he should join the party. 'I joined the Communist Party relatively late, in 1974. The management invited me to join because I had good working results and excellent organizational skills. I am still a member of the Communist Party.'

Despite Vasilčo's high earnings, there was little to spend the money on in Czechoslovakia's failing economy. 'My wife says that many times she had to stand in a queue to get things the family needed. We mined 24 million tons of coal, rolled 16 million tons of steel, Czechoslovakia always had the money for this, but there was no money for importing goods or fruit from the southern hemisphere for people. Sometimes it was laughable.'

In November 1989, after the Velvet Revolution, a local branch of Václav Havel's Civic Forum criticized the fact that a portrait of Vasilčo hung in pride of place in the office of the director of the coalmine. The painting portrayed him in heroic mode, dressed in full regalia with all his medals on display, including his gold star. They said it promoted a personality cult, so they ordered it to be taken down and put into storage. Vasilčo offered to buy the painting, hoping that they would give it to him for free. They asked for 6,600 Czechoslovakian crowns, eventually agreed on 2,000, and the painting was moved from the coalmine's headquarters to Vasilčo's house. 'History is written by the victors,' said Vasilčo. 'In 1989, when the so-called Velvet Revolution started, those who were at the front, like me, had to go to the back. I cannot imagine how I could promote a personality cult. I was not to blame for the picture hanging in the office; it was the decision of the management, not mine.'

Vasilčo doesn't want to return to how things were before 1989; he accepts there were things wrong about that period. He does miss aspects of life then, though, and he has stayed loyal to the Communist Party. 'What I miss and what I hear my friends are missing, is the friendly spirit in the team. This spirit has simply disappeared.'

MARIE KOŠNEROVÁ

COMMUNISM WAS UNFOLDING in the countryside too. Just as factories were nationalized, so were farms. In Czechoslovakia, the communist regime of Klement Gottwald set about 'winning over the village for socialism'. In practice, this meant the forced nationalization of land along Soviet lines into collective farms and the destruction of the livelihoods of relatively affluent farmers.

Marx considered peasants to be incapable of grasping the meaning of communism. For their part, most East European peasants knew little about Marx's doctrine and cared less. Wealthier farmers had a lot to lose. In the new system, no one could own more than 50 hectares of land. Farmers generally were viewed by the regime with suspicion and seen as a source of political opposition.

Many suffered as communism in the countryside was brutally enforced. The authorities used whatever means necessary to force people into the collective farms and to give up their own land: enticement, blackmail and imprisonment. Sometimes people were murdered.

And collectivization did not work, only surviving through massive government subsidies. The farms were hugely inefficient, greatly overmanned enterprises and few peasants felt a real sense of collective ownership. But there were some enthusiastic supporters.

Marie Košnerová lives in the village of Vyhnanice in southern Bohemia. Over half a century ago, she joined one of Czechoslovakia's collective farms that went by the initials JZD (*Jednotné zemědělské družstvo* or Unified Farming Cooperative). The creation of her collective and Marie's part in it was recorded in Vojtěch Jasný's 1952 film *The Extraordinary Years.*

Someone like Marie had nothing to lose by joining the collective farm. Her family owned little land, had scant machinery to work it and limited labour resources. Poorer peasants were on the whole keener on collectivization and the communists used them to help create a local momentum. 'The farm collective was a kind of salvation for me. My dad was a blacksmith and he worked for the whole village and he did a good job. After he had three children his right arm was chopped off in a cutting machine and he couldn't work any more. We had four hectares of land, which we couldn't survive on, so we went to work on other farms. There we didn't get much either.

'My sister got married and left, my brother left for military service after the war and I grazed cattle together with my dad. So for me and for the whole family the collective came to our rescue. It saved my life and changed it for the better. Before the cooperative started we sowed wheat and we harvested thistles. We had to do everything manually. I'd had enough of hard work raising cattle. But when the collective started everybody was better off. Everybody.'

Like most young people in the village she joined the Communist Party and was on the committee that set up the cooperative. Throughout Czechoslovakia's countryside, a campaign to recruit members for collective farms was under way. Every peasant received a personal invitation to attend. Those who failed to display the necessary enthusiasm for the new venture found themselves in trouble. They might be publicly denounced, subject to extra taxation or find they were no longer able to obtain supplies. But Marie had no such problems. She was keen on the collective from day one. 'I had no idea what was going on in politics. But I was a member of the SM (Czechoslovak Youth Union), everybody was. There were 40 of us in SM from our village. Because I worked hard I earned three weeks out in Poland. We also went on trips to Germany by bus and all that we had for free. The cooperative paid for everything. Now there's nothing like that.

'I was a member of KS (Communist Party of Czechoslovakia) but I didn't understand it much. My husband also was a party member. And we had a good life. You know, back then, a worker had his say. In the cooperative I worked in the milking barn. First I did the milking then I looked after the calves and the pigs. I stayed there till I retired. We had 70 sows and 200 pigs. I miss everything. We had such a good collective. We were such a great team.

'We got everything from the cooperative. They loaded the grain on a tractor, took it to the mill, and distributed it around the village according to how much everyone did… We could take milk from work, plus everyone had a cow at home.

'When the cooperative started we got a lot of flour so mum baked a lot of bread. It was our salvation. They were really the extraordinary years. I wish to get back to those years. That would be great.'

VOJTĚCH JASNÝ

THE DISTINGUISHED CZECH film director Vojtěch Jasný made *The Extraordinary Years*, in which Marie Košnerová appeared playing herself. Part drama, part documentary, the film promoted collectivization. Jasný was a member of the Communist Party and was always aware that the party ultimately called the shots. In case he was in any doubt the general secretary of the Communist Party and president of Czechoslovakia, Antonin Novotný, made clear to him during an outdoor reception where the limits of his creative freedom in such matters ended. 'My wife and I were drinking cognac, were holding glasses in our hands when Novotný came to us with a glass of vodka. I had been observing him and discovered he allowed others to fill his glass, but he spilt it on the grass every time. He only had a sip once in a while, so he wouldn't get drunk. He came to us and said, "Jasný, now you can make whatever films you want, but if you stand up against the party, we'll take action..." and he made a sign as if killing a rabbit by breaking its neck. I said, "Mr President how could I?"'

But in time Jasný was persuaded by events to make a more truthful film about collectivization and the suffering it brought to many farmers. It was called *All My Good Countrymen* and was finished in 1968. Although Novotný's regime wouldn't allow it to be made his successor, Alexander Dubček, gave Jasný the go-ahead. 'Dubček called me personally and said, "Now you can make the film, nobody will oppose it. You will get all the necessary finance." That's how it was. Thanks to him I could make the film. Dubček was a wonderful person.'

Shortly afterwards, Warsaw Pact forces invaded Czechoslovakia. To the communist hardliners who replaced the reformer Dubček, the film was anathema. 'They minded about everything; the whole idea, how I showed the truth and the way I pictured how they liquidated the good farmers. What I wanted to show was how the harmony in the countryside was disturbed. I am not against collectives, but in this case it was done violently. They killed a lot of people. They didn't like that I said it. After the Soviet occupation they wanted to destroy the negative and all copies of the film. They wanted to burn it, burn it, burn it.'

Jasný was then called in to see his boss and told he had to collaborate with the new regime or face prison. He had to express support for the Soviet invasion, retract his criticisms and condemn his own movie. He refused to agree to what he called 'moral death'. The film was put on a list of those 'banned for ever' and Jasný went into exile.

HERBERT HÄRTEL

WITH UTOPIA CAME plans for new cities for the Marxist workers of the future. The first in East Germany was Stalinstadt (Stalin City), on the river Oder near the Polish border. Ideology, architecture and the demands of the economy all figured in its conception.

At the Third Party Congress in July 1950 it was decided to build the Ironworks Combine East (*Eisenhüttenkombinat Ost*, or EKO), which would form the nucleus of the 'first socialist city in Germany', near the old town of Fürstenberg. The ironworks would use coal from Poland and iron ore from the Ukraine. To house the workers for the EKO, they started to build houses in January 1951.

In May 1953, two months after Stalin's death, Walter Ulbricht, the leader of the SED, attended the opening ceremony of Stalinstadt. In 1961 it was renamed Eisenhüttenstadt after Stalin's fall from grace. The town attracted large numbers of people, drawn to its good wages and housing. No church was allowed in this new town by the atheist regime but there were schools, hospitals and shops.

Architecture under socialism was about politics. The town's architecture was supposed to emphasize light and sunshine, and the integration of cultural and social facilities into a community. In the 1950s times were hard but hope was prevalent as people felt they were striving towards a better life. There was also a sense of collective belonging, of having a stake in the utopia they were building.

Herbert Härtel came to Stalinstadt in 1955 as the deputy to the chief architect, Willi Stamm. In 1958 he became the town's main architect, designing among other things the Leninallee, the main thoroughfare that connects the community with the ironworks. He still lives there 54 years later. In the early years, the architecture was strongly influenced by Stalinist and neoclassical architecture and was not undistinguished. Later on, to save money, the style was what was called *Plattenbau* ('Panel building'), or in other words tower blocks made out of prefabricated concrete. Härtel believes the 1950s was an amazingly creative time to be in Stalinstadt, even if it was politicians who had the final say on the blueprints. 'Stalinstadt was a simple concept because it was based on a simple need: to populate the agriculturally underdeveloped Oder region with as many people as possible and as fast as possible.

'Walter Ulbricht was very interested in town planning and urban development. That meant there was not one single important city that could have planned the building of its centre without the agreement of the Politburo. The party examined the plans, not only of city centres, but also of individual buildings. I was a member of the party. My political beliefs were formed here in Stalinstadt. As a young comrade, life is the stage where political attitudes are formed. I never separated my professional skills from my political views.'

In July 1950 the East German government set out 16 architectural principles, which were supposed to form the basis of all public architecture. Accordingly, architecture had to be in line with the national traditions of the country. These had originated in German Classicism. According to SED ideologues, Classicism had been the last important architectural movement in history. 'Eisenhüttenstadt was built on the basis of these 16 principles. These principles originated from the premise that urban construction was all about harmonic satisfaction of the human need for working, living, culture and recreation. I believe that urban planning cannot be formulated on a more beautiful and more classic goal.

'Certainly those principles also originated in the DDR's socialist ideology and policies, and so took the social structure of the population into account. This presents quite an essential difference to present city planning. Based on the knowledge that three- and four-storey houses were the most profitable to build, you could set a target to accommodate 80 to 85 per cent of the inhabitants of such a new-founded city in that way. Social discrimination was avoided. On the contrary, a worker lived in one and the same block of flats with doctors and teachers. As a consequence, the flats had to meet the needs not only of the working class, but also of the middle class and the intelligentsia. That was the challenge.

'This first socialist city has a number of characteristics that clearly distinguish it from any capitalist city. The construction of a socialist city was completely planned throughout, focusing on the city as a whole, every aspect of it. Such planning is a socialist characteristic. In capitalism you have "island planning" which doesn't focus on the city as a whole, which means that connections, relationships between different parts of the city are not recognized or worked out or even considered. This is the result of the inability to plan.

'My Western colleagues have always envied the fact that in socialism you could dispose of the land according to the interests of the majority. In socialist Stalinstadt, I never had to worry that a certain territory would not be available for building on because it was in private hands.

'Another difference was the economic structure of the socialist city: all the businesses were located on one big industrial site and the ones that needed to be within easy reach of the people were situated within the housing estates.'

The first housing blocks of the city were constructed by 1956. In communist propaganda these apartments were described as 'palaces for workers' but they were far from that and Walter Ulbricht recognized the problem, calling them *Schnitterkaserne* or 'barracks for the Grim Reaper'. In later plans ceiling heights were raised and central heating was included.

Härtel recalls a number of rather heated meetings with early residents of Stalinstadt – meetings that caused the authorities to look again at their plans for the city's development. 'We climbed up Diehloer Höhe, a hill in the southern part of the city. We then looked at the city from above and saw that it was dominated by a relative monotony: all buildings were three and four storeys high. There was little differentiation in the height, all the buildings had flat roofs, they were all painted yellow-grey. There was a certain similarity of forms. It's true that the architecture left great spaces for details and subtleness, but only when seen from the streets. From a bigger distance the city looked boring. It also lacked greenery. That was the first thing my predecessor and I changed upon my arrival in early 1955. We went to two schools and recruited pupils of the 10th, 11th and 12th grades to help us plant trees during the weekend.

'At a number of rumbustious town meetings the debates at the assemblies always centred on quantity. People wanted more flats, more facilities for the community, and they wanted to get them quickly. Very little importance was attributed to the look of the buildings. I don't think that the first buildings corresponded to the taste of their inhabitants because tastes diverged massively. People came from all over East Germany and from every social background.

'My wife was horrified when she first visited me in Stalinstadt, despite the fact that she came from the bombed Chemnitz and so wasn't used to anything special. She doubted whether we could ever feel at home here and raise our daughter. But eventually she got used to it. Unfortunately, good building was limited to a few social constructions only. In the 1970s and 1980s remarkable things were built in the DDR, but they were limited to the centres of certain cities.'

WALTER WOMACKA

THESE NEW CONCRETE utopias became gigantic display cases for the people's art. Walter Womacka is one of East Germany's most distinguished artists and in 1955 he became art director in Stalinstadt. He is especially known for his murals. *Our Life* on the House of Teachers is one of the most prominent features overlooking the Alexanderplatz in the centre of East Berlin. In Stalinstadt, he created a 125-metre long and 7-metre high mural inside the town hall called *Our New Life*. It is designed to represent an idealized version of the development of the country after the Second World War, with pride of place given to the workers. Having lived through the bombing of those times, Womacka, like many of his generation on the left, identifies socialism with peace. His style is consistently that of the Socialist Realist, a style whose purpose is to promote socialism and the working class.

Womacka remains an unreconstructed Socialist Realist to this day. 'Certainly you can term it Social Realism, as the Soviets used to call it. I would describe myself as a socialist artist and, most of all, as an objective painter. I do not want to just paint for myself but I want the public to understand my works. I want to communicate that I am for peace and against war. It's a very broad topic and actually the most fundamental of all, because all life depends on it. Everything else follows from that.

'Eisenhüttenstadt, the former Stalinstadt, was the first socialist city that was built from out of nowhere. It was very fascinating, but not always beautiful, because things had to be done quickly. One beautiful aspect was that it was full of young people who were employed at the ironworks. That was nice. For me it was clear that I should include in the painting [*Our New Life*] the developments of this new country, East Germany, and the relationship between the people and the state. It's a complicated topic but it was a big wall for a mural.

'I wanted to display reconstruction and the attitude of elderly people after the war, and how the young people coped with the hand fate had dealt them. That is why female workers are also represented. There's a woman who has survived the war but who has since sunk into poverty. Next to her stands a young couple. He is rolling up his sleeves and is ready to do the reconstruction work. I featured a character I call "Rubble Woman", picking up the stones from bombed-out buildings, as well as the construction workers who built this new town.'

Womacka appreciated that socialist East Germany was committed to public art that was accessible and understandable. 'A certain percentage of the building budget – at that time it was three per cent – had to be spent on artwork. I have met many members of the Politburo. I knew Walter Ulbricht very well and he asked me to paint his portrait. When you portray someone, you build up a special kind of relationship. Walter Ulbricht was in favour of murals like *Our New Life* because this kind of art is democratic art, made available for everyone. He was very interested in establishing city centres, and for them many works of art were created. So art was at the centre of the general development of this new life for working people.'

VLADIMÍR REMEK

THE WORKER WAS also associated with the future and with science and technology. The achievements of the Soviet space programme and its cosmonauts represented not only a space race but also an ideological conflict with the West. From the 1970s onwards the Soviet Union allowed a select few would-be cosmonauts from other socialist countries to train at Star City outside Moscow as part of its Interkosmos programme. Of these, a handful made it into orbit.

Thirty years ago Vladimír Remek became the first man who wasn't a Soviet or an American to go into space. As a result, he garnered a number of awards, including Hero of the Soviet Union, Hero of the Czechoslovak Socialist Republic and the Soviet Order of Lenin.

He made his space flight between 2 and 10 March 1978, as research cosmonaut on the spaceship *Soyuz-28*, together with Soviet cosmonaut Alexei Alexandrovich Gubarev. They were in space for seven days, 22 hours and 16 minutes.

Remek, son of a Czech mother and a Slovak father, with an impressive record in the Czechoslovak Air Force, started space training in 1976. *Soyuz-28*'s mission happened ten years after Soviet tanks had invaded Czechoslovakia to crush the reforms of the Prague Spring. Many believed that the Soviets selected a Czechoslovak cosmonaut to help assuage anti-Russian feeling in the country. Whatever the reason for the choice it was, for Remek, the fulfilment of a boyhood dream. 'Try and imagine a time when nobody and nothing flew into outer space. I was nine years old when Sputnik was launched. It was an enormous event for those who remember it, especially for me as a boy. Then came Yuri Gagarin and then the others, Soviet and American astronauts. And I succeeded in achieving the same thing just before I was 30.

'When we sat in the spacecraft at the tip of the rocket, I knew I was about to experience something exceptional. I felt I was embarking upon something that could help my country enormously. I remember well that the immediate moment of weightlessness occurred after the engine in the third part of the rocket got disconnected. It was euphoric. Then the real work started, consisting of various tests and screenings of the equipment to prepare the spacecraft for the connection with the space station.

'I felt that I was doing it for my country. When I spoke to people on Earth, I felt I should say something that would go down in history. Nobody told me what to say. So I tried to summarize my own feelings and to express the thoughts that I had. I said we had a good chance of living in peace for a long time.'

Soviet leader Leonid Brezhnev and Czechoslovakia's president, Gustáv Husák, greeted the cosmonauts by radio during their mission. Husák's sign-off to Remek was, 'Long live socialist internationalism!'

Remek accepts there were propaganda aspects to his mission, but feels what he helped to achieve went beyond that. 'Every flight into outer space up to then was considered by the whole world to be something of an event that had political or if you like propagandistic or PR value. You could not expect our flight to be any different. For me it was very heart-warming and in a certain sense it moved me when we were flying over Latin America and we were able to receive local radio stations. It was very uplifting to hear my name in connection with Czechoslovakia on the opposite side of the world.

'Of course, to say that it was only a matter of propaganda for the communist leadership is misleading. I think it gave joy to many people on Earth, in Czechoslovakia and elsewhere. The fact is that Czechoslovakia was the third country in the world after the two superpowers to have a man in space.'

On his return the party had arranged a series of 'welcomes' throughout the country. 'I never expected such a reception on my return. Some say that people were forced to attend meetings with me. It is, of course, possible and I don't want to rule it out. But there was the cavalcade through Prague flanked by thousands of people, I visited thousands of different groups in factories. Of course, at school pupils were invited to come and meet a cosmonaut. I also visited children's summer camps. It was quite difficult to find a place in which I could be alone.'

After 1978 Remek continued with the Czechoslovak Air Force before becoming the director of the Museum of Space and Aircraft in Prague. After that he became a diplomat in Moscow. He left the Communist Party in 1990. In 2004 he was elected a Member of the European Parliament. Yet those seven days in space remain the most influential period of his life. For him, it showed what ordinary working-class people could achieve under the scientific creed of socialism and, even more importantly, it altered his view of everything. 'I can say it fundamentally changed my life. I realized at the age of 30 that planet Earth has a finite dimension. It takes about an hour and a half to fly round it at the height that we did. It influenced the way in which I saw things. It deepened my belief in working for peace on this planet. Of course, it also influenced me in that I tried to see things from a greater distance, to keep a wider perspective.'

KAREL GOTT

THE WORKERS' AND Peasants' States of Eastern Europe created their own superstars of popular culture. When such artists achieved the success and popularity of Czechoslovak singer Karel Gott, the communist regime had to deal with someone with a greater following than the party itself.

Gott is the best-known Czech singer of all time, the so-called 'Sinatra of the East'. He managed to thrive before, during and after the Warsaw Pact invasion of 1968 remaining popular with both party and people. Today, he remains the Czech Republic's most famous celebrity.

The crooner from Pilsen has been a fixture on the East European music scene since the mid-1960s, performing a mixture of pop, film musicals, jazz and balladeering. He was used by the regime and, in return, kept silent about politics. The regime was wary of how he was treated because of his massive popularity, and because they appreciated the foreign currency he earned for them through sales of records and concert tours in the West and the Soviet Union.

In 1967 Gott performed for six months in Las Vegas at the New Frontier Hotel and Casino. It was part of an agreement with the hotel and Czechoslovakia's Ministry of Culture. The ministry would provide 'cultural employees' for the world capital of gambling and the party would gain badly needed foreign currency.

Gott's trip to the United States made a big impression on him. 'I objected to the way they announced me: "Ladies and gentleman we proudly present straight from behind the Iron Curtain Mr Karel Gott." I said it wasn't nice and I asked them not to introduce me in that way. The American organizers said I should leave these decisions to them as they knew what they were doing. I should understand that I was the first communist to sing in Las Vegas. I said, "But I am not one, I have never had anything to do with the party."After my performance the women in the audience were standing there saying, "Look at him", as if I was a monkey.

'When I went for my first interview on a radio station in Las Vegas, the presenter told me at the beginning that I was in a free country and that I could say whatever I wanted. I thanked him for the information and then he asked me the first question. "Mr Gott, we know you like American music, who are your favourite American singers?" I answered, naming all black singers. The presenter said, 'Mr Gott, I heard you want to sing in Las Vegas for half a year. It's a long time. I would recommend that you say you like Frank Sinatra. Understand? I asked him to explain to me why Frank Sinatra… I liked him but he was not exactly my kind of voice. And the presenter said, "He helped a lot of people here." It was a kind of a Don Corleone, Godfather-type answer.'

After a subsequent tour in West Germany, Gott decided for the moment not to return to the Czechoslovakia, a country where censorship and other restrictions had been reimposed in his absence by the regime of Gustáv Husák during the period known as 'Normalization'. Gott's family back home immediately came under pressure from the Czechoslovak secret police. 'I knew there would be a pressure put on my parents and there was. Immediately the gentlemen of the StB (secret police) came and moved all my things out from our house; they took books, my collection of albums, about 2,000 of them… simply everything that belonged to me. That was the first thing my parents had to deal with. Then the authorities said I was a political idiot; they told my mum I was a political *stupido*, a moron. Then the leader of the communist party, Gustáv Husák, went on national TV and said, "Let Karel Gott sing for the bourgeoisie". That was on live TV, and of course the whole world heard it: "We will make our own new stars over here", said Husak'

Nevertheless, Husák realized that Gott was too popular and too much of a money-spinner to be banished. 'Surprisingly, through a diplomatic route, I was invited to a trade mission in Frankfurt and I was told there that if I came back to Czechoslovakia the "biggest boss" guaranteed that there would be no pressure on me and that I wouldn't be punished. He guaranteed that, "nothing would happen" to me. The regime could do two things: they could either arrest me or award me. And they awarded me. They decided it would be better if I earned foreign currency for them.'

Eventually Gott accepted Husák's offer to 'come and deal' and he returned home where he was more successful than ever. It is said that during this period he earned more money than Skoda cars but he says most of it went into party coffers. 'My wage for a sell-out concert at a sports stadium was 600 crowns. You could buy a nice dinner for two for that; and it was a sold-out sports stadium that in fact made 1.5 million crowns.

'The audience didn't expect me to put politics into my lyrics. And that saved me. If I had brought my politics into my performances I would have had to express clearly which side I was on. And if I had stood against the system I would have been finished as a singer.'

5
SOCIALIST YOUTH

'The child needs to be moved to the deepest of love for East Germany, and the deepest of commitments to its socialist agenda, and to passionate disdain for the imperialistic enemies of our people'

Instruction manual for Pioneer teachers, 1970

SOCIALIST SOCIETY NEEDED to rewire its population. Instead of competitive self-seeking individuals like those populating Western capitalism there had to be socialists working selflessly for the collective good.

These utopian ideals forged in the minds of old, grey men required the enthusiastic participation of the young. To achieve them, it was deemed that young people needed a 'socialist personality', officially defined as having a 'class outlook' based on a Marxist-Leninist world view; they were to be 'imbued with collective thoughts and deeds' and possessed of 'excellent mental, physical and moral qualities'.

Thus the upbringing of socialist youth became a political and ideological matter. Collective goals took priority over individual wishes and the party was more important than the family. Lifestyle, fashion and hair length were things that mattered to the communist authorities.

The education system was also designed to reinforce these aims as it was especially geared towards the working class, with subjects like Marxism-Leninism on the syllabus and Stasi informers in schools to ensure compliance with socialist goals. Eduation was also concerned with meeting immediate production needs. Individual career choices were subordinate to the economic priorities of the state.

Academic achievement was not enough to ensure access to further education. Political conformity, working-class credentials, atheism and active involvement in communist youth movements were also important requirements.

The party created mass organizations to control and channel the energies of young people. In East Germany, the Free German Youth organization (*Freie Deutsche Jugend* or FDJ) co-opted youth over 14 for political ends. For East Germany's younger citizens there was the Young Pioneers for those aged six to ten and the Ernst Thälmann Pioneers (named after a communist killed by Hitler's regime) for ages ten to 14.

There was plenty that was good about these groups as they organized holidays, sports events and even ran discos. But such organizations also provided a training ground for future leaders. Both Erich Honecker and Egon Krenz, two East German Communist

Party leaders, had previously been heads of the FDJ. East Germans joined these organizations in considerable numbers in what has been described as a 'participatory dictatorship'. By 1952, two-thirds of people in the relevant age group were members of the FDJ. After various peaks and troughs, membership rose gradually from the late 1960s until the second half of the 1980s. Membership started to decline in 1987 as the situation became more difficult in the DDR.

Although membership of youth organizations was not compulsory, not joining could have serious consequences for educational and career prospects. Refuseniks did exist, however, usually acting on religious grounds.

The FDJ also assisted the state police and Ministry of State Security through FDJ disciplinary squads. These were targeted at unacceptable behaviour such as *Rowdytum* (a term denoting anti-social behaviour which often involved listening to or watching Western media channels), missing work or being under the influence of Western imperialism of the 'class enemy' generally. One prominent operation involving the FDJ was the 'Ox Head' campaign of September 1961 in which members reported those with television antennae pointing towards the West. FDJ squads were dispatched to repoint the aerials back towards the East.

In 1954 the communists revived a secular ceremony, the *Jugendweihe*. This was a coming-of-age ceremony for 14-year-olds as the atheist regime sought to replace religious Confirmation ceremonies. Its reintroduction was controversial at the time but the practice had become widespread by 1989.

Those who took part in the ceremony would dedicate themselves to the ideals of the state. Included in the 1985 pledge were the words, 'Are you prepared, as true patriots, to deepen friendship with the Soviet Union, to strengthen the brotherhood with the socialist countries, to fight in the spirit of proletariat internationalism, to protect peace and to defend socialism against every imperialist attack?' This was one of many questions to which young people replied, 'Yes, we pledge!'

HAGEN KOCH

ULTIMATELY, HOWEVER, THE force of international cultural trends and the power of individual desire held sway over all attempts to produce a one-size-fits-all 'socialist personality'. Hagen Koch was a Young Pioneer at the height of the Stalinist period in East Germany's history. In 1960, aged 19, he joined the Ministry for State Security, the Stasi, and was held up by its leader Erich Mielke as a role model for socialist youth. As with so many others in East Germany, family history played a crucial role in shaping the young Hagen's future.

His father Heinz served in the German army during the Second World War. He returned to eastern Germany, became a schoolteacher and founded the local chapter of the centrist Liberal Democratic Party. He ran for mayor in East Germany's first post-war elections and easily beat the Communist Party candidate. Instead of taking office, however, he was interned in a former Nazi concentration camp by the Soviets. There he was offered a deal: his freedom in exchange for joining the communists. He accepted and brought up his son Hagen to accept communism 'like a religion'.

'We were told that the DDR's Young Pioneers would build bridges of friendship among people who had fought against one another during the Second World War, in order to create peace in the world,' remembers Koch.

'We knew that there had been the Hitler Youth during the Third Reich. When the Pioneer organization was founded, many adults were opposed to it because it reminded them of the Hitler regime. But my father was a teacher and had the task of recruiting children for the Pioneer organization. Children of that age aren't concerned with political issues. They simply like to wear badges, caps and uniforms.

'In August 1952, 80,000 Young Pioneers were invited to Dresden because we, the children, had to carry on socialism. At the age of 12 I was proud to attend.' He was, he realizes now, the ideal age to soak up the party message.

On 13 February 1945 the historic city of Dresden had been levelled by English and American air force bombs. Thousands of people were killed. 'They showed us around cemeteries with mass graves,' Koch recalls, 'They said, "That's what the American imperialism has done!" And we children would do anything to ensure such things never happened again.'

The party message extended from perceived war crimes by the Americans to outrageous propaganda. 'I came from a little town which had many potato fields and many potato beetles which destroyed the crop. In Dresden they told us that it was the Americans who had unleashed those potato beetles. They told us that the very same aeroplanes that had bombed Dresden had also unleashed those potato beetles.'

Among the atmospheric ruins of Dresden 80,000 children pledged that they would not go to war. 'I was 12 years old and I made that promise, not with my mind but with my heart. That had such an emotional impact on me. I told myself that I would do anything; I would study with diligence, I would believe in what the politicians told us.

'We wanted the Americans to get out of West Germany. We didn't even think about the Soviet Union at that time. We were told that imperialism and capitalism had been restored in the West. At school I learned that everything was destroyed and wrecked because of capitalism, that if we didn't want to be involved in a war again, we mustn't be capitalist, but socialist instead. As a child I made the equation: capitalism equals war, socialism equals peace.

'Stalin was our role model because he had destroyed Hitler's fascism. We children idolized Stalin. He was a god to us. When he died in 1953 the world collapsed around me. We would put portraits of him on the wall and adorn them with a black ribbon and flowers. We would hold a minute's silence in his memory and we would cry. It was as if a member of our family had left us.'

Like his friends, Koch was chiefly worried about who would step into Stalin's shoes. At school he embraced socialist politics and achieved high grades. 'They knew that I was passionate and convinced about the idea of a socialist DDR. The Ministry for State Security took notice of the young man I was then. Their spies would tell them what I was thinking, what I felt, what I believed in. No one could ever apply for a job at the Stasi. Everyone who did that instantly became a suspect; they would wonder why someone would want to work for them. It was they who decided who to employ.

'In the spring of 1960, when I was 19 years old, a Stasi officer approached me and told me that I was worthy of working at the Stasi headquarters in Berlin, on the front line for maintaining the peace and for protecting our home country. I was amazed and accepted with conviction. On 5 April 1960 I went to Berlin and became a soldier within the Stasi guard regiment. The city didn't have any wall or barbed wire at that time.

'Only four days after my arrival, I was asked to give a speech at the SED party conference on why I and others had voluntarily joined the army. Military service was not compulsory then. During that speech I talked about my childhood and my adolescence, and about the Pioneer meeting in Dresden. I condemned the Americans and their potato beetles, and ended with the words, "Better a thousand drops of sweat under peace than only one single drop of blood under war. That is why I am here and why I put on this uniform."'

Afterwards, Koch was swiftly promoted to director of the department that drew topographic maps. 'I didn't know anything about the job. I had studied to become a draughtsman for mechanical engineering. But the Stasi knew that I was keen on studying atlases and maps. It was like a dream coming true.

'On 13 August 1961 the construction of the Berlin Wall began. Two days later, I was ordered to take my maps to a group of people including future party leader Erich Honecker and head of the Stasi Erich Mielke, and outline where the border should be drawn.

'The decision to construct a border within the city of Berlin was taken at short notice: there were no detailed construction plans. We took the maps and walked through the whole city from the Bernauer

Strasse to the Brandenburg Gate and Potsdam Square. In the afternoon we reached the border-crossing point at Checkpoint Charlie. People in West Berlin would demonstrate and throw bottles and stones from there. I was ordered to paint a thick white line on the street at that border-crossing point. I stood with one leg in the West and the other one in the East, and my assignment was to show to the evil people in the West, "so far and no further. Capitalism is over there and here is socialism."

'I painted that line still firmly convinced that the border would avoid a third world war. At the very same time, the first border guard to defect jumped the barbed wire in the Bernauer Strasse. Many people were against the Wall. But I was not the only one who was for it. There is a German proverb that says, "Where wood is chopped, splinters must fall". That was my justification at that time. "It is unpleasant and terrible, but in principle it's good."'

From 1970 to 1985 Koch was employed as officer for culture within the Stasi. One the the films he used to show Stasi recruits was *The Day of the Jackal*, starring Edward Fox as the would-be assassin of General de Gaulle. It was screened to prepare soldiers for the extent and nature of Western perfidy. It was part of his role to 'educate' and entertain soldiers and youth organizations. 'I showed them many films about life in the DDR, its nature and landscapes, its beauty. But many young people started wondering why they were shown only the beautiful aspects of the country. Obviously, we had to show Soviet films about the fight against the Hitler regime and also a lot of Soviet literature.'

The gradual discovery that Stalin was evil rather than good was a blow for Koch, as was the growing realization that there was a lot the East German state was not telling its people. 'We knew that wherever there's a white, there must also be a black somewhere. We were told that our ideology in the DDR was socialism – our ideology or, to put it another way, our world view! But we couldn't "view" the world at all. We knew about it through books, but had never experienced it ourselves.

'As a young man I enthusiastically loved the DDR. We had tried to make better things, to make a utopia come true. There's a saying, "Who isn't a communist as a young person doesn't have a heart. Who is still a communist as an adult doesn't have a brain."

'I cannot answer questions about guilt or innocence. I tried to live correctly with regards to what I knew at the time although I would feel guilty if I kept silent today. The knowledge I have now, but which I didn't have back then, should help to warn people against supporting such kinds of dictatorship. I cannot deny my involvement. But I'm only to blame for believing the wrong words.'

RAINER PENZEL

LIKE KOCH, RAINER Penzel was a model pupil until one act of juvenile defiance cost him his freedom. On Wednesday 21 September 1961, Rainer, a leading figure in the local FDJ, together with his classmates from the sixth form of Anklam school near Neubrandenburg, decided as a protest against recent political developments to arrive at school wearing black and proclaiming that they were, 'bearing their future to its grave'.

The previous month the Berlin Wall had been erected, effectively imprisoning East Germans inside their state. Even more recently, the East German parliament had passed a law introducing compulsory national service in the National People's Army. But no one could have predicted the repercussions that followed this mild act of rebelliousness.

Seventeen-year-old Rainer was charged with treason and sentenced to five years in jail. Another 'ringleader' was also arrested and imprisoned. Others were expelled from school and so prevented from taking the school-leaving exam, a requirement for university entrance. Some teachers were fired. Parents were forced to undergo self-examination and admit their shortcomings in the political education of their children.

The Politburo received an account of the 'counter-revolutionary' activity at the school. Personal copies of the report were sent to party leader, Walter Ulbricht, and future party leader, Erich Honecker. The Communist Party organization within the school was deemed to have failed, the local FDJ was criticized for its 'politically negative role' and links between some teachers and the former Nazi regime were highlighted.

Political conditions inside schools across the country were then subjected to a major investigation. But for Rainer it was a personal rather than a national disaster. He was part of a cheerful gang that was concerned more with having fun than with the politics of the day. 'I think everyone thought about studying first then getting married and starting a family. Everyone thought that everything would work out.'

But the prospect of conscription and being penned in by the Berlin Wall changed everything. 'Already on the first school day they were recruiting for the army. We didn't want to join. But the party and the headmaster tried to brainwash us and urged us to sign up for the army. The headmaster even said that if we didn't join the army, we wouldn't be able to attend university. This blackmail was the reason why we eventually signed up, but we did it only on condition that we would be allowed to study.'

Not content with that, the headmaster compelled those who had signed up to sing a Pioneer song at the daily flag muster. Rainer – who would one day be a headmaster himself – and some of his sixth-form colleagues refused to sing and looked down at their feet instead.

That evening the pupils decided to further their protest by wearing black the following day. 'Black wasn't a common colour for clothes at that time, so we had to wear jumpers and tracksuits or things we had borrowed. The girls weren't supposed to participate, but they insisted on it and organized some clothes for themselves.

'When we entered the classroom, the teachers were gobsmacked. We looked like mourners at a funeral. The maths teacher said, "Well, I hope that today your performance in maths won't be as black as your clothes." The geography teacher said, "Well, you can't be serious!" They were quite relaxed about it.

'Our schoolmates and the younger ones asked why we were all dressed in black. And one of us, Gerd, answered, "We are carrying our future to its grave".' The Stasi later used that as evidence of counter-revolutionary activity.

Only one teacher, the party secretary of the school, took exception to the protest and immediately reported what was going on. Word of it soon reached Berlin. 'Later on, I went to a sports festival, which was being held on the sports ground. After it had finished we wanted to eat something at school. I went into the school and suddenly I found myself handcuffed and marched off. I thought that they were crazy. They arrested us, me first, and two others, who I saw in court. Our class was disbanded and the teachers dismissed.

'They took me to the Stasi office in Anklam in the Ellbogen Strasse. They interrogated me there. I just said, "We did wear black, but we never intended to overthrow the government." They didn't know what to do with us and so they transferred me to the Stasi prison in Neustrelitz that very evening.

'Back in those days, everything was highly symbolic; they would make a big affair out of every piece of trivia. I knew that they had searched my parents' house. My mother had an old gardening catalogue, which her sister must have brought over from Hanover during a visit. They suspected that the catalogue was a code. For three or four hours my interrogator insisted that I had to admit that there was a deeper meaning attached to it, and that it wasn't simply a present from her sister.

'Before my sentence, I was put in solitary confinement. There were no books, no radio, no light, no newspapers, no table, no chair. The wall was made of bricks, there was no window. I only had a 40-watt bulb and a bucket. I wasn't allowed any contact with my parents. I didn't see a lawyer, no one… I was forced to behave like an animal. They used to beat me up if I didn't sign the interrogation notes.

'Before the trial started, I was transferred to another prison. The food was better; they fed me up a little because I had become very skinny. The trial was on 13 January 1962. There were three defendants, Dietmar Tietböhl and Peter Klause, my two schoolmates, and I.

'The prosecutor depicted our depravity in the darkest colours and tried to prove that we were dangerous. The others were sentenced to three and a half years, and I was sentenced to five years because my actions had threatened the entire nation, and because I was seen as the leader of this counter-revolutionary activity. We were dumbstruck. We weren't able to think any more. Nobody cried, but we were completely poleaxed.

'Then I was put on a train and sent to prison in Cottbus then in Leipzig. The number of detainees in Leipzig was so high that they couldn't put us into cells, we had to sleep in the corridors at night and were watched by guards with machine guns. The prisons were that overcrowded.

'Then we were sent to Torgau in Saxony. One area was designated for juveniles. We were 20 in one cell, or more. But the political offenders were the majority and thus we would take over all available positions like food distribution, filling in of worksheets and so on; we would regulate all that... You can't compare it to the conditions in today's prisons; drugs didn't exist at that time.'

Rainer and his fellow prisoners were trained for menial jobs so they could be integrated back into the working class. He was finally released after two years and nine months. 'From the moment of my sentence onwards, I saw the DDR as a nation which needed to be eliminated. I realized that it was omnipotent and that its need for security was unnatural. We had got involved and had to somehow get out of it. We had to rely on ourselves and stand our ground.

'For me, communism was a utopia. Like any utopia it can only be tested when it is translated into reality. Even Christianity failed with that. We had to live with that national doctrine of communism and to occupy the niches we could find. Such was our life in the past. It was an inner emigration.'

ANDREI DUBAN

ROMANIAN YOUTH PLAYED a key role in promoting the Father and Mother of their nation, Nicolae and Elena Ceauşescu. Schoolchildren would spend weeks practising for athletic or theatrical displays in their honour. After being screened for disease, some would be allowed to approach Nicolae and Elena and present them with gifts or flowers. Andrei Duban was a child actor and star of such propaganda parades and displays. From the age of eight he performed regularly on television and in person before the Ceauşescus. 'I started reciting poems when I was in school. There was a famous festival called "Ode to Romania" where favoured children showcased their talents. I would recite poems. There were heats at different levels and I got through to the national final.

'After that they started calling me to recite poems for Romanian television, the only television channel at the time. Of course, they were patriotic poems. The first show had something to do with spring and the equinox, and after that the so-called "homage" shows to the Ceauşescus started.

'At the same time I got into movies, and I was also appearing on the radio in a daily broadcast called *Good Morning Children*. Slowly things started to snowball for me. This is how I started.

'During the homage shows there were various performances – dance, choirs, patriotic songs – and among those were the poetry recitals. There were two categories of recital; some were performed by adult actors and some by children. Even the children were divided into boys and girls; boys would dedicate their poems specifically to Elena Ceauşescu and the girls were reciting to Nicolae. There were thousands of poems, all very similar to each other, hailing the couple's amazing qualities.

'The message and the meaning of the things I was doing only revealed themselves to me later, when I was older and I came to realize where I was living, what kind of country it was, what other things were going on around me. But in that period I was very busy with all these activities, and it all seemed perfectly normal to me.'

As a reward for his work Duban and other gifted children went to camps, both at home and abroad, though usually in Eastern bloc countries, but once, in 1984, to Paris. Sometimes he enjoyed special privileges. 'In school you weren't allowed to wear your hair long. The test was that the teacher would put her hands through your hair and it couldn't be longer than the teacher's fingers. But I was allowed to have my hair long. Of course, all the other children hated me for it. Some of the teachers could be quite strict with me as well.

'At that time, you weren't allowed to do anything different from everyone else, and everything was very regimented. My relationship with other children was a little bit strained, precisely because they saw me as privileged. But I was working doubly hard to keep my grades up in school.

'It's true, I didn't have that many friends, except two boys who lived in the same block of flats as I did. Apart from them, my friends were grown-ups and the other children I was working with who did the same thing as me. We knew each other very well because we spent so much time together over a few years and participated in the same shows. We invented ways to play and use up our energy. The same group of children did all the shows, so we were practically growing up together.

'Often, I was excused from school. When the final rehearsals started for one of the homage shows, I would be allowed to miss classes, but this did not mean that I was allowed to miss the exams at the end of the year. None of the teachers would let me pass if I hadn't studied just because I was performing for the Ceauşescus.

'There were two categories of participants at these homage shows. There were the regular people, who were normally working in factories and plants; they quite enjoyed the shows because they were missing work. Even today we say about those communist times, "They were pretending to be working and the employers were pretending to be paying them".

'Then there were us children. We were treated differently, we didn't have to stand in the sun for hours on end [like the rest of the assembled audience] because we were actually artists, and we weren't just a faceless mass of people. But it's true that there were children who were exploited, and sometimes they would faint.

'Sometimes I did enjoy the shows, sometimes I didn't. Some of them were boring. As I got older, they all started to become boring and annoying and I started to realize how pointless they were. But all you could do was swallow your frustration and find the inner strength to go on because if, God forbid, you were to refuse, it would create problems for the entire family, including you.

'Like any children, we imagined all sorts of things and we got up to all sorts of nonsense. For example, we were participating in this well-known event called "The Plough", and there was always a very young child involved. Maybe he was three or four years old, he had to be very young and very light, and he represented the "New Year". He was dressed in a one-colour suit from head to toe, and the coming year was written across his chest.

'Ceauşescu would pick up this child representing the New Year and lift him in his arms, showing the world that we had crossed over into the New Year. And the people would cheer for another year under the leadership of the great Ceauşescu.

'One year, there was a problem because the suit the little child was wearing was very slippery. As soon as Ceauşescu picked him up, the child started sliding down and the scene was absolutely hilarious. The president was struggling to show how prosperous the New Year would be, but the child kept sliding down from under his arm. He picked him up and continued his speech, but the child slid down again, so he did it over and over again. We were laughing (subtly, because we could not have done it in front of everyone).

'Of course, this shouldn't have happened and I do not know who got sacked after that, but I have to tell you that everyone was sniggering. It was meant to be broadcast on television and the producers had to cut the scene so as to avoid any embarrassment.

'There were some very old members of the Central Committee who would fall asleep during performances. They must have seen the same performances over and over again, so many times.

'There were no instances of someone refusing to do something, or doing it badly intentionally, no way… It was out of the question. All the performers were carefully screened in advance. They would not bring in complete strangers, and they wouldn't use people who could not speak or who had any psychological problems… Moreover, everyone was so frightened of doing something wrong that they didn't get any ideas, they just couldn't make any mistakes. The fear was so great that they all gave their best performance.

'The only breaks we got were when we were playing cards and at that time I became a master at whist. I had whole years of practice at this game… I also really enjoyed imitating Ceauşescu, blissfully unaware of the risks. So when I was in a small group, with the door closed behind me, I would impersonate him giving a speech, or I'd find a dead moment and start talking like Ceauşescu while we were playing cards. I'd start saying, "Dear comrades and friends, I'd like you to deal the cards faster because otherwise you will be in trouble" in a Ceauşescu voice.

'It was pretty easy to imitate Ceauşescu because his pronunciation was unique. He was easily imitated because he had all these particularities, because of his diction; because of the way he pronounced words, which sounded hilarious at times. It was entertaining precisely because you were doing something so dangerous. You were playing with fire as you could lose your freedom for mocking comrade

Nicolae Ceauşescu. This type of humour was very dangerous indeed, that's why everyone enjoyed it so much.

'Gradually, I started seeing in Ceauşescu the cause of all our fears and problems – that food was rationed, that the electricity would get cut off, that we only had two hours of TV a day, that children only got to watch two or three minutes of cartoons per week, every Sunday. We were unbelievably happy if we got to see a *Tom and Jerry* cartoon that was longer than four or five minutes. All these things happened because of one person.'

On one occasion Andrei had problems about reciting a poem to Elena Ceauşescu. 'The poem said she was a good, loving and protecting mother. As a child, my own mother was the one who was loving! So I found it quite difficult to relate to those verses. I told my mother that I couldn't recite the poem because I didn't believe in it. I couldn't say that Elena Ceauşescu was a good, loving and protective mother. Luckily, my mum had a brilliant idea which saved me. She told me to imagine that when I was looking at Elena Ceauşescu and reciting those words that I was actually seeing my own mother's face. Her advice helped me overcome a situation which could have become quite dangerous.

'As a child, I saw the Ceauşescu couple as a bit of a pantomime. I saw these homage shows for what they actually were: soap balloons. The shows were very artificial, the people involved only put in physical effort and there was no faith involved. Nobody believed in what they were saying, no one believed those slogans, but the fear of not being able to see your family, or be close to the ones you love, made you take part in these artificial shows and treat them as the real thing.'

NICU COVACI

GUITARIST NICU COVACI is the leader of a legendary Romanian rock band called Phoenix. He's an iconic musician in his country and although now in his 60s is still immensely popular. Today he lives in Spain, but since 1990 has returned regularly to Romania for concerts.

Phoenix were launched in 1962 when Nicu was still at school. The band soon began doing cover versions of Beatles songs, but they were forced to change their style after Nicolae Ceauşescu visited the Far East in 1971. He toured North Korea, China and Vietnam and, inspired by the hard-line communism he saw there, instituted a mini cultural revolution on his return. He told the Executive Committee of the Romanian Communist Party that culture should be ideological, militant and anti-Western.

The communist regime suggested that all rock bands should draw their inspiration from Romanian culture. These restrictions forced Covaci to look towards Romanian folk tradition, pagan rituals and mysticism for his inspiration and, in doing so, he came up with a unique sound.

By the mid-1970s Phoenix were hugely popular inside Romania, largely due to their music but also because of their thinly veiled criticism of the communist regime. The Securitate increasingly harassed members of the band and in 1976 Covaci married a Dutch woman and left the country. Returning to bring in relief aid after a powerful earthquake in 1977, he managed to arrange the escape from Romania of all the other band members bar one. Before their defection Phoenix had sold over two million albums, a huge number by Romanian standards.

Even adopting the long hair that was the trademark of rock stars in the West caused Covaci and his friends problems. 'We had big problems – at school, as well as in the street. We were sent home from school to cut our hair and to shave. They even gave me money saying, "Go get a haircut!" I went home, I put some oil in my hair, fixed it tight behind the ears, so that the ears were visible, and I got away with it for a while.

'There were members of the Communist Youth Union who would take you by force to have a haircut. Police would take away your ID papers and would only return them if you had your hair cut.'

However, as regular performers for the Communist Youth Union, Covaci believes they received some kind of protection. 'They could have harassed us more because we were going against the stream but somebody must have protected us. It's possible that the children of the party elite liked us, and that helped.

'When I was still a student the Securitate summoned me to a special office – I didn't even know that they had a Securitate office in our faculty. And there was a big guy there – twice as big as me – who said, "Comrade Covaci, I hear that you threatened to raise hell among the students". "I never said such a thing, but I like the idea!" I replied. Then he started to threaten me. I said, "I know very well that every third person around me is your spy. I don't care and I'm not afraid. I've got nothing to hide. You can hire as many spies as you like. I'll tell you to your face what I've got to say." And I left.'

Covaci resisted all efforts to make him a member of the Communist Party, telling fellow students through a microphone in the university main hall, 'Thanks for your trust but I don't think I'll be up to the task. And I'm not that interested either.'

'Throughout our career in Romania we used to have gigs at the seaside. We spent three to four months there every year. Of course, we met girls from Sweden, Norway, Germany, Holland – from everywhere. And they brought us everything we wanted. We discovered whisky and all sorts of drugs because the girls always had some with them. But nothing tempted us into addiction.

'The fact was that we had the best instruments and dressed as we pleased. People would turn their heads in the street to look at us. All this was proof that we had chosen the right path, and that gave us strength. These were our joys and our fun. On top of all that we had money – more than now.

'And we had become a symbol for protest. We had found a way to protest more subtly in our lyrics and everyone identified with us. And this is what made us so hugely successful. At a certain point the country was divided in two – on the one side us and the ordinary people, and on the other side the leadership that lived on another planet.

'On the other hand, we were so successful from a commercial point of view that state institutions, like ARIA (the official artists' agency) and ELECTRECORD (the state recording house), made more money than they ever dreamed of. And the money earned by us was used to finance the recording of Ceauşescu's speeches on vinyl discs. In other words, we financed other stuff. Football teams, for example. We were the goose laying golden eggs for them.'

Raw emotion and an inner fury contributed to the Phoenix sound. 'We were angry about all the things we weren't allowed to do. For all the narrow paths we were forced to follow. The fact is that for us the West was another planet. We studied geography, we learned many things, but we couldn't step beyond the frontier. When Ceauşescu returned from North Korea and passed the "June laws" that stipulated that all Romanian art must draw its roots from authentic Romanian traditions and folklore, we were accused of "importing foreign influence".

'According to those new laws we had no choice but to sing in Romanian. However, we thought, "You want folklore, you'll have folklore", and we started to study thoroughly the authentic folklore – old traditions and rituals which are older than any Christian tradition.

'So, we took advantage of Ceauşescu's new laws and we created a new musical style – world music as it's called today. It was a powerful music, forceful – like rock music – but it drew its roots from the pre-Christian Romanian folklore. This was happening in the early 1970s.

'Of course, after discovering our authentic Romanian "values" and roots, we weren't interested in mimicking Western culture any more. But, as we sang in Romanian, using an archaic vocabulary they couldn't put us on a par with the Western bands.'

Despite growing harassment, Phoenix were still sanctioned to perform publicly in order to raise funds for the regime. Soldiers and undercover police mingled with audiences to crack down on dissent.

'The biggest slap on their cheek was when we defected from under their noses. If they captured us, they would have killed us. No doubt about it. We took that risk and that was our greatest victory.'

Covaci had been interrogated for two weeks in 1976, after which he renounced his Romanian citizenship; he was also given a passport after marrying a Dutch woman and was therefore permitted to leave the country. 'I had been warned, "Watch out because you are in great danger." It was so easy to end up in a madhouse there, tied to a bed, with them saying, "He was taking drugs". I left the equipment, everything, and just said, "Keep rehearsing boys".

He returned in 1977 with a truck full of aid after the earthquake. Following a few concerts he suggested to his fellow band members that he smuggle them out of the country inside a set of loudspeakers. He had already stripped out the speakers and his mother – the only one who knew about his plan – had made black covers to disguise their backs. He gave Valium to the three band members who agreed to go, and they had to adopt compact yoga positions for the whole journey.

'I planned that we would cross at the best-guarded Romanian border checkpoint, the Danube dam at Turnu Severin at night, when there's no queue, when nobody would have imagined that somebody could try such a thing.'

As expected, Covaci was challenged by the guards, who searched the truck while he ate sausages and drank wine. Eventually they joined him, swallowing large amounts of alcohol. They discovered wolf and boar furs, cigarettes, whisky and money, all of which they confiscated as Covaci had planned. But they failed to discover the hidden human cargo. 'One of the band members had a soldier sitting on the box he was in. And the soldier was drunk and singing and kicking his heels on the side of the box.

'On the Serbian side it was thick fog. By 6 a.m. we were on top of a mountain and I could only see the tops of the trees. I stopped and let the boys out. They kept asking, "Where are we?" I said, "In heaven." You should have seen their faces.'

CITIZENS AT PLAY

'Since the hand of the State penetrates even to the inside of its citizens, every genuine struggle for one's soul becomes an openly political act.'

Václav Havel

ACCORDING TO MARXIST-LENINIST ideology, capitalism and communism took very different attitudes to leisure time. In the West it was simply a cathartic release from the burden of work. In the East, however, it offered the perfect opportunity to develop state socialism through the enhancement of health, creativity and, especially, sporting excellence.

That said, the East German Communist Party was also wary of the subversive potential of leisure time. Western society was considered a bad influence on socialist youth, and its iconic elements – rock'n'roll, long hair, Levi's jeans – were viewed as products of the class enemy. To counter this, long-haired youths would sometimes find themselves arrested and given a compulsory short-back-and-sides. The state even devised its own versions of trendy youth culture, such as an officially approved dance called the 'Lipsi'. It never caught on.

Above all, the party sought to control its citizens' time off through participation in vast, government-run leisure organizations. Holidays were often run by youth organizations or approved trade unions – in East Germany, for example, 70 per cent of all schoolchildren and apprentices took organized holidays. Most did not involve going abroad and the maximum stay in factory- and state-owned holiday centres was 13 days.

This mass ordering of leisure served as a 'transmission belt' through which the Communist Party exercised control of the population. Pressure to conform and a fear of being penalized at work or at home were powerful factors in someone's decision to join a leisure organization. Yet there is also evidence that people enjoyed their association with organizations and were even able to shape what was on offer. In this way the system was enabling as well as coercive, and many activities had little or no political baggage. Indeed, in their leisure activities many people found a sense of normality to balance the demands of communist doctrine.

One activity was extolled above all others. Sport was an easily organized, healthy, empowering medium and most work brigades and factories had competitive teams. This provided a vital military and economic dividend because socialism required a fit population to defend the homeland and achieve productivity goals. But, more importantly, sport was an ideological weapon that could demonstrate the superiority of the communist system. And East Germany's athletes didn't let their leaders down.

Between 1972 and 1988 the country won 384 Olympic medals. At Montreal in 1976 the DDR's haul was an astounding 40 gold medals, turning a nation of 17 million into a sporting superpower that for a time rivalled the United States. The key to this unprecedented success lay in the performance of East Germany's female athletes – achieved through the deployment of a top-secret doping system that bypassed individual choice and would eventually permanently damage the health of competitors. Side effects included hair growth, expanded musculature, deepened voices, liver and heart disease, depression, cancer, infertility, gynaecological problems, miscarriages, birth deformities and sexual confusion.

Girls as young as 12 would unwittingly take the drugs and two million pills – mostly steroids and male-hormone boosters – were doled out to athletes each year. These were often described as 'vitamins'. The administration of this vast cheating machine was carried out by the government's elite sports federation under State Plan 14.25. And, just to keep everyone on message, the Stasi was given a monitoring role.

ANDREAS KRIEGER

ANDREAS KRIEGER WAS one of East Germany's star athletes. At the European Championships in Stuttgart in 1986 he won gold with a shot-put of 21.10 metres. Only back then Andreas was called Heidi and was officially a female. Looking at him today with his muscular, broad shoulders and facial stubble, you wonder how the DDR ever got away with it.

In 1979, aged 14, the then Heidi received an invitation to join the prestigious Dynamo Sports Club and Boarding School in East Berlin, which was sponsored by the Stasi. Towards the end of the second year her coaches prescribed a course of bright blue vitamin pills and almost immediately her body began to change. Her clothes stopped fitting, her muscles expanded, her facial features broadened and her moods became volatile. By the time she was 18 she weighed 220 pounds and was developing male sexual characteristics. Trainers would privately refer to her as 'Hormone Heidi'.

Of course, those bright blue pills weren't vitamins but androgenic-anabolic steriods called Oral-Turinabol and known colloquially as 'blue beans'. Available only on prescription, they helped athletes build muscle by enabling them to train harder. In 1986, the year she won gold in the shot-putt at the European championships, Heidi was fed a massive dose of nearly 3,000 milligrams of anabloic steriods – that's about 1,000 milligrams more than the disgraced Canadian sprinter Ben Johnson received in 1988, the year he 'won' the 100 metres at the Seoul Olympics.

Krieger recalls how he was talent-spotted in 1979 following four years at a training centre in Pankow. By the age of 16 his coach was providing packs of 'supporting substances', including blue pills wrapped in silver foil, with instructions on daily dosage. 'He would tell me, "These are to help you. Everyone takes them." I trusted him. Soon I was able to practise more and to lift heavier weights. Lifting weights was part of throwing – it was normal to build muscle

– and I didn't perceive how abruptly I had bulked up. I've always had a somewhat coarse voice and neither my mother nor I realized that my voice had become even deeper. When our grandmother phoned and I answered she would always say, "Frank? Detlef? Thomas?" – they were my three brothers – and I would have to answer, "No, it's Heidi". That was always funny and made us smile. But I would also have terribly unpleasant experiences, which made me prefer staying at home rather than going out to let others bully me on the street. People would call me a transvestite or a queer, which I found incredibly hard to cope with.

'The curious thing about it was that for a very long time I didn't recognize myself. I attended boarding school for a year but didn't know what to do with the girls and that entire environment. I wasn't interested in boys and I wasn't interested in fashion. All I wanted was to sleep, to eat and to be let alone. However, I would have emotional conflicts from time to time; I would always feel that I didn't belong with the others. I so wanted to belong and yet I didn't. I didn't know what to do with that pain. I then started hurting myself so I could start to feel something.

'I would scratch my hands and invent the maddest stories to explain why they were bleeding. Once I absconded from boarding school and my mother couldn't comprehend this. She would tell me, "That is what you wanted. You wanted to practise sports. Now stick to it!" She misinterpreted my plea for help. And I wasn't able to express myself or tell anyone about my problems. The only solution we found was for me to commute on a daily basis between home and the sports field.

'I was self-harming early on but when I had my first success people would pat me on the back and congratulate me. Those who had previously ignored me would suddenly take notice and that was enough to make me feel better. I would get the feeling that I belonged with the others. It would all turn out to be illusory: people only saw my achievements, not me [as a person].

'But those first achievements really boosted my self-confidence. I realized that I didn't have to justify why I didn't conform to the norm. "I am Heidi Krieger. I am the one who for the very first time won two competitions at the Youth Competitions of Friendship (*Jugendwettbewerbe der Freundschaften*)." I had fulfilled my plan. This made me grow in confidence. But the crazy thing was that if someone asked me about emotional issues I would turn into an insecure mess. I also became more aggressive. They would send me to a psychologist and I would tell him, in confidence, all the things I didn't like or didn't approve of. Then I'd go to training and the coach would talk to me about those very same things I had just told the psychologist. It made me realize I couldn't trust anyone.'

By 1991 Heidi's career was over. Damaged joints, tendons and vertebrae meant she could no longer compete, and she felt emotionally and sexually confused. But it wasn't until she finally sought medical advice in the mid-1990s that a doctor suggested she check records to establish what she'd actually taken. Gradually the awful truth emerged. 'It was only after the Berlin Wall came down that things became clearer to me. Then I realized I was in the wrong body, that something wasn't right. I didn't even know how to define my situation up until then because although I liked women

I knew I wasn't lesbian. The word "transsexual" meant nothing to me until 1995.

'Looking back I loved being a sporting champion for the DDR. I was proud of my country on that score, and believed that we athletes strengthened the socialist republic with our achievements. I wasn't aware of being confined because I was able to go abroad. I learned how athletes in other countries had to earn money from sport to finance their studies. In the DDR that wasn't the case. Those little details made me feel happy to return home.

'The only problem was that I didn't know what to do with guys. And I wasn't allowed to officially start something with a girl because to be lesbian was absolutely unacceptable in the DDR, at least officially, and certainly not in public. Basically, I started hiding my feelings and became more aggressive because I wanted to be left alone.

'Around 1987 I did have a relationship with a woman. We tried to keep it very secret but I believe some comrades from the club knew about us. The Stasi had a finger in every pie. They might have tolerated it because I was good at shot-put but if life had continued like that and the Berlin Wall hadn't fallen, I wouldn't be alive today. After I was done with athletics I basically didn't have any support left. There was a huge void, a huge gap. I felt as if I was losing ground. I was neither fish nor fowl and I didn't relate to my body any more.'

Over a 20-year period up to the fall of the Wall in 1989 more than 10,000 East German athletes were doped. The government knew that steriods had the greatest impact on women's performances, and every sports organization in the world was wise to the competitive edge they gave. Yet, amazingly, only one DDR athlete was officially caught (that was Iolna Slupianek, a shot putter in the European Cup in 1977, who tested positive for steroid use). The doping programme was hushed up by forcing coaches and doctors to sign confidentiality agreements; a measure enforced through a network of 3,000 informers within the sporting establishment. The athletes were also secretly tested before international competitions and those whose results were positive did not travel abroad.

Although more than 300 former sporting officials have been convicted of doping offences since the fall of the Berlin Wall, many athletes are still waiting for justice and compensation. In May 2000, Krieger – by then known as Andreas following a sex-change operation – was in court to confront East Germany's former top sports official, Manfred Ewald, and leading sports doctor, Manfred Höppner. Both were convicted of being accessories to the intentional bodily harm of athletes. Ewald was given a suspended sentence; Höppner got probation.

A chance encounter while working in a pet shop in 1995 gave Krieger renewed hope. A young colleague revealed that he was a transsexual who had gone through a sex-change operation. 'He explained that transsexuality had been a recognized illness in Germany since 1978, and told me how he had airbrushed his past. He didn't keep old photos and nobody was allowed to use his old name.

'They operated on me in mid-March 1997,' Two months later I received a letter from the Central Investigation Authority for Governmental and Reunification Criminality (*Zentrale Ermittlungsstelle für Regierungs – und Vereinigungskriminalität*) with regard to the proceedings against Ewald and Höppner. I had arranged for a news embargo about my operation to prevent anyone from identifying me as Heidi Krieger. But I realized then that it wouldn't work. Heidi still existed. My decision to give evidence at that trial, to join the action against those people and to say, "Yes, they ought to be punished for what they have done" made it clear to me that it was not possible for Heidi to disappear. Heidi still exists. I am still a bit "Heidi". That is my life. I used to be a woman and I will always remain a woman up to a certain extent.

'I knew that if I gave evidence someone would inform the press that a former female shot putter had turned into a man. It would be far better if I appeared upfront and tried to take charge of the publicity myself in order to avoid the voyeuristic approach of the commercial broadcasters. I wanted to prevent a scandal and avoid having the press swarming over me.'

Before the trial started Krieger contacted Professor Werner Franke, a molecular biologist and author of *Doping*, a highly acclaimed book on performance enhancing drugs. He explained that, for some teenagers, sexuality wasn't fixed during adolescence and that the pills Heidi took had acted as a catalyst, which enhanced her 'masculine' side. 'Suddenly my situation started making sense,' said Krieger. 'I told the professor I wanted to come forward before somebody exposed me in public, and he agreed to deliver a medical commentary on the effect of the substances and consequently what had happened to me. I wasn't a doctor – I wouldn't have been able to talk about this stuff. We appeared together in public and I really appreciated that.

'The damage those pills caused was horrendous. People got cancer even though no one in their family had ever suffered from the disease. There were adult women with uteruses like 11-year-olds so they couldn't get pregnant. I remembered how older female athletes had to take a "baby year". If they wanted to become pregnant they had to make a formal request, which the sporting authorities had to approve. Then an athlete had to live without any pills whatsoever.

'They would check to ensure women conformed. They feared the second generation might be damaged, and I believe some malformed children were born. There must have been female athletes who said to themselves, "I want to be pregnant, but I'm not going to ask permission from my coach".

'In addition to the blue pills I had to take birth control pills. Afterwards I learnt that male and female hormones needed to be balanced but at the time I didn't see why I needed birth control pills. So after six months I simply stopped taking them and my breasts started hurting very badly from sclerosis. The doctor was completely unsympathetic and just sent me home saying, "Well, you did what you wanted and now you have to live with the pain".

'In retrospect you realize what was going on, how narrow-minded you were, what tunnel vision you had, how my sport and the sports forum were the only things that mattered. You would ask yourself, "Am I allowed to do this?", "How am I supposed to move?", "Am I allowed to go now?", "Am I allowed to stand up and wash my hands?" – you weren't yourself; you merely functioned. In German the word *dressiert* means "trained" as applied to animals. That is the right word. They trained me well.

'I look back, horrified, at the way the whole, perfidious doping system functioned; how the cogs of school, sports scout and sports club linked together and how in the background they analyzed every detail for keeping athletes focused. When I tried to escape from boarding school they pushed me back because they had seen my potential. They enforced this without pity. East Germany took my life away from me – the ability to make my own decisions – and without asking me. They made a lab[oratory] rat out of me because they saw my potential. I wasn't allowed to decide for myself what I wanted to become.

'When I won at the European Championships it seemed incredibly easy. I had trained well, my technique was very good and that four-kilogram shot just flew. I hit 21.10 metres and I beat everyone who mattered. But when I stood on the podium and heard the anthem, I thought, "Damn, now they want to always see this!" And I didn't know if I was able to do it.'

Despite his ordeal, Krieger admits that he didn't see the fall of the Berlin Wall as cause for celebration. He recalls how during the final days, when demonstrators were besieging the Wall, Home Ministry officials arrived at his gym seeking to put DDR athletes on standby in case of trouble. The idea was for them to stand beside police officers and appease the masses. Athletes who had previous engagements could choose not to go and Krieger wasn't slow to excuse himself. 'To be honest, I was afraid,' he said. 'I didn't understand why people were on the streets wanting to have that crazy Western lifestyle. Just to have Milka chocolate rather than Crack chocolate? Stuff that! Now I don't miss the DDR, although at first

I had great difficulties in coping, in finding a personal place in the new society and realizing that everyone had to think for themselves.'

During the Ewald/Höppner hearings in 2000, Krieger met female swimmer Ute Krause who was also there to testify. They got married in 2002 and today they live together in Magdeburg where Krieger runs a clothing shop. His gold medal from the 1986 European Championships has been used to make a trophy in the shape of the molecule in Oral-Turinabol, which is competed for each year by German athletes in the fight against doping.

'These days, apart from normal bodily wear and tear, I feel incredibly well' Krieger said. 'In Ute I have found a wonderful person from whom I don't have to hide, who knows how to handle me – because I sometimes see myself as very complicated – and who doesn't judge me. I feel like I won top prize in the lottery and married it. I have what I wanted all those years ago when I tried to be part of a group through athletics. I have a sense of belonging.'

JARINA ŽITNÁ

IT IS EXACTLY this sentiment, the need to feel part of a successful – even powerful – organization, that inspired Sokol ('Falcon' in English), a sporting organization founded in Czechoslovakia in the nineteenth century. Sokol was closely linked to nationalism and democracy. Its festivals, or *Slets*, proved immensely popular with Czechs and Slovaks and its membership grew to over a million between the two world wars. Sokol also represented the last mass resistance to the communist takeover when, during the 1948 *Slet*, its members symbolically turned their heads away from the communist leadership as they passed the central podium. The state government banned Sokol after 1948 and it was not permantly restored to the fabric of national life until 1990.

In communist Czechoslovakia Sokol was replaced with the highly regimented Spartakiáda festival. Held every five years, Spartakiáda featured thousands of gymnasts performing in consort before some 200,000 spectators in Prague's cavernous Strahov Stadium. The event's whole *raison d'être* was to emphasize the value of group dynamics over individual prowess, and it was considered very important to the communist regime. It helped to underline themes important to state propaganda – building socialism, individual sacrifice for the collective good and national unity.

For many Czechoslovaks, whether they were interested in mass gymnastics or not, involvement in Spartakiáda was akin to a political endorsement of the regime. For this reason it became a blasphemy to some Sokol enthusiasts.

Jarina Žitná was no communist but she was heavily involved in Spartakiáda. She composed and choreographed the massed ranks of senior girls at three different Spartakadias (1975, 1980 and 1985) and among her greatest accomplishments was choreographing 16,000 young female gymnasts in the stadium for perhaps her signature work – *The Buds*. 'Spartakiáda was an effort to present communism as an enormous force that influences everything and takes care of its people,' said Žitná. 'People from abroad should realize that during 40 years of communist rule schools were teaching, doctors were curing people, the health service worked, sportsmen were running and jumping, singers sang, actors acted and we all exercised. We knew for sure that the state machinery was in a way abusing us; abusing the work of ordinary people in order to boost the image of a socialist physical education. But the gymnasts didn't give a damn.

'We realized that we had to exist somehow. Spartakiáda was a social bond – despite what many may think – and the young people who started there had the most beautiful experience of their lives. As for *The Buds*, it is a unique piece, a Czechoslovakian pop music legend. It generated chanting from the audience and had beautiful lyrics that children could easily understand, such as, "My only aim is to grow and to blossom". So it was nice all round.

'One trainer walked the girls to the train station on the outskirts of town and they started singing the song they had just performed along the way. If the gymnasts take to it in this way then you know it has an incredibly emotional impact on them. And their mothers sang along with them. The sense of – let's call it – fraternity was enormous. Unfortunately, the media interpreted it as an achievement of the Communist Party.

'I think that we – the trainers, the teachers and the organizers who dealt with the practical side of Spartakiáda – have nothing to be ashamed of. We brought about great progress, we brought a lot of beautiful things to so many people, and as for the so-called political abuse, of course, anything can be abused. It's interesting that no one asks questions about our Olympic winners yet everyone points a finger at our children doing a performance in Strahov Stadium. That's downright garbage. We reconciled ourselves to this attitude because we knew there's nothing we could have done. We wouldn't have been able to teach, put on a performance or anything.

'Our gymnasts didn't care about building socialism. They wanted to be there, to perform, even though it wasn't cheap. Some people were assisted by their companies – I once got sponsorship for a skirt – but that was all; 99 per cent of the people attended because they had the zest for it.

'I was born into a Sokol family. It provided a moral profile, taught the virtues of personal responsibility and courage and formed you both spiritually and physically. I think the communists were afraid of Sokol because it involved people with strong convictions who were not used to keeping their mouths shut, as was demonstrated at the Sokol parade in 1948. At that time the communists still thought they might preserve the Sokol organization under a different label. But it didn't work out.

'From the point of view of people deeply harmed by the system, Spartakiáda was contributing to the honour and glory of the communist regime. On the other hand, I believe, the positive aspects of our work completely balanced this out. You can't blame everything on 40 years of communism; you also need to consider the many negative things that came from the West. The exaggerated individualism, where everybody is a hero, this is certainly not good.'

DR VOLKER PETZOLD

THE CZECH ATTEMPT to hijack Sokol and replace it with Spartakiáda was typical of the communist battle for young hearts and minds. In East Germany the battle began at an even younger age through a home-grown animation series on telelevision, *Sandman*

(*Sandmännchen*). Created in 1959, the show soon established iself as a firm favourite with children and adults alike. Featuring an animated puppet figure called Sandman it was designed to send East Germany's children happy to bed and to win their hearts for socialism. For generations of East Germans, Sandman remains an icon to this day

Dr Volker Petzold, an East German academic and a leading authority on the programme, says its animators had a firm belief in the ideology of socialism. 'They didn't do it because they were forced to, but because they enjoyed it,' he said. 'They had a vision of socialism and communism – the creation of a better world, an ideal world. Obviously, that was part of DDR ideology. You only have to watch a couple of episodes to see the political aspects.

'You find parades, sometimes the army, sports, technology, and you find outer space. Space exploration, and the achievements of the Soviet Union cosmonauts, were reflected in the series because this reflected progress; it was believed that communism would also flourish in outer space. Belief in technological progress was the strongest feature of *Sandmännchen* especially in the 1960s and 1970s. And that is what made it so very popular. It transmitted the belief in technological progress to children. Clearly, there is nothing negative about space exploration. And it made socialism appear victorious.

'One very early episode is set in Africa, in 1964. When you watch it today you think that it's something exotic, set in the jungle. The Sandman even arrives in a Land Rover – it's written in the script that the vehicle type should be a Land Rover. Some monkeys and some little African children jump around and the children learn about the liberation of the oppressed nations of Africa.

'There were other episodes featuring the Arabic world. The DDR had cultivated an amicable relationship with Iraq, and Iraqi television worked with German broadcasting to collaborate on two episodes set in Iraq. The Sandman travelled there on a flying horse and a magic carpet in the style of the *Arabian Nights*. It was noted in the script that Iraqi viewers should be able to recognize their country. That obviously had something to do with politics.'

Sometimes the Sandman's adventures had to be reworked according to the changing political landscape. 'In 1961, the year the Berlin Wall was built, one episode was plainly and simply called "Sailing Boat",' said Petzold. 'The Sandman arrives at a children's home on the Baltic Sea by boat. You can see the open sea in the background. But when I saw that episode in a later, filmed version I realized that it didn't show the sea any more but a lakeland area in Mecklenburg. That change was necessary because after the Wall was completed on 13 August 1961 sailing on the Baltic Sea was banned. That is a typical example of how politics exercised a negative influence on *Sandmännchen*.'

One later episode proved controversial. It featured a paraglider, although paragliders were banned in East Germany to prevent people using them to escape across the border.

DIVERTIS

WITH EASTERN EUROPEAN society so closely orchestrated by the state an urge to rattle barriers was inevitable. The trick was to find a counterculture that could mostly be tolerated by government yet remained anarchic enough to offer an escape from conformity. Comedy, particularly underground comedy, became a powerful tool of rebellion. Behind the Iron Curtain it offered a running commentary on daily life and a voice for the non-ideological majority.

Telling jokes could also, of course, get you imprisoned and there were limits even to oblique criticism of a regime. But humour provided a language through which the populations of Eastern Europe could converse with themselves. Even the party elite told jokes and occasionally sanctioned jibes directed at the regime, realizing that discontent needed a safety valve.

And so communism created its own brand of humour; coded references to political leaders, an absurdist perspective on the ever-widening gap between ideology and daily reality, and a heady sense of danger achieved through veiled critiques of communist rulers. It was an enclosed brand of humour that would eventually die alongside the political system it lampooned.

Toni Grecu and Silviu Petcu are two members of a Romanian comedy group called Divertis. Formed in 1981, Divertis performed at student gatherings and other shows subject to official censorship. From 1988, when conditions became extremely difficult, the group appeared in the closed environment of underground clubs or private parties, telling jokes about food shortages, housing conditions and Elena Ceauşescu's illiteracy. While these events were not censored the general public had no access and the occasional filmed footage was never shown on Romanian TV. The last Divertis show under the Ceauşescu regime was on 14 December 1989, a week before the revolution started in Bucharest and two days before the unrest in Timişoara.

'At the time we weren't interested in taking a clear political stance against the government,' said Grecu. 'We just wanted to deride the stupidity of communist ideology and the way it was imposed. We were fresh out of school where we'd had propaganda shoved down our throats. From the president of the country to the most insignificant party member the basic vocabulary was the same, "We must give as much as we can to our country," "We must work as effectively as possible," "We must always come first" and "We must always exceed our targets".

'All these things represented a fantastic source of humour for us because lying had become pervasive in our society. The entire press was hailing our standard of living as fantastic and praising our progress towards building communism in our beloved motherland when, in fact, the truth was tragic: we did not have food, we did not have heating during the winter, we had electricity only a few hours a day.

'We couldn't mention names because if you were to target a party leader, especially Ceauşescu and his wife, you would be sent straight to jail or maybe worse. So we would hint at things. We had a humorous language based on innuendo and the public would look for hidden meanings, even though at face value our statements seemed completely innocent. But we never considered ourselves as dissidents in any sense of the word, either at that time or even now. It was our way of having fun and we had a good laugh about the sheer stupidity of that period.

'It was enough to say the word "food" on stage and the public would burst into applause because they thought you were being very brave using a forbidden word. It got to the point where the Ministry of Culture and Communist Education decided such words were not allowed on stage, not in shows, TV, newspapers or anywhere else. Neither were you allowed to say the word "dollar". It was thought that someone who used the word "dollar" must have a hidden agenda; he must be the enemy of the regime, the enemy of the working class and be seeking the downfall of the country.'

Such was the surreal nature of Romanian censorship that Divertis was sometimes able to incorporate a censor's demands and actually produce a better script. 'We gave a performance in 1986 in Cluj,' recalls Petcu. 'The censorship people checked our script and found one joke which mentioned dollars, so we thought we'd say roubles instead. They were outraged by this, crossed out the words and wrote in pencil "any other currency". And so we said exactly that: "We bought this piece of machinery for 300 any other currency." The public burst into hysterical laughter, it was funnier than either roubles or dollars.'

By now Divertis, along with other radical comedy groups, was being closely watched by the Securitate. The group's name had been flagged up following a student festival performance in 1983 at which they parodied a Romanian fairy tale about Prince Charming and Princess Ileana. Censors insisted that Ileana's name should be altered because it too closely resembled that of Elena, wife of Ceauşescu. But when Divertis changed the character's name to Maria Cosánzeana the reaction of the audience was extraordinary.

'Maria Cosánzeana was hilarious for a Romanian audience because they were used to Ileana being in this fairy tale and they

VERA OELSCHLEGEL is a distinguished actress and theatre director who was married to a member of the East German Politburo. The picture above shows her (right) on holiday in the Crimea with party leader Erich Honecker and his wife Margot. 'All of a sudden I was forced into this elite circle.'

JÜRGEN KRAUSE was Erich Honecker's cook. He is pictured, second from the left, after a deer hunt. 'I was brought up as a communist, as a servant of the government, and it actually made me very proud. Communism is a good thing when it's done right.'

ERIKA RIEMANN pictured (left) last year at Sachsenhausen. Under the communists, she spent part of a prison sentence at the former Nazi concentration camp for drawing a bow on a picture of Stalin when she was 14. The inset shows her as a teenager.

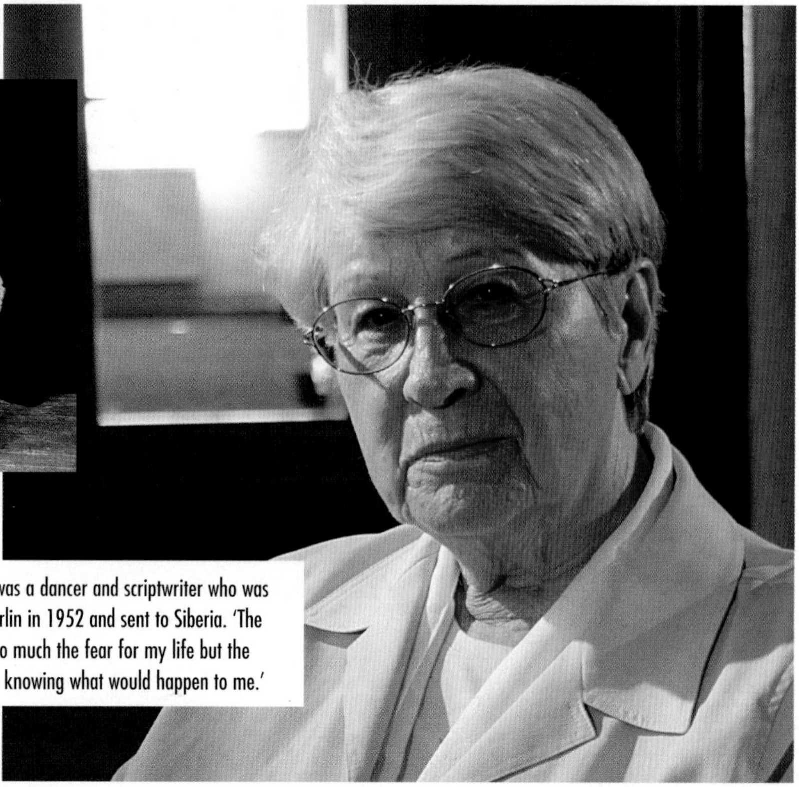

URSULA RUMIN was a dancer and scriptwriter who was kidnapped in East Berlin in 1952 and sent to Siberia. 'The worst thing was not so much the fear for my life but the hopelessness and not knowing what would happen to me.'

VLADIMÍR REMEK was a Czechoslovak cosmonaut. In 1978 he became the first man who wasn't a Soviet or an American to go into space. 'I felt I was embarking on something that could help my country enormously.'

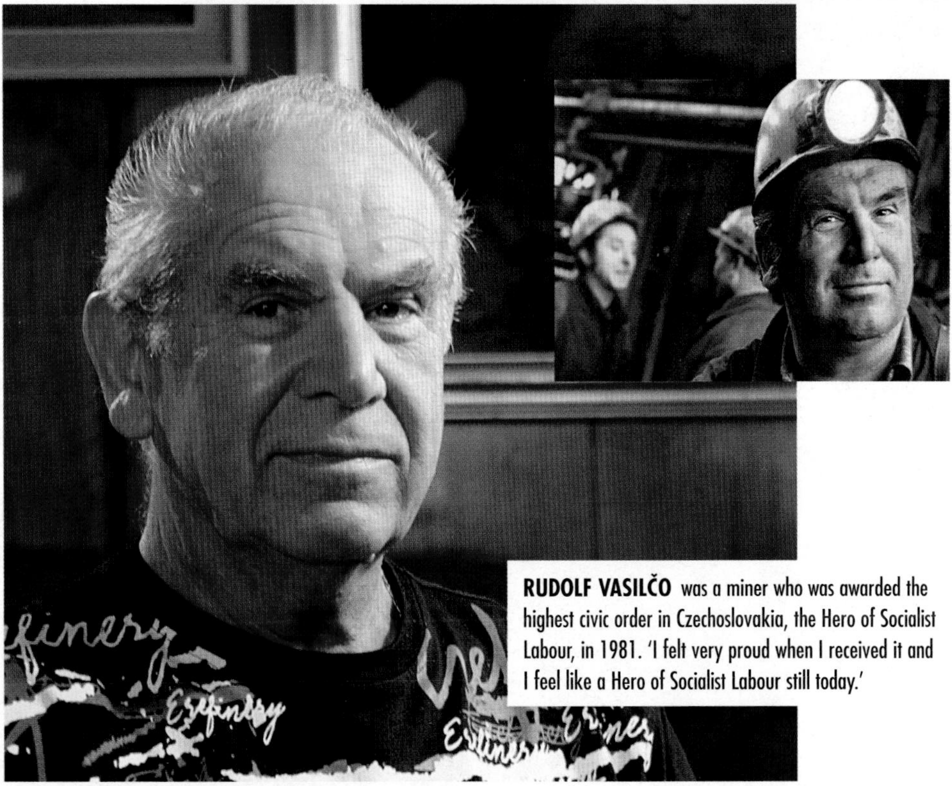

RUDOLF VASILČO was a miner who was awarded the highest civic order in Czechoslovakia, the Hero of Socialist Labour, in 1981. 'I felt very proud when I received it and I feel like a Hero of Socialist Labour still today.'

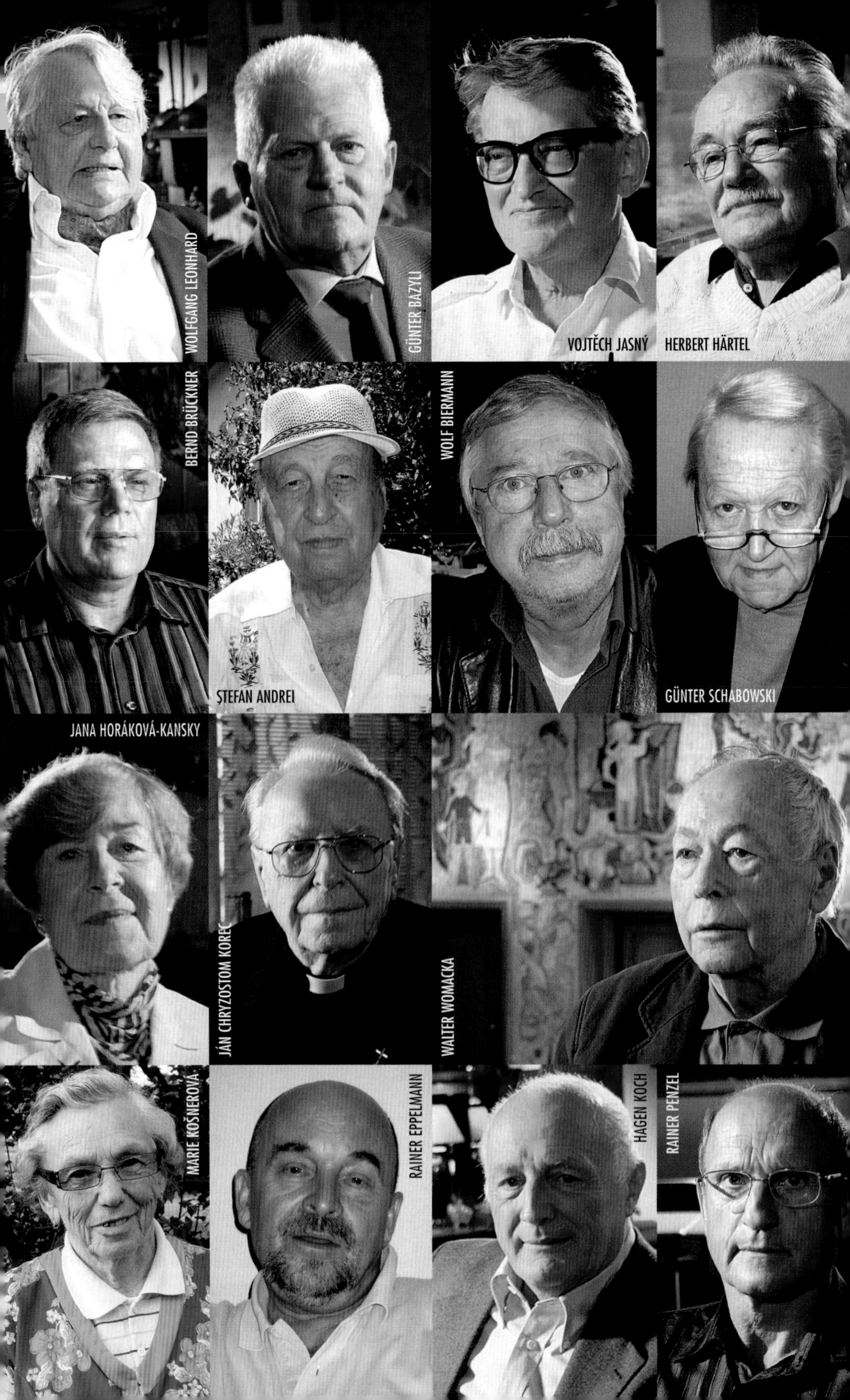
WOLFGANG LEONHARD
GÜNTER BAZYLI
VOJTĚCH JASNÝ
HERBERT HÄRTEL
BERND BRÜCKNER
ŞTEFAN ANDREI
WOLF BIERMANN
GÜNTER SCHABOWSKI
JANA HORÁKOVÁ-KANSKY
JÁN CHRYZOSTOM KOREC
WALTER WOMACKA
MARIE KOŠNEROVÁ
RAINER EPPELMANN
HAGEN KOCH
RAINER PENZEL

PAUL MUNTEANU
HORST KREETER
VASILE PARASCHIV
DIETMAR SCHÜRTZ
DANIELA DRAGHICI
VERA LENGSFELD
REGINA AND UWE KARLSTEDT
JOSEF JANÍČEK
KURT STARKE
VÁCLAV HAVEL
JUTTA GALLUS FLECK (LEFT) AND HER DAUGHTER
MILOŠ JAKEŠ
DAN VOINEA

WOLFGANG WELSCH organised escapes out of East Germany and became a target of attempted murder by a Stasi agent. 'I found out that I was the number one enemy of the East German state.'

JARINA ŽITNÁ was a choreographer at Czechoslovak mass games known as the Spartakadia, performed every five years before 200,000 in Prague's vast Strahov Stadium. 'Spartakadia was an effort to present communism as an enormous force that influences everything and takes care of its people.'

MARTA PUŠKOVÁ is a Romany woman who was forcibly sterilised by the Czechoslovak state. 'I think they wanted the Romany people to stop "spreading"; they wanted us to disappear.'

HEIDI WITTWER was an East German stripper. 'Striptease wasn't a common thing in East Germany. But then it suddenly started booming. I made loads of money.'

KAREL GOTT is Czechoslovakia's best-known singer, and was a big money earner for the communist regime, who tried to keep politics out of his act. 'If I had stood against the system I would have been finished as a singer.'

ANDREAS KRIEGER (formerly Heidi Krieger) was one of East Germany's star athletes and an unwitting victim of a state-sponsored doping programme. 'East Germany took my life away from me. They made a lab rat out of me.'

understood the reason for this change,' said Grecu. 'Our colleagues got a bit scared because the public was reacting in an unusual fashion. They weren't just applauding or laughing at a good joke. They were screaming their approval. As we got to the end of the story I knew what was coming, and I was trying to persuade my colleagues to get off stage immediately. I wanted us to stop before the ending because I thought we might actually get shot by the Securitate people.

'We were in front of an audience of about a thousand people and I was trying to communicate to my colleagues, who were also on stage, that we had to get out of there. But neither one of them looked in my direction. Then came the last line, "And so the two old people lived happily ever after, reconfirming the old Romanian proverb, 'A long life leads to the poverty of the people'." As soon as that line was uttered, the audience fell completely quiet; a silence that just didn't seem to end. We were frozen in front of our microphones and then all of a sudden they started slowly clapping, like in one of those cheesy American films. The whole audience joined in and started screaming and congratulating us.'

Petcu recalls, 'We ran off stage and we went straight home. We didn't stick around there because we realized the enormity of the situation. They looked for us; there were people who suffered because of this, some local party leaders were forced to resign. Many years later we found out that a recording of that show had been analyzed by the Securitate people, and that was why we were monitored closely afterwards. After 1987 we had to go underground and so the only people who knew about us were show organizers from the university, a few professors and obviously the students. We were not approved of by party officials.

'From 1988 onwards we weren't even mentioned in publicity material and we relied simply on word of mouth. It was never officially announced that Divertis was going to participate in an event; people were told, "Just come along and you'll see".

'On an earlier occasion we appeared at an event that drew a large audience – not just students – at the seaside resort of Costinesti. This was a festival called "Feasts of the Sea" and it included all sorts of games for young people holidaying in the resort. The atmosphere was very pleasant, relaxed and uninhibited. Even the Securitate officials were less vigilant – perhaps they had suffered sunstroke or something.

'Silviu was playing the role of Neptune, god of the sea. We had this idea that Neptune would resemble the "most beloved son of the people", the great leader Nicolae Ceauşescu, and this attracted the attention of the party officials, who had to do their jobs and justify their salaries and their mere existence. Neptune's travels were similar to the sort of international trips comrade Ceauşescu took to places such as North Korea, Sudan and Uganda, and various other African countries that even now are still dictatorships. This created a big scandal and soon the Securitate began looking for a recording of the show. They began to ask questions: who said the words, who wrote the script, who committed the crime, who recorded it? We only learned about this later.'

Petcu believes the group was extremely lucky to escape unscathed. 'The Neptune sketch had been recorded by Mr Partos, manager of Radio Holiday Costinesti,' he said. 'He received a call from the gate warning that the Securitate had arrived, and in that instant he started to record folk music over the only tape of our performance. The folk music was recording while he was talking to the Securitate people and by the end of the conversation the tape was completely erased and the evidence destroyed.'

In the last days of the Ceauşescu regime Divertis found itself playing the Winter Ball at the School of Electronics and Communications in Iasi. The city was a hotbed of student protest; anti-regime leaflets had been dropped in Unirii Square and police were massed, ready to stamp out trouble.

'On our way up to the performance hall we met three or four professors – all members of the Communist Party and all in charge of something within the polytechnic institute,' said Petcu. 'They told us, "Boys, today will be more difficult than any other day. Be extremely careful what you say on stage." It was the first time that someone had openly warned us.'

The show unfolded in what had become a highly charged atmosphere, and eventually officials barged into the group's dressing room ordering them to 'stop and go home'. 'We knew about what was happening in Timişoara because we were listening to Radio Free Europe,' said Grecu. 'Things were very, very tense. But we didn't realize exactly what was going on in Iasi on the night of 14 December until a week later.

'The people who came to our performance that evening were behaving very strangely. They weren't laughing at our jokes; they were laughing in an ostentatious way. It was unnatural for a student show. Our jokes had an underlying meaning aimed at the leadership of the Communist Party and the public's reaction was exaggerated, unusual. There was something strange floating in the atmosphere of that cultural hall.

'We were told, "Go straight home! Do not wander around the streets in big groups, do not congregate anywhere." We had never heard anything like that before. Then, on 16 December, the protests started in Timişoara and spread to Bucharest. I was living in Bucharest at the time and took part in the revolution, or whatever it was. It's still not clear what actually happened. Did we have a revolution? Did we participate in a *coup d'état*? Or did we take part in a show, a spectacle, with many actors and a lot of shooting? Sadly, we still don't know.

'The policies of the communist regime were so insane, especially after 1988, that you didn't feel like laughing any more. The censorship was so strict, the situation so dire and the lives of the ordinary people so unbearable that it became harder to laugh at these things. The Ceauşescu jokes and the unflagging belief that something would eventually change were the only things that could keep our spirits up. Without humour, Romanians would have had a much harder 45 years of communism.'

7

THE MEN WHO ABOLISHED GOD

Religion is the sigh of the oppressed creature, the heart of a heartless world, and the soul of soulless conditions. It is the opium of the people.

Karl Marx, 'A Contribution to the Critique of Hegel's Philosophy of Right' (1844)

COMMUNISM IS AN atheist ideology. When the 1917 Bolshevik revolution occurred in Russia the boast was that every church would be turned into a museum. The communists saw, quite rightly, that religion offered rival systems of belief and political power. Accordingly, all the communist regimes of Eastern Europe sought, at different times, to suppress, co-opt and control organized religion, with varying degrees of success.

Some religious bodies were more biddable than others and, after the fall of communism in 1989, revelations about Church collaboration with communist regimes and their secret police surprised many. This was especially true of the Romanian Orthodox Church. But, on other occasions, organized religion flexed its political muscle or acted as a catalyst for others to do so. The Protestant Church in East Germany was one of only a few institutions to achieve a degree of autonomy.

In Czechoslovakia there was the emergence of the highly influential 'Hidden Church', an underground movement that included clergy and lay people, predominantly from the Roman Catholic but also from the Orthodox and Protestant Churches. In 1948 the communist leadership of Czechoslovakia had described the Catholic Church as 'the last and most dangerous enemy'. Consequently, it bore the brunt of the communist assault on religion. Communists passed a law seizing most Church lands. They banned Catholic schools and the public wearing of crucifixes.

The Communist Party also spawned a number of pseudo-religious groups. In 1949 Catholic Action was formed but the Vatican excommunicated its members. In 1951 came the Peaceful Movement of Catholic Clergy (MHKD), followed 20 years later by Pacem in Terris. All three organizations were prepared to do the regime's dirty work.

In March 1950 there was a show trial of Catholic priests after secret police planted weapons in a monastery as evidence of their subversion. After being tortured, the accused all confessed to espionage and sabotage and were sentenced to many years in prison. Shortly afterwards, on the night of 13 April 1950, all 216 monasteries in Czechoslovakia were closed down. Some 2,400 monks from 28 orders were interned in 'concentration cloisters'. Later on that year most of Czechoslovakia's 339 convents were seized by the state. Over 12,000 Roman Catholic nuns were detained. Most clergymen were jailed, sent to labour camps, or forced into military service. Some were even murdered. It was the continual persecution of the Roman Catholic Church that led to the creation of the underground or 'Hidden Church'.

Remnants of the 'official' Church soon became a collaborationist, or at best dormant, entity. In these difficult circumstances, the Vatican gave permission for the creation of new priests and bishops who would work 'underground'. Men were now secretly ordained and led double lives. During working hours they were manual labourers in factories or on farms, and they carried out their religious duties behind closed doors.

The instruction from Rome decreed that there should always be two bishops, *uno nascosto, uno attivo* ('one hidden, one active'). The movement was especially strong in Slovakia where Roman Catholicism was robust. Consequently, government reprisals were more severe there.

JÁN CHRYZOSTOM KOREC

HAVING JOINED THE Jesuit Order in 1939, Ján Chryzostom Korec was involved in this underground religious movement from the start and soon became its leader. His journey into a covert religious life began when all Czechoslovakian male religious orders were shut down. The action had been planned in secret some time beforehand with all the precision of a military operation. It was code-named Action K, but it was to become known as the 'Night of the Barbarians'.

Korec recalls the events of that night. 'We were woken up by loud banging on our door. There were two of us in each room. We were ordered by a militiaman, wearing his militia cap and with a machine gun in his hands, to get dressed. We all had to gather in front of the chapel. We were given 20 minutes to pack our things. Some of the brothers protested and they were told that if they weren't silent immediately they would be put up in front of the wall and shot.

'Finally, we were put on the two buses that were waiting outside. By now, it was 1 a.m. We had no idea what was happening; we thought we were on our way to Siberia. But just after Košice we stopped. We got off at the monastery at Jasov. But there were no monks. It was completely empty. We stayed there for ten days.

'After that they took us to Podolínec where we stayed a little longer in a 'concentration monastery'. The youngest men were drafted to work on dam-building sites and those who had gone through military service were taken away as soldiers. A lucky few of us (five, me included) with no military experience were released. We were told to go and find a job and earn a living.'

Korec went to his brother's house in Nitra. The following year he became one of the world's youngest bishops at a secret ceremony, but continued working in a series of manual jobs. 'The statement of approval of our consecration along with several signatures was written on a small piece of white fabric. Each of us sewed it into a suit or article of clothing or a handkerchief so that it could not be found during body searches.'

In May 1951 he moved to Bratislava. It was there that he first realized he was being monitored by the police. 'I dedicated my life to the Church knowing I could be arrested or executed at any time. It was really hard but we had our internal, spiritual support. We prayed daily and it helped us a lot. For instance, when it came to being put in prison, we believed our being there was helping to fulfil the mission; we knew we were in the right place and that God knew about us.

'I was very strict and very serious with the secret ministry, and that applied also to the sanctifications. I spelled out to all those who were to become priests and bishops what it really meant "not to tell anybody!" They couldn't mention who had ordained them or where and when it had happened. I told them to take it seriously for the sake of the Church. Overall, I ordained about 120 priests. I had a younger friend, a Jesuit too, who sorted out the requests. He arranged everything: places, timings and so on. All I needed then were the first names of the priests and bishops to be; I didn't know the surnames of any of them. He also checked out if all the requirements for the applicants to become a priest or a bishop had been fulfilled. The ceremonies themselves were usually held in my flat. As a bishop, I didn't write anything down. If I had been taking notes and somebody had found them, it would have been the end, a disaster.'

Even Korec's mother didn't know that he was a bishop. The first she knew of it was when he was put on trial. On 11 March 1960, he was arrested by the secret police. He was bundled into a Tatra 603 and taken to the police headquarters in Račianska Street in Bratislava for interrogation. 'When they arrested me I was still wearing my working clothes. I was surrounded by about 11 policemen who were shouting and screaming at me. I tried to remain calm. But after about two hours of brutal interrogation I said if it was going to continue that way I would not say anything any more, and I stayed silent. They persisted in shouting questions at me but I just looked straight ahead.

'My brother had been in prison in Nitra for ten years already and he had told me about some tablets called Veritex they put in the food there, to make you talk. They took me out of the room around 9 o'clock in the evening; I was given some food and I was worried they had put a pill in it. So very carefully I ate a few of the larger pieces of potato and didn't touch the gravy.'

However, after six further hours of questioning Korec himself began to feel 'talkative and boastful'. At 1.30 a.m. he was taken to a prison cell in the Palace of Justice. At his trial in May 1960 Korec was accused of treason. 'In court, there were two witnesses against me, both of whom I had ordained and who didn't keep the secret they had been entrusted with. I was looking at them and they hesitated, so the prosecutor told me to turn away. After I did that, they spoke out. They sentenced me to 12 years in prison.'

Realizing that re-educating Korec was unrealistic, the authorities sent him to the isolated Valdice prison in north-east Bohemia, which held many political prisoners including 250 priests. There he was put in the so-called 'third department' which was actually an isolation area. The priests shared this section of the prison, and sometimes their cells, with murderers and the criminally insane. However, they still secretly performed Mass. 'I found out that the priests had discovered how to make wafers from wheat, flour and water, and wine from grapes or even raisins. In prison I had a medicine bottle that held about a hundred drops of wine so that I could serve Holy Mass.'

Later, Korec was transferred to the glass-grinding section, a factory in the prison that produced Bohemian crystal that ended up in chandeliers for export. Throughout this period, his interrogations continued.

Eventually, in 1968, the reforms of Alexander Dubček and his 'socialism with a human face' brought some comfort to political prisoners. Many priests and monks, including Korec, were released and 'rehabilitated'. On 24 June 1969, Bishop Korec was judicially rehabilitated. He travelled to Rome where he was granted a private audience with Pope Paul V1 and thanked for his secret ministry.

However, when the period known as 'Normalization' started the attitude to religion hardened again. Bishop Korec wasn't allowed to conduct pastoral work and once again the secret police followed him everywhere. 'They used to come to check out my flat secretly and put bugs all around the place. I caught them twice when they were trying to get into my residence. For seven years we couldn't speak openly in my flat. We only whispered quietly through a long tube, so the secret police in the flat above, who were listening to us, couldn't hear what we were talking about. I lived under pressure all the time, was watched all the time and was put in danger many times too.

'Once, they even loosened the front wheel lug bolt on my car, another time both screws on the car axle. A few times each year I was interrogated.'

During the late 1980s the number of faithful prepared to

publicly acclaim their religious faith was on the increase. This became apparent in 1985 on the 1,100th anniversary of St Methodius's death, when 200,000 pilgrims converged on the town of Levoča. Huge religious meetings followed.

The first demonstration organized by Roman Catholic dissident groups against the communist regime in Czechoslovakia came on 25 March 1988 in Bratislava, the capital of the Slovak Socialist Republic, when a peaceful assembly of 10,000 people asking for religious freedom was suppressed by police. 'It was a heroic action,' recalls Korec, 'because the people knew what might happen. The water cannon made them wet and dirty all over, and in that filthy condition they were dragged to police stations. The people knew about the consequences of their actions, but they remained calm, they held their own. They only prayed, holding lit candles in their hands. Unfortunately, the huge spiritual capital we gathered there is vanishing today.'

It was only after the end of communism that Korec was finally allowed to practise his religion in peace. On 6 February 1990, Pope John Paul II appointed him bishop of Nitra, and on 28 June the following year Bishop Korec became a cardinal of the Roman Catholic Church.

RAINER EPPELMANN

IN EAST GERMANY, 1989 is sometimes referred to as the year of the 'Protestant Revolution' because of the prevalence of pastors and prayer in the events leading to the demise of the communist regime there. Certainly, the Protestant Church had always been a dominant political force. Although its membership declined under communist leadership, by 1989 it was at the forefront of the campaign for change. It had enjoyed a degree of tolerance.

However, for the Communist Party it was largely a question of holding your enemies even closer to you than your friends. The Stasi made extensive penetrations into the Church, its followers and their activities. At certain Church synods a quarter of the members turned out to be unofficial informers.

Rainer Eppelmann was one of the most spied upon figures inside the Protestant movement. He was a Lutheran pastor based in East Berlin, who became a well-known opposition figure inside East Germany and, subsequently, carved out a career as a politician. He was born in what later became East Berlin, and his father had been a member of the SS during the Third Reich and served as a guard at the Buchenwald concentration camp. Rainer went to school in West Berlin until the advent of the Berlin Wall. Eight years later he began to study theology and in 1974 he became a Protestant pastor in East Berlin where he famously organized Masses that featured blues music.

He is a firm believer in the role played by 'people power' in the fall of the Berlin Wall. 'I was born in 1943. I remember that life was hard in the post-war years. I was one of those children who wasn't a member of the Young Pioneers. I went to religious classes. I was Confirmed, but I didn't take part in the *Jugendweihe*, the communist youth ceremony. Consequently, I wasn't allowed to take my A-levels in East Germany. West Berlin used to have two schools for East Berliners who had good results at school, but who, like me, weren't part of the Young Pioneers or the Free German Youth (FDJ) and who had received Confirmation.

'But it was like that only until 13 August 1961 when the Wall was constructed. That meant school was over. Added to all this my father, who used to work in West Berlin, remained there and left his wife back in the East with their four children.

'My father never told me that he had worked in Buchenwald concentration camp. My mother told me after he had passed away. All I knew was that he had been an SS officer, and my sister and I used to quiz him about it. One of the reasons why I refused to take the soldier's oath later in my life was my father's past; I believed I was not able to vow obedience to any man after learning about Auschwitz. This I still firmly believe.

'I then worked as a roof tiler. After a year I was allowed to take an apprenticeship as a bricklayer. I didn't find it demeaning to earn my living having to use my hands. Later on, as pastor, I was very grateful that I had spent several years earning my money from manual labour, because that turned me into a comradely person and prevented me from having feelings of superiority or arrogance towards ordinary people.

'My original plan had been to study architecture. I completed my bricklaying apprenticeship and, surprisingly, was offered a place at technical college to study civil engineering. But I abandoned that after only three months because I couldn't stand it. I had been spoiled by three years of schooling in West Berlin where I had learnt to ask questions and look at things with a critical eye. But that attitude would only cause me trouble at the technical college.'

Eppelmann was drafted in 1966 and opted to serve in a non-combat construction unit (*Baueinheiten*). 'I was lucky in that during that period the National People's Army let young men choose whether they wanted to carry guns and be trained to use them or not. The Church had urged the army to do that.' The construction soldiers wore uniforms and were under the command of army personnel, but they didn't have to carry weapons. They had a symbol of a spade on their uniforms and undertook building work.

The communists remained suspicious of these units for conscientious objectors. Although construction soldiers did not bear arms they still had to take an oath saying they would fight all enemies and obey their superiors unconditionally. Eppelmann refused to take the oath.

'When I refused to take the soldier's oath, I was court-martialled and sentenced to eight months in jail due to repeated insubordination. For them it was all about my insubordination; my conscientious reasons weren't taken into account at all.

'But those eight months didn't do me any harm. If you had asked me in the late 1980s about the most relevant experience and period of my life, I would have told you that it was those eight months in prison. The first days were very hard, and although I was already over 20 years old, I cried, because I realized that I was locked up and couldn't get out. But the longer I stayed there the more I got used to it, and to my surprise I realized that it didn't break me, especially when I thought about the reason why I was in there. That was a crucial point.

'After I got out I worked as a bricklayer. But when we realized that the Wall was not just going to be temporary, I seriously had to ask myself what I wanted to do for the rest of my life. That's when I decided to study theology. I began my studies at a professional school for theology because I had no A-levels. And that's how I became pastor in the borough of Berlin-Friedrichshain.

'In retrospect, I realized how risky it was to commit to a job about which I had only the vaguest notion. I only found out later that it was exactly the right job for me: I had to deal with people, and, by DDR standards, I had incredible freedom.'

One day in late 1970 a musician called Günter Holvers knocked on the church door asking if he could give a blues concert there. 'I told him that it wasn't possible to give concerts in churches because the DDR constitution dictated that they had to be regulated by the Concert and Performance Department. But I said that if he was willing to find a way to combine his music with biblical content, we could talk about it. And that's what we did. At the beginning we collaborated with the pastor of the neighbouring community and 250 adolescents attended the services. Usually that number only came on Christmas Eve and possibly on Christmas Day, and for Confirmations. We recognized the missionary potential. The number of people attending doubled without us advertising, simply by word of mouth. Many of these new members of the congregation, some of whom liked to smoke and drink during the proceedings, had never been inside a church before.

'Also, we used to discuss the social situation and the political flaws of the DDR. At our best we attracted several thousand teenagers, not only from Berlin but from all over East Germany.

'That aroused the interest of the Stasi. I know now that over 40 unofficial collaborators were spying on me, my flat was wired and my mail and telephone calls were monitored. They positioned men with movie cameras on the roofs around the church so that everybody could see them. They wanted people to know that they were being recorded on camera, to spread fear and unease. They positioned soldiers at the nearby railway stations. They stopped adolescents on trains and on the streets asking them what they were doing there. They had cars with darkened windows so that you couldn't look inside but knew that somebody was watching you. Sometimes they even opened the car door in order to let you see that somebody was sitting there and filming you.

'The meanest thing they did was to throw stink bombs into a full church. That was very irresponsible because it might have started a panic. They constantly tried to put pressure on the Church, especially on the dean of Berlin, Hartmut Grünbaum. They urged him several times to shut down the services. Luckily for us he would never ban the controversial services. If the Stasi wanted to impose a ban, he said they had to do it themselves.

'We started with the "Blues Masses" in the late 1970s and continued until 1983 or 1984. Then their frequency diminished. Many people outside the parish came because it was their only chance to meet like-minded people and to discuss environmentalism, human rights in the DDR, peace matters and so on.

'When I checked my Stasi file after the Wall came down I saw that they knew that I and seven other people once sat in my studio to organize one of the Blues Masses. Six out of those seven had informed the Stasi about that.

'Today we know that among the salaried officers of the Church, including bishops, pastors and deacons, there were surprisingly few who collaborated with the Stasi. The people I had organized that Blues Mass with were all members of the community. I knew them all by name but that was all. We didn't ask them whether they were SED (Socialist Unity Party of Germany) or FDJ members. Most of them probably were. That was of no importance to us. It would have been ridiculous to ask them whether they worked with the Stasi because even if they had, they would probably have denied it.'

Things got considerably worse for Eppelmann in 1982 after the publication of the 'Berlin Appeal'. This document was co-authored and publicized by Eppelmann and the prominent dissident Robert Havemann, and was a plea for disarmament and dialogue on behalf of the burgeoning peace movement. 'The stockpiles of weapons in East and West will not protect but annihilate us,' it declared. Significantly, the appeal called for the removal of 'all occupation troops from Germany'. It was sent to politicians in East Germany and the Soviet Union as well as to Western newspapers.

'The Stasi had plans to murder me,' recalls Eppelmann. 'Apparently that was after the publication of the Berlin Appeal. A senior Stasi officer asked his colleagues to work out how to turn Ralf Hirsch, a colleague, and me from the living to the dead, making sure that the Stasi could not be blamed. They thought about making Ralf drunk and then leaving him lying in a snow-covered forest in wintertime to freeze to death. And they wanted to tamper with my car so that I would be involved in a fatal car crash. Luckily a Stasi officer didn't approve the plan because of the threat to innocent people. I used to drive to Robert Havemann's house in the evenings together with my wife because she enjoyed Robert's company. It was probably her presence that saved my life.

'I did fear for my life. I got involved in an accident at a (controlled) traffic light where somebody had not respected my right of way. That might have been the Stasi. Also, I once picked up my car from an auto shop and a while later the wheel came loose. Luckily, we were driving in a forest at walking speed when that happened. If it had happened at a speed of 50 or 60 kph a family with four children would have been wiped out.

'After the publication of the appeal, they simply arrested me during a Confirmation service and carried me away. The Stasi interrogated me for three days but they had to let me go. From the way they were interrogating me I understood that they had planned to forcefully expatriate me. But they didn't do it because I clearly stated that they had to put me into prison if they deemed me culpable, because I wouldn't leave the country. Then the Church started supporting me, probably because they didn't want to be reproached for having stood by and done nothing about the expatriation of a pastor who hadn't done anything wrong on a professional level.

'I was opposed to East Germany because it was a dictatorship. Reading the papers was like a red rag to a bull. Every day I read how wonderful life in the DDR was. I knew that the republic they were describing was a different republic from the one I was experiencing. I used to ask myself if they themselves believed in what they were writing, in something that was so far from reality? My second question was: do they think I believe in what they are writing? Are they asking themselves what I might think about it, or worse, don't they even care about what I'm thinking?

'It was an untrustworthy, mendacious and corrupt system that worked against the will of the majority of its citizens, I was firmly convinced of that. The moment I liked East Germany best was upon completion of my academic work because I had just left the ideal world of theology studies. But then I had to deal with the problems of parishioners and their children. They used to tell me what worried them most or why they couldn't bear the situation any longer. I have spoken with hundreds or perhaps thousands of people who were agonizing over their exit visas for weeks, months or years.

'I was starting to get well known and I was economically independent. I knew that even if they had arrested me for political reasons, I would still have received my salary so I didn't have to worry about the financial situation of my wife and children. So I felt that I had to make good use of the freedom I possessed.

'I was one of the co-founders of Democratic Awakening. We realized that others too had started doing something; that the situation in 1986 and 1987 was different from the way it used to be ten years earlier. For instance, we, very ordinary citizens, did things that we wouldn't have dared to do ten years earlier when we would have had to face years in prison for our deeds. In 1986 or 1987 it could happen that you were detained for a couple of hours or a day or two, and that they interrogated you, but afterwards they would have had to let you go. We had grown accustomed to that and so it didn't impress us.

'Candlelight vigils were held and we didn't know if we would go home afterwards. But we knew that if we were arrested they would have released us after 48 hours at the latest. Otherwise they would have had to initiate proceedings against us, but what would they have charged us with anyway? We were backing a cause that was supported by two-thirds of the population, and we showed our support by standing on the street with candles in our hands. I remember that earlier everyone was scared of the Stasi, but towards the end we used to make fun of them.

'We wanted more civil rights, we wanted a system of administrative courts, we wanted every citizen to be allowed to lodge complaints against political decisions – for example, in relation to schools and jobs. It made us happy to know that we felt we had the right to do things, which we hadn't dared do earlier. That made us feel more adult, so to speak, and more self-confident.

'Our hope was not for a total change of the system, but for it to become a little more colourful, humane and efficient than it was at that time. We used to think of ourselves more as reformers than as revolutionaries. When those who wished to leave the country joined our movement in 1988 and 1989 – for years we had been less than a thousand people in the whole of the DDR – our movement grew to several thousand, and from then on we constantly grew bigger. That's how that revolutionary atmosphere came about. Lenin once said that a revolution comes about when those from above can't cope anymore and those from below don't want to cope any more.'

On 9 November 1989, at a live televised press conference, the SED politician Günter Schabowski announced measures to lift East Germany's travel restrictions. His message flashed around the world, bringing thousands of people, including Rainer Eppelmann, on to the streets of Berlin and up and down the length of the Wall. 'All the people who went on the streets didn't know whether they would come back home safe and sound that night, or what it might have meant for their professional careers or the destinies of their children. Nevertheless, two million people dared to go on the streets! And I think that this was one of the reasons why everything happened so fast afterwards.

'We headed for one of the border crossings. When we arrived 50 or maybe even 100 people were already there. If people had stood there only one day earlier, they would have been chased away with shouts or they would have been asked for valid travel documents. But that day no one had documents; they simply stood there talking to the border guards.

'We heard people saying, "Come on, open up! Schabowski said that we could go through." But the guards didn't show any reaction. They stood there in a very weird way. After having observed them for a little while, I realized they were standing like that because they were not armed. Usually, a self-confident German soldier stands upright with his legs apart. But these border guards looked very different; they looked lost and helpless. And actually it was very mean to expect those 18- or 20-year-olds to solve the problems of the DDR – and without weapons.

'Well, that was the situation and nothing happened for several minutes, until we realized that apparently they weren't allowed to open the border and so we had to do it. And that's what we did. It was so easy. And we went through. My friend and I walked for about

20 metres and then stopped. All the others crossed the Bornholmer Bridge into the West.

'Apparently the people from West Berlin had had the same idea and they wanted to see what was happening after they had realized that more and more people were crossing the border. They too started to cross. The two of us stopped and watched the scene. To see those people and their faces filled with joy or incredulity or incomprehension. People were hugging each other. It was unbelievable. It is important for me to say that it was the people from Berlin who did that. It was a further step towards self-liberation.

'Every morning that I wake up in good health I can exclaim "Hallelujah" with firm conviction. I always carry this quote with me: "Hope is not the conviction that things will end well, but the certainty that something makes sense independently from how things will end."'

PAUL MUNTEANU

IN ROMANIA THE Ceauşescu regime tightly controlled all aspects of religious worship within the country. The main religious body was the Romanian Orthodox Church to which 80 per cent of Romanians belonged. When the communists came to power in 1947 the Orthodox Church was purged through killings, arrests and intimidation. By the mid-1960s the Church was an ally of the newly established Ceauşescu regime. Its close identification with expressions of Romanian nationalism proved useful to the communists who now had effective control of the national religion. Many priests were collaborators with the regime and informers for the secret police, the Securitate. This close alliance remained in place until the fall of the Ceauşescus in December 1989.

When Ceauşescu demolished or relocated around two dozen historic churches in Bucharest the Orthodox hierarchy remained silent. The Romanian leader was seeking to rebuild central Bucharest to implement his vision of a new civic centre based around the House of the People and the Boulevard of the Victory of Socialism. The relocation and demolition of churches was a consequence of these projects.

One of these relocated churches, the St Ioan Pia, was built in 1740. It was situated in the heart of Bucharest in Piata Unirii, not far from Ceauşescu's House of the People (*Casa Poporului*). In 1983 Ceauşescu ordered the church to be moved. Paul Munteanu was a priest at this church. Imprisoned by the regime in the 1940s, he was present during the period of his church's enforced 'relocation'. 'Generally Ceauşescu couldn't stand religion and the Church because he was a communist and an atheist. We knew he was very much bothered by our church because each time he passed it we had to make sure that there weren't people standing outside and the doors had to be closed. We had to fix metallic shutters in the bell tower so that nobody could shoot at him from there. The church was seen as a spot where he would be vulnerable when he was driving by. So they decided to move us so that we were hidden between two blocks of flats.

'I think that it was a miracle the church survived because all the churches around us were demolished. Somebody – a member of the commission – had accompanied Ceauşescu when he'd said, "Demolish this or that". This man said he'd seen a church like ours in Switzerland that was praised for its architecture. "OK, then move it," Ceauşescu said. And with that the church was saved.

'And when we found out that it would be moved we were very happy that it wasn't being demolished. But work began with just three days' notice. It was very difficult for us to move everything out so quickly – chandeliers, furniture, pews and so forth. Outside, in the Unirii Square, no traffic was allowed and we had to carry everything on our backs.

'We received notice to evacuate the church at the beginning of October 1985. The work to prepare the moving of the church lasted until May 1986 when they actually moved it… by approximately 23 metres. Ceauşescu seemed unable to appreciate a historic monument like this. They'd already demolished St Friday Church, St Spiridon Church and so many others. One couldn't intervene. One couldn't negotiate with a man who had a gun pointed at one's head.

'The furniture and the pews were taken to the Caldarusani Monastery. But the abbot gave many of them to the gypsies, in winter, to burn them. We lost many treasures but we saved whatever we could. Regarding the conservation of the valuables fixed inside the church, we were extraordinarily lucky to have an engineer called Iordachescu – he coordinated the move. He helped us to save the altar, the pulpit, the rood screen and the bishop's pulpit. These are invaluable objects made of wild rosewood and specially sculpted. The altar – brought to us from the Sarindar Monastery and dating from 1711 – was saved at great risk.

Under the church they found the bones of some of its founders, from the eighteenth century. We saved as many as we could but most were thrown away. I couldn't guard the church all night. Many bones were loaded into cars and taken to the rubbish dump.

'It took four hours to pull the church 23 metres. I was in here for two hours. I couldn't see anything. Mr Iordachescu also moved an eight-storey block of flats with everybody in it – they woke up in the morning in the new location.

'I had feelings of pain, of regret, of course, because the church had been there since 1740 and now it's hidden between the blocks of flats. And it was very difficult to keep the front entrance because they wanted to close it and make us enter from the back.

'I felt repulsion for everything Ceauşescu did. If you said something you'd end up in prison. I spent two years in prison because I spoke out against the communist regime. In 1948 I was arrested along with many other students because during a meeting I talked against the party and its activities. In prison I had many beatings, bad food and I was treated like a criminal for expressing myself.

'As to the Ceauşescus' execution, it didn't give me any satisfaction. I viewed it with regret that they ended like that – being shot like dogs. God doesn't want the sinner's death. God wants the sinner to right himself. But this one couldn't change because he was so stubborn.'

SECRET POLICE

'Trust is good but surveillance is better.'

Unofficial motto of the Stasi

ALL THE COMMUNIST states of Eastern Europe were secret police states. But the most active secret police were in East Germany where they fostered a pervasive culture of paranoia.

The Stasi – *Ministerium für Staatssicherheit* (Ministry for State Security) – was the self-proclaimed 'Shield and Sword of the Party' (*Schild und Schwert der Partei*). When the regime collapsed it had 102,000 full-time officers organized into 29 departments, each with its own responsibilities. But perhaps more significantly there were also around 189,000 informers, known as *Inoffizielle Mitarbeiter* or IMs (unofficial collaborators), on its books when the Wall fell. Since many records were destroyed the exact number of informers will probably never be known, but half a million has been cited as a reasonable estimate.

No other population has been so spied upon by its government. In Stalin's Soviet Union it is estimated there was one KGB agent for every 5,830 people. During the Third Reich it is estimated there was one Gestapo agent for every 2,000 citizens. In East Germany, if all part-time informers are included, there was approximately one informer for every six people.

And the Stasi's tentacles extended to every nook and cranny of public and private life in East Germany: sport, religion, the bedroom, the punk scene, the dissident movement, even inside the Politburo. Industrial plants, apartment blocks, schools, universities and hospitals were infiltrated by Stasi spies. In the 1980s eight per cent of salaried pastors and administrators of the Lutheran Church were on the Stasi's books as unofficial collaborators. By the late 1980s the state kept files on around six million East Germans, a third of the population.

The Stasi developed its own language which included a whole host of terms surrounding its own agents and *feindlich-negativ kräfte* or 'hostile negative forces' – a cover-all term for anyone it suspected. It included: IMs – unofficial informers, IMBs (*Inoffizieller Mitarbeiter zur unmittelbaren Bearbeitung*) – penetration agents, and OIBEs (*Offiziere im Besonderen Einsatz*) – deep-cover agents in high positions of important institutions. The IMs were organized by OMs (*Operativer Mitarbeiter*) – case officers employed directly by the Stasi. The work of the IMs had three main focal points: collecting information about certain events or people in their working and social environments, active fighting against enemies, usually by carring out investigations into susupicious persons and contribuiting to their elimination; and, finally, logistic tasks like making their homes or telephones available for the use of Stasi agents. The full extent of this complicated web of deceit was revealed in 1992 when the post-Unification German authorities began an official investigation of the Stasi archives and published a lexicon of terms approved personally by Erich Mielke, the DDR minister for state security from 1957 until the collapse of the regime in late 1989.

In all, records show that over 200,000 people were imprisoned for political reasons and there was little or no information about those in detention. The Stasi even developed plans to assassinate its enemies, and in one documented case that went to court it nearly succeeded. Over its lifetime, the Stasi's focus moved from the enemy without to the enemies within. The state's interest in the lives of others created a morally devastated society. Hardly any family was untouched by the Stasi: it was either working for them or being spied on by them – or both.

The Stasi also developed its own special surveillance techniques. For example, it collected the body odours of East Germans thought to be hostile to the state and kept them in smell jars so that sniffer dogs would have something to go on in the future.

Although inefficient and ineffective in many ways, as testified by its collection of vast amounts of irrelevant and often inaccurate information on the East German population, it rightly foresaw the demise of the communist regime it served. Right up until the end in 1989, the Stasi was standing by to clamp down with martial law. Thirty-five concentration camps were planned to receive the intake of arrests of 400 people an hour across East Germany, from a target list of

85,000 of its citizens. But by then the state the Stasi had sustained had lost its will to govern.

East Germany's surveillance society was created by the Soviets and the SED (Socialist Unity Party) and implemented and enforced by the Stasi. But the East German people themselves lent their eyes and ears to the enterprise. The fact that so many did cooperate with the Stasi, whatever the degree of coercion, is one reason why coming to terms with the past has been so difficult for so many citizens of the DDR.

VERA LENGSFELD

THE MARRIAGE OF former dissident Vera Lengsfeld to the poet Knud Wollenberger was shattered when Vera learnt in 1991 that her husband had spied on her and been a Stasi informer, code-named Donald, since he was a teenager.

Lengsfeld joined the SED in 1975 but was expelled from the party in 1983 for protesting against the stationing of Soviet nuclear missiles in East Germany. Throughout the 1980s she was a leading figure in the peace movement. In January 1988 she was arrested for her part in a demonstration in East Berlin. After she was finger-printed, Vera had to sit on a piece of fabric. This was later placed in one of the Stasi's smell jars as a record of her odour. Subsequently she was convicted, imprisoned then deported to the United Kingdom in February 1988. She returned to Germany on 9 November 1989. She was a member of the German Parliament until 2005 and plans to run again in 2009.

Lengsfeld recalls, 'In the late 1970s and early 1980s the USSR started stationing their nuclear rockets, SS20s, on DDR soil. At that time military classes started being taught in schools. For both of these reasons the Protestant Church awakened from its years of deep slumber and a number of pastors spoke out against these things. As a consequence, many worried parents started going to church again. That was the founding pillar of the opposition movement of the 1980s.

'We founded the so-called Berlin–Pankow Peace Circle in autumn 1981, and it very quickly became the largest peace association in East Germany. During its best years it counted 100 active members and around 300 supporters. It was simply a matter of time until the Stasi found out who attended the meetings. People active in those associations often had to face harassment.'

As part of her peace work Vera took posters that quoted a line from the East German constitution, 'Every DDR citizen has the right to freely and publicly express his opinion', to a major annual rally. She believed her husband's attempts to dissuade her from attending that rally were related to the impending threat of her imprisonment. 'My husband later told me that he had been working with the Stasi, and because he was concerned about me and he thought that thanks to his collaboration he would get to know early if I was in any danger. And I believe him. If he had behaved differently and maybe even tried to encourage me to attend the demonstration… but he tried everything he could to prevent me from going.'

Revelations about her husband's role in the Stasi appeared in the German press after the end of communism. Initially he denied involvement, believing all the evidence incriminating him had been destroyed. But when Vera confronted him he admitted his guilt. 'My marriage ended straight away. He was one of the few people to admit that he had worked with the Stasi. He had actually been working for them since he was 18. The only unclear point remains the question of whether the Stasi engineered our meeting each other so that he could spy on me or if we met each other by chance. I don't know that and I will not ask him.

'In total 49 unofficial collaborators spied on me. I was very surprised about the comprehensiveness of those activities and about the things they deemed worth reporting. For example, they noted down which washing-up liquid I used although we really didn't have much of a choice in the DDR. We had only two or three brands anyway.

'I forgave Knud long ago. He wrote me a letter asking me for forgiveness and explaining why he had done it. I believe him because he really had tried to keep me away from that demonstration. You cannot change the past. In retrospect I find it worse and more damaging to our relationship that at the moment when he was exposed he didn't come clean. I don't know whether that would have saved our marriage but it would have saved us much pain.'

FIT OF RAGE

ONE LEIPZIG-BASED punk group in the early 1980s was Wutanfall (Fit of Rage). Their story is fairly typical of what happened to the punk scene when the Stasi turned up the heat. Wutanfall's lead singer was called Chaos while its bass guitarist went by the name of

Zappa. Two decades ago they were best friends. It was only after the collapse of East Germany that Chaos discovered Zappa, his best friend, had been a Stasi informer.

Recently Zappa has explained his delicate political position. 'When we first set up the band it was not our general aim to get involved with politics. It was more that we were young and wanted to have some fun and that we were also critical of the DDR, some more and some less. Some of our lyrics were fun and others were critical.

'We wanted to fight the boredom and the frustrations of our desolate lives. It was not cool to live in East Germany. We didn't want to be conformists. It simply sucked, living according to imposed guidelines. We wanted to live differently... we just wanted to be true to ourselves.

'Somehow the authorities had the feeling that I was the weak link in the group and thus I was constantly summoned and asked to give them information. During fairs in Leipzig, the police would always be in front of my house.

'After I had already been summoned two or three times they told me I had to sign something. They dictated to me a two-page-long text full of gibberish. I wrote it all down, but then said that I couldn't sign it, so they threatened to arrest me. The following day they said, "OK, leave out the things you don't agree with and sign the paper anyway". I thought that I'd sign it and then they'd let me go and I'd be done with it – but they had that lousy signature of mine. Consequently they continued to approach me and say, "You've signed it, so now you have to tell us when the concerts take place". So I had to agree to do it.

'My code-name was "Captain". They gave me a phone number and told me that when I called I should say, "Captain speaking". After each concert I was summoned. "Tell us when the concerts are, otherwise we can't treat you differently and you will go to prison." I have not experienced pressure like it in my life since. Obviously, I didn't tell my mates everything; I simply said that I had been with the Stasi again. I never told them that I had signed that paper. It was horrible.

'At one concert they gave me some money, which we exchanged for alcohol straight away and paid for the transport of our equipment. Then, in fact, the Stasi gave me a flat. I had to swear that I would vote in the next elections. The elections were not real elections, they were rigged, but in spite of that they wanted as many people as possible to vote. So I voted, I went there; I kept my promise to vote in the elections.'

By 1982 Chaos was also being summoned twice a week by the Stasi to 'clarify' certain circumstances. He was deprived of his documents and occasionally beaten. 'One interrogation which I cannot forget was the one which lasted over 17 hours. Four or five different interrogators questioned me. My protocol was over 60 pages long. I had to sign all 60 pages, which were then torn up, and I then had to go over the same story from the beginning. At the end I was so exhausted that I had difficulty in writing my own name. This was one of the methods used; there were also other times where brute force was used.

'My house was searched during my absence which happened after they took my key during an interrogation. They turned everything upside down in my place; at the same time they searched my old room at my parents' house'.

'I felt I was permanently controlled. I knew that no matter what I did I could be observed. I didn't know if I was bugged, I had no idea. After all, everything was possible. There were surprise visits at 3 o'clock in the morning. I was accused of sheltering fugitives and stuff... I was constantly bullied. Because I was a punk and looked like one I was also bullied by normal people in the streets and at work. I got rid of my frustration thanks to our music and my band and the fun we had together. That was what kept me going. But certainly I also had depressions.

'According to my files one of our band members was an unofficial collaborator of the Stasi. I didn't know about it at that time. I didn't suspect anything but I felt it during the interrogations. I couldn't explain it at that time. I didn't think it was possible. For example, the Stasi knew the dates of our concerts, which only we could have known. Now, of course, everything makes sense.'

When he discovered Zappa was an informer Chaos was greatly disappointed about the breach of trust and what he sees as Zappa's cowardly behaviour but, in fact, the bass player was only one of nine unofficial informers tracking him. Looking back, Chaos realizes that he had no chance of a normal life. 'East Germany was simply a dictatorship. Only for small things like founding a band and looking different, your whole life got screwed. I could never have succeeded in the DDR. That's why I eventually applied for an exit visa.'

WOLFGANG WELSCH

THE STASI WENT further than observation and harassment in the case of Wolfgang Welsch. In 1994 former Stasi agent Peter Haack was jailed for six and a half years after being convicted of trying to murder him.

Welsch became a target thanks to his success in helping people escape from East Germany. In 1964 he had himself served time in an East German prison for attempting to flee. Released to West Germany in 1971, he was responsible for over 200 successful escapes, mainly of intellectuals and professionals like doctors. 'The Stasi tried to kill me by using all possible means,' said Welsch. 'Initially, they planned my assassination in 1979 when they planted a bomb in my car. The bomb was rigged to explode when I reached a certain speed. It was supposed to look as if I had a fatal accident.' The bomb did explode and the car crashed but Welsch survived.

Later that year, Welsch met Peter Haack – a Stasi agent who was posing as a photographer – on holiday in Greece. They became friends and kept in touch for the next couple of years. 'In 1981 Peter Haack invited me to Israel. He said that he had some work there as a photographer for the French station Antenne 2, observing the fighting in the Golan Heights and the damage caused by Katuscha rockets in the town of Kiriat Sh'mona. He told me that he only had to work for a short while and afterwards we could rent a camper van to explore the country. It sounded very interesting and I travelled with my wife and daughter to Israel. He picked us up from Tel Aviv airport. It was baking hot, I remember, and we travelled around various places.

'One day we stopped and Peter told us to go for a swim while he cooked some food. We had swum to an island, which was only about 80 metres from the beach. After a while he called us back to the camp. We sat down at the wooden tables that were placed there for tourists and ate the burgers and salad that he had prepared for us.

'It was mainly me who was eating because I hadn't eaten much for the last few days. I was very hungry. My wife and daughter didn't eat much. After the meal we decided to drive to Jerusalem, which is a bit further north. My wife, who was sitting next to me in the passenger seat, became acutely sick as we drove across the West Bank towards Jerusalem. Eventually she stopped vomiting and felt a bit better.

'Three days later, I felt a kind of prickling in my legs. It was painful. We were driving through the Negev Desert and were near Beersheba when the pain became extremely intense and I could hardly move. I could not drive any more and we spent the night at the Desert Inn Hotel.

'I saw two doctors but they were puzzled; they did not know what was wrong with me. I was in agony and I could not sit, stand or lie down. The only position in which I could endure the pain was a sort of Muslim prayer position – on my knees with my head on the ground. This was the only pain-relieving position. I obviously could not remain in this position for long. The only other place I could stand the pain was in the swimming pool. I was in the pool from 5 o'clock in the morning. This continued for days and I suffered from the so-called "washboard syndrome" – skin softened by water. It was more or less tolerable in the water and I was drinking a lot of weak Israeli Maccabee beer. The combination of being in the water all the time and the increased consumption of liquids saved my life. That is what the doctors told me later.

'When we arrived back in Germany, we went straight to the accident and emergency unit in Mannheim where I was examined by the senior consultant – a well-known toxicologist. He did not detect anything wrong with me and asked if I had any psychological problems. Luckily, they took blood samples, which they sent to a number of institutes for analysis. It was almost too late when the last blood analysis came back from the Fresenius Institute in Oberursel (a large food chemistry institute). The institute concluded that the person from whom the blood sample was taken was suffering from a life-threatening poison. I was only half-conscious when the ambulance arrived with its blue light flashing. I was taken to the intensive care unit and they started the only possible therapy – a high dosage of thallium antidote. I was in a coma for three days. It turned out that the burgers Peter had prepared for us contained ten times the fatal dose of thallium.

'I woke up in the intensive care unit. The chief consultant came to visit me. Since he was a toxicologist, he apologized that he had not detected the poison. He told me that they saved my life at the last minute – another half an hour and I would have died. He also said that the paralysing effect of the poison had already affected my breathing. The consultant told me that the intake of such a large dose of thallium does not happen accidentally. Thallium does not have any taste or smell but he said it was beyond coincidence.

'I found out later that my supposed "best friend" Peter was involved in the assassination attempt and that I was the number one enemy of the East German state. It is not an overstatement. That is how I was viewed.'

PETER HAACK

FOR HIS PART, Peter Haack – code-named 'Alfons' – was living in West Berlin in the late 1960s when he met and became involved with a woman from East Germany. Later on he was approached by the Stasi and pressured into working for them. 'I would often bring things over for this girl which I hadn't declared at East German customs. The Stasi somehow found out about what I was doing. They said, "We know these things, and we can cause trouble for you. Otherwise, you can do a few things for us."

'In the course of one or two years the tasks became more and more detailed or more specific, and it turned out that I was working for Department 6 of the Stasi, responsible for passport control and travelling. I grew into the job, so they didn't need to blackmail me to do it any more.'

'Afterwards I worked for them all the time, almost always on the borders with Germany, later on in other countries, Czechoslovakia, Hungary, and afterwards in the whole of Eastern Europe. It was clear that I wasn't in the police service, I knew I was involved in spying. But I didn't know to what extent the Stasi was a criminal organization. I wasn't interested. I wasn't concerned about it. In the beginning it was about getting to know where drugs and forged money was going. Later it was about escapes.

By 1974 Haack was working full-time for the Stasi, getting an allowance and a bonus. 'I worked undercover as a tourist. For example, I had to investigate why East German tourists travelling to Romania by car or aeroplane suddenly disappeared. Many East Germans would fly to Romania as East Germans and then leave the country as citizens of West Germany. I found out how travel documents were faked there.

'I first heard about Wolfgang Welsch in 1978 in connection with these escapes through Romania. I was told to travel to Greece because we knew that was where Welsch would go on holiday. I had to get into contact with him. Such was my task. He was a kind and sociable person and we got on well together.

'The Stasi's aim was to turn the tables on him. They knew he was trouble for them. His main goal was to help intellectuals escape the country, causing a brain drain from East Germany. They wanted him to reveal the names of those who wanted to leave the country. The talk was of "turning" him to work for the Stasi or to damage him financially.

'It was just part of my job. I used to report back on my meetings with Welsch and I was told that I should convince him to travel to Israel in my company. The Stasi had several people spying on him, not just me. That was when preparations started and when I was kitted out and provided with a cover story. I had to pass myself off as a photographer for a photographic agency in order to give Welsch a plausible reason for my travel to Israel. That disguise worked very well.'

When the case finally came to court in 1994, Haack admitted that he did prepare the meal that poisoned Welsch but he claims that someone else must have added thallium to the food. 'We were somewhere near the Dead Sea. It was a very hot day. I decided to cook these meatballs I had made. He was poisoned with thallium the day of that big dinner.

'Welsch dropped me off at the airport in Tel Aviv where he complained that he didn't feel very well and that he was in pain. I took a flight from Tel Aviv to Cairo and then to London. Once in London I was ordered to Berlin. When I got back to the DDR my superior instructed me to write a postcard to Welsch stating that I was in South America so he wouldn't wonder why I didn't keep in touch with him.

'The following years I worked in East Germany and the Eastern bloc. Then I was arrested in 1993. At that time I lived in the southern part of Germany, in Baden-Würtemberg. The police arrived and told me that I was suspected of murder.'

Despite his betrayal of Welsch and his subsequent jail term, Haack has few regrets about joining the Stasi. 'It happened to thousands of employees that they realized only afterwards that what they did was against the law. It was just a job for me. Apart from the operation in Israel my job was a normal one. I was punished for my guilt and sentenced for it, and I accept that. Other culprits are still walking around freely and receive good pensions.

'There were no baddies and goodies within the Stasi. It was all Stasi. The Stasi was an institution infiltrated by political dreamers and bureaucrats, who took illegal action against anyone they didn't like. Such institutions are to be condemned and need to be eliminated. The persons in charge need to be called to account. But unfortunately that is not what happens.

'I found out after the fall of the Berlin Wall that the Stasi, and especially the people of my former department, weren't the people they had pretended to be. They were neither comradely nor ready to help. Every one of them cared only about their own advantage and and were prepared to succeed at somebody else's expense. Today, I feel very much exploited by the Stasi when I think about what was going on in there.

'Life in the DDR was not bad at all and I was doing well too. But now I realize that I was part only of the lower middle class in terms of accommodation and participation in public life. My salary was 800 marks plus expenses and thus not as high as any sales representative. I thought it was a pity that after I was sentenced my so-called friends and colleagues all just made excuses and said nothing to support me. They simply left me out in the cold. What do I do today? Well, my hobby is repairing clocks and watches.'

REGINA KAISER AND UWE KARLSTEDT

REGINA KAISER GREW up in a communist family. Her parents were committed communists and her sister worked for the Stasi. At 19 she began to question the way her country was governed. At 21, she married a fellow dissident. Together they wrote anti-government pamphlets and smuggled them to the West, unaware that another member of their circle was an informer.

On 6 April 1981, at the age of 31, Regina was arrested with her husband at their Berlin flat and taken straight to the Stasi headquarters. 'I was brought into a room with only one guard; the people who had accompanied me disappeared. The guard stood there and didn't say a word. I sat down on a chair. I lost orientation because the windows were darkened. I was very nervous. Also, because I didn't know what had happened to the third member of our group, I was still hoping that I could somehow inform him about what had happened to us. These were all frantic thoughts.

'At one point the door opened, someone went past me and hung up his coat. That was my interrogator, Uwe Karlstedt. That was when we first met. I was still wearing my own clothes. And he explained that I was brought there because the facts of the case needed to be clarified. But I didn't believe a word of what he said.

'At first, I didn't look at my interrogator. I looked down but I noticed that he was frantically going through documents. He was highly tense and nervous. I then looked at him and I think he looked at me at the very same moment. That was the moment I just thought "Wow". I don't know why, maybe it was his eyes, and I knew that it was an inexplicable magic. I was absolutely shocked and looked down immediately. I had never experienced anything like that before. I felt completely out of it. For some seconds I heard angels singing or something like that.

'After I had composed myself and realized that there were no angels singing and that the interrogation had started, he was neither likeable nor unlikeable, he simply remained factual. He was very young; I had always imagined that Stasi interrogators were elderly men. I had never imagined that someone so young could sit there, someone who was probably younger than me and who had soft features. I thought that he was miscast because of his outward appearance. I didn't understand why he started laughing when I told him that I wouldn't say anything and that I wanted to see a lawyer. I thought his behaviour was completely inappropriate, and looked at him as if he was stupid. He was embarrassed and stopped laughing at once.'

Uwe Karlstedt had grown up in a loyal socialist family. His father was a party secretary and many of his siblings worked for the Stasi. So when Uwe was offered a job with the Ministry of State Security he seized the opportunity. After six months training he joined Department 9, dealing with investigations and interrogations.

From his side of the desk Uwe, aware of his junior rank, was preparing to deliver some tough questioning. But he had been expecting someone more hostile and unpleasant than Regina. 'I instantly thought that she looked wonderful and fell in love with her. I had to struggle to compose myself. But luckily Regina looked down again so that we didn't have to look each other in the eyes and I was able to concentrate on my job. I wanted to repress my feelings.

'We fell into our roles quickly. I told her that her friend had been arrested. The fact that all three of them had been caught was the hardest thing for her to bear. The facts of the case were clear. I went out and told my supervisor the results of the interrogation. The decision to arrest her was taken instantly. I told her that a preliminary proceeding had started against her and that she was under arrest. She was taken to the prison in Hohenschönhausen and I drove there too. Regina had to be registered and then I continued with the interrogation, which lasted for nearly the whole night.'

Despite her feelings Regina tried to take the moral high ground with Uwe. 'I ignored the impotence I felt. I was aware that I wouldn't be released and that I'd have to face a trial and time in prison. I drew strength from the fact that I never denied my actions. I tried to turn the tables and present myself as being a morally better person than him. I told him that I thought what I had done was right, that it had to be done for the country.

'At one point we argued about who was the better socialist. I said that I wouldn't be in prison if he were the better socialist. I never got the impression that he was a person who took pleasure in arresting people. As I looked at him sitting in front of me and applying his strategies, I felt like I was watching myself a couple of years earlier. I could tell that he'd had the same upbringing as me and probably thought exactly as I did about our country. I believed that his sincerity and commitment were genuine and that he actually was convinced that people like me needed to be arrested because I had collaborated with the enemy.

'Right from the first interrogation there used to be a notepad and a pencil on the left-hand side of the table. Uwe told me that I could use it for writing down personal notes or things that might come to my mind. But I said that nothing came to my mind. However, during the first interrogation, while he was writing his report, I wrote the sentence, "Despite everything and again and again eleven and twelve". I don't know how that came to my mind.

'I hadn't figured out anything beforehand. I just reacted instinctively. Eleven stood for "you are beautiful" (*du bist schön*) and twelve "I love you" (*ich liebe dich*). This "code" was made up of the number of letters in those phrases. It came to me in a flash. I thought he looked wonderful; he was just my type. And I was very much in love with him and writing it helped me to blow off steam and to calm down. I wrote that same sentence after every interrogation either in very small letters or I drew some decorations around it in order to make it unreadable. That was absolutely childish and schizophrenic, but then, I wasn't under normal conditions anyway. At times when I wasn't angry at him, that was the only means to cope with the pressure.'

Mystified by the notes left by Regina, Uwe decided not to pass them on to his superiors. Although he couldn't understand their meaning he felt sure they contained some kind of personal message. 'Shortly before the end of the interrogations, it was me who declared my love to her. Up to that moment I just left her notes alone, probably because I feared that she wouldn't tell me what they meant or that I would be disappointed if I learnt that they didn't have anything to do with me.

'I was in a similar situation to her because I was totally in love with her but wasn't allowed to show it. That was most difficult to handle in situations where I knew that Regina wouldn't answer or when I knew that her declarations weren't what the Stasi wanted to hear.

'Then the end of the proceedings was near, only three more interrogations needed to be done. By then we didn't see each other on a daily basis any more, and the periods between each interrogation grew longer. I knew that I wouldn't see her any more once she went to prison, and I couldn't do anything to prevent her from being sentenced.

'After the final interrogation had ended and she was signing the report, I said, "Could you imagine loving a person like me?" Obviously, I wanted to make it sound as vague as possible so I could step back in case she wasn't interested in me. But I hoped that her answer would be direct. At that moment Regina didn't appear to understand what I was implying. I realized that I had to ask her more directly, so I asked her if she could imagine kissing someone like me. That was very direct. She said she could imagine that. So I stood up, went over to her table and said, "Here I am..." Then I asked her about the meaning of "Eleven and Twelve" and she told me. I was immensely happy.'

Regina was taken by surprise by the unexpected declaration of love. 'That situation made me realize that I wasn't as courageous as I had thought. I was simply non-committal. He asked to hold my hand and I held it out. He simply put his hand on mine and in that moment I felt something like an electric shock and we kissed very quickly. After that, we simply sat there and didn't say a word. We didn't even look at each other; we simply stared in front of us because neither of us was prepared for that situation.'

Despite his feelings, at that time Uwe couldn't condone Regina's actions. ' I absolutely couldn't identify with what Regina had done. Although I was in love with her, I thought that she had collaborated with the enemy. I didn't accept the fact that she wanted to leave the country. Love didn't change that. After all, secret service is secret service. I was part of a closed circle. I didn't have any friends outside the Stasi. Everthing revolved around the Ministry of State Security and that's where my world view was formed.'

Regina was sentenced to three years and two months, most of which she served at Hoheneck, East Germany's most infamous women's prison. There she hoped for intervention from West Germany to bring about her release. It finally happened two weeks before the end of her sentence.

It wasn't until 1997, when she saw her files, that she learned the name of her interrogator. She scoured the telephone book to find him but when he took her phone call Uwe, married with children, refused to acknowledge that he was the man who had interrogated her, although he remembered who she was. 'I wrote him a letter the following day and reassured him that it wasn't revenge I was looking for, but that I was hoping for a dialogue between the two of us. He responded to that.

'When we saw each other it went "bang" again! That was the moment when our love for each other started. We hugged strongly and then drove over to a nearby cafeteria. We weren't able to do anything else but embrace each other again for a long time.'

This curious romance came to its final denouement when the couple, both divorced from their former partners, married on 16 October 2006.

NATIONAL HEALTH

The foetus is the property of the entire society. Anyone who avoids having children is a deserter who abandons the laws of national continuity.'

Nicolae Ceauşescu

CENTRAL TO CONTROLLING and shaping people's lives under communism was the range of health services available to a state's citizens: doctors, maternity wards, research centres, GP surgeries and hospitals were all used by communist authorities to further their political ends. At times, security forces and their spies worked alongside medical staff to ensure that communist ethos was enforced.

Nicolae Ceauşescu had grand plans to expand the population of Romania. He decided to achieve this by nationalizing the reproductive process itself to ensure his citizens had a multitude of children. In this he was helped by his wife, Elena. As head of the

National Women's Council, she played a key role in the regime's campaign to persuade women to breed for socialism.

Communism also warped existing health services for other political purposes. Ceauşescu sometimes dealt with dissidents by having them diagnosed as mentally ill and committed to psychiatric hospitals. His answer to an unwelcome disease like HIV/AIDS was to deny its existence in Romania. Meanwhile, in Czechoslovakia, the regime designated its Romany population as 'unhealthy' and tried to curb it through the enforced sterilization of Romany women.

In 1965 abortions in Romania reached sky-high levels with four abortions for every newborn. The following year Ceauşescu began a drive to boost the population by introducing a new ban on abortions under a law known as Decree 770. He was concerned that, with a virtually zero growth rate in the population, the labour force needed for his vision of an industrialized Romania would not exist.

Under Decree 770, abortion on demand was banned. Women over 40 or who had at least four children were exempt, as were abortions following rape, incest, congenital deformity or if the mother's life was endangered. Otherwise, carrying out an abortion was a criminal offence punishable by imprisonment. At the same time contraception was banned.

The severity of this legislation was underpinned by an Orwellian apparatus of enforcement. Police and militiamen were placed in hospitals, on wards and in operating theatres, breathing down the necks of physicians and patients alike to try to ensure that those abortions now deemed illegal did not happen. Informers were recruited among medical and nursing staff.

The decree remained in place for 33 years until the fall of Ceauşescu. Over the years, requirements permitting an abortion became more restrictive. By 1985 a woman had to have five children and be over 45 to qualify, and a representative of the Romanian Communist Party had to authorize every procedure. Furthermore, there were compulsory gynaecological examinations for schoolgirls and women factory workers. The government also checked the progress of pregnancies to full term and carried out investigations into childless couples.

Ceauşescu set Romania the target of increasing its population from 20 million in the mid-1960s to 30 million by the millennium. Women who had five or six children were awarded a Maternity Medal; for seven to nine children they received the Order of Maternal Glory and for ten children or more they joined the ranks of the Heroine Mothers.

Socialist competitions were held to see which area of the country could produce the highest birth rate, and single women were encouraged to have children regardless of the social consequences of illegitimacy. This was all reinforced by a system of financial rewards.

On the other hand, there were fiscal penalties if you failed to procreate for your country. A couple who remained childless beyond the age of 25 saw their tax bills increase and had their sex life scrutinized by government inspectors.

Initially, Ceauşescu's drive had some success as by 1967 the birth rate had almost doubled, from over a quarter of a million live births to over half a million. These babies became known as *decreţei* or 'children of the decree'. But the baby boom was short-lived. By the early

1980s the number of legal abortions was greater than the number of live births, which stood at pre-decree levels despite massive investment. Women were just not prepared to have more children when economic conditions and standards of living were in rapid decline.

During the 1980s, sources of illegally acquired contraceptives – including Chinese condoms via Russia, IUDs from Hungary and contraceptive pills smuggled in from the West – began to dry up. More than ever, Romanians were left with withdrawal, celibacy or illegal abortion as the three main options for birth control.

There was a heavy price for all this. It is estimated that at least 10,000 Romanian women died due to complications from illegal abortions. Nor was there sex education for women or men. In particular, nothing was done to inform Romania's male population about their responsibilities. The consequences of sexual activity fell squarely on the shoulders of Romania's women. Unsurprisingly, many of them felt a state of undeclared war existed between themselves and the communist state.

DANIELA DRAGHICI

DANIELA DRAGHICI WAS an educated, middle-class Romanian woman living in Bucharest in the 1970s. She still cannot forget her first compulsory gynaecological examination, which happened while she was in high school. 'I was 18. It was the 1970s and I was graduating from high school. I was getting ready for the entrance examination for the university and before that we were told in high school – only the girls, not the boys – that we needed to have a gynaecological examination to prove that we were fit for this entrance examination for the university.

'We were just lined up in the hallway waiting to go inside the medical room in the school to be examined by a male gynaecologist. We knew he was a doctor but we didn't really know what he wanted from us. There were rumours, and we knew he was looking at a certain part of our body that no one had ever looked at before.

'We were afraid of what they might say, what they might write down after that kind of examination, of what they might tell our parents. We were ashamed. We felt our dignity was snatched away from us while waiting in the hallway to go in that room, being lined up like that. And that was only the first time.'

Such control over the most intimate aspects of women's lives for political not medical reasons created an oppressive climate, as Daniela recalls. 'We were concerned at that time mostly about being able to have sex and enjoy it rather than being afraid all the time. There was just this permanent fear that we might become pregnant no matter what we did because access to contraception was restricted.

'The preferred method of contraception at the time was withdrawal, that's what people knew how to use. We had some access to mostly Chinese condoms. There were people who would sell contraceptives illegally and these were smuggled in from the Soviet Union and from Hungary, but most of the time there was nothing.'

At university, Daniela got pregnant for the first time. As with so many Romanian women, an illegal abortion was the next step. 'I was lucky to be connected to the underground abortion network that existed. The first thing everybody did was to drink shots of some unpleasant mixture, and you had to get these shots in somebody's apartment not in a medical facility. It was all very secretive.

'A week went by and I was not rid of that problem. So one horrible evening I was taken to a house far away, outside Bucharest. There was this old woman. I'm not sure she was a medical person but she appeared to know what she was doing. She was boiling some sharp instruments on a stove in her house.

'She asked me to get up on the kitchen table. You knew whenever you had to have something done to you like that there was always a kitchen table involved. So, I got up on the kitchen table and she started using those sharp instruments and she did not give me any anaesthetic, because she didn't have any. So I had to suffer and, because of the neighbours, in order to prevent me from making any noise she put a rag in my mouth so that I would bite on it when it hurt.

'After a few days I noticed I still had morning sickness, and I was confused as to how I could still be pregnant after I'd just had an abortion. Then I was lucky to be taken to a real doctor who finished the job on a different kitchen table. I remember I left the place with the conviction that I would never have sex again.

'There was always some underground movement going on. That's how most people survived communism: by having an abortion network, by having connections with people who supplied illegal goods, by having a video and being able to watch movies, by listening to Radio Free Europe, by having a parallel activity.'

Daniella felt that Ceauşescu's brand of communism was particularly inimical to the interests and rights of women. 'It was a kind of communism against women. Women had no right to their bodies or their minds. They were totally controlled. Women were not supposed to have access to contraception, or to sex education. Women would go to prison if staff in the hospital found out they had done something to stop a pregnancy. It was always women. They were the victims who were punished all through the system.'

DR ADRIAN SÁNGEORZAN

IN THE 1980s the regime tightened restrictions on abortion and further developed its methods of enforcement. Compulsory gynaecological inspections of women aged between 16 and 45 at their workplace were introduced in 1985. Dr Adrian Sángeorzan, a gynaecologist based in the city of Braşov, took part in these examinations, the main purpose of which was to detect undeclared pregnancies. 'Ceauşescu decided that gynaecologists would go into the factories and do a gynaecological check-up on women. I realized this was just a mockery; they did it to intimidate the women.

'I used to go to this big factory near Braşov; it was a huge so-called "bicycle" factory. But we all knew it was an armaments factory; they made cartridges, rockets and cannons, and had countless numbers of women workers there.

'Every Tuesday I had to go over there between midday and 2 o'clock and see between 40 and 60 women, which was hard to do. It was not done at their request. And when I asked one of them what would happen if she didn't show up, she said she wouldn't be paid that month.'

Although other tests were performed and doctors like Adrian Sángeorzan did cervical smears and tried to detect other gynaecological problems, the real purpose of the inspections was clear to all. 'I knew it was a mockery because I took cervical smears but never saw any test results. The main reason we had to do this examination was to check on women who were possibly pregnant because in a factory it was easier to constrain them and force them to have the check-up.

'And for this reason I think the women hated us. But I just tried to do my job, and, during these check-ups I found many pregnancies which I did not report. I also found cancers and other diseases with which we were able to help.

'The way the check-up was done was really surreal. I had to see the women two at a time. They came in their uniforms in their lunch break. They got undressed and they had no gowns to put on. Everything looked like a grotesque ballet. They had to stand on this cold cement floor with bare feet without a gown. And I remember pictures of Ceauşescu were right there, presiding over us. Years ago he declared basically that every physician was like the property of the state. So everything about this gynaecological check-up was a masquerade and I really felt guilty. It clearly had a political message.

'And after each visit there were always a few pieces of underwear and stockings which were never claimed because everything had to be finished by 2 o'clock when they had to go back in the factory. Basically, the word "privacy", or the word "intimacy", was not in our dictionary. For women who were exposed to this kind of exam, it was humiliating, and I felt it every Tuesday when I went there.'

PARASCHIVA NEAGU

IN BUCHAREST, PARASCHIVA Neagu was forced to undergo one of these gynaecological examinations at her workplace. 'There were compulsory gynaecological check-ups every three, four or six months. They summoned three or four girls from each department. They took us to the consulting room and we'd go in one by one. They'd check us and then told us what was wrong with each of us.

'We were afraid that we could have been pregnant and we'd be recorded as such. Because once you were recorded as pregnant you had to have the child. There was no choice. They found me pregnant once. Then they sent me to the surgery because the GP used to come to the factory's consulting room to collect the lists. Or the nurse would take the lists of pregnant women to the GP.

'After the examinations I was ashamed. But what could I do? It was compulsory to get undressed. Sometimes the nurse would shout at me saying that the doctor was waiting for me to get undressed, to get on the table. The nurses were rude. I was dragging my feet, one of them said. They would shout at me that I was wasting the doctor's time, that there were other girls queuing outside. And the doctor would shout too if he didn't like how we lay on the table. They called us names, said "You act as if you've been born in a stable", or "You peasant". Even now I don't go to the doctor because I'm afraid.'

Unlike Daniela, Paraschiva was a poor, working-class woman who lived in basic, rented accommodation in Bucharest. The house was made of earth and the roof of cardboard. When it rained the roof leaked. At night the electricity was cut off. For water, she had to use a pump in the street.

Paraschiva was married and ended up having three children. She worked in a furniture textile factory earning a meagre wage. In those days most food, apart from bread, was rationed and Paraschiva and her family found it difficult to get by. The last thing she needed was more mouths to feed. 'Ceauşescu wanted people to have as many children as possible in order to torment them, because people had no means to raise them. There wasn't enough food, housing was scarce and three or four people had to live in one room. The decree wasn't right. He should have allowed people to have as many or as few children as they chose or as many as they could afford. Ceauşescu wanted a large population but he didn't think about how they'd be able to live. I suffered because I had a few abortions.'

ANUŢA TIMIŞ

ANUŢA TIMIŞ WAS a peasant woman living in a small village in the north of Romania. She did abortions on herself, advised other women how to perform them and on one occasion assisted in one herself. 'I had three abortions which I performed on myself. I had them because life was difficult then: there was no money and we lacked so many things. We just couldn't afford many children. In Ceauşescu's time we did them in any way we could. Everybody did it – not just me.

'I used a medical probe made of stainless steel like a radio antenna. Somebody had made it. It wasn't mine. I got it from other friends who also did this. I put the probe in medical alcohol. That was all. And I put it inside my uterus. It worked immediately. We borrowed that probe from each other. We disinfected it and passed it around. We boiled it and wiped it with medical spirits.

'The aborted foetus would come out. It took about a week. There was some pain, of course. Then I buried it by the electricity pole in my backyard where nobody could find it. Nobody knew about it. If I were caught, I would go to prison. Even our husbands didn't know we were having abortions.

'I did help one or two women. I gave them the probe and I explained to them, just as others explained to me before, how to use it. Of course, some women died and many ended up with haemorrhages in hospital. But then there weren't condoms as there are now because they were forbidden. If you talked about abortion in Ceauşescu's time, they'd arrest you on the spot.'

Timis was tried and convicted for her role in an illegal abortion. Three months pregnant for the second time, she was sentenced to prison. While she was there her child was born and then forcibly removed from her, an issue that still causes her pain today. 'I was in prison for one year and ten months. They took me to Jilava hospital in Bucharest and I gave birth to my baby girl there. Three weeks after that they told me I was to be sent from Jilava to a women's labour camp. And I asked them to let me see my baby. With great difficulty some policemen did allow me to see my girl. I kissed her and I never saw her again.

'When I left the prison I asked, "What about my baby, where

should I go to pick her up?" And they said, "Make enquiries when you get home." But after I got home I couldn't find out anything. All the people I asked knew nothing. They took her without my knowledge. And today I still don't know what happened to her.'

DR ADRIAN SÁNGEORZAN

DESPITE THE KNOWN risks, the number of illegal abortions continued to rise. Gynaecologists like Dr Adrian Sángeorzan at the hospital in Braşov had to deal with the medical fallout. 'If a woman doesn't want to be pregnant, nobody will be able to prevent that woman from having an abortion. She will do whatever is necessary to get rid of the pregnancy. Ceauşescu wanted us to multiply like rabbits but he did nothing to increase our standard of living. Life here in Romania became tougher, starting mostly after 1979. It became unbearable after 1984.

'The tragedy was so vast that I don't think there was a single family in Romania that did not have a woman who had an illegal abortion during those years. I helped many women by sending them to Bucharest where I knew a friend, who knew a friend, who had another friend, who knew a gynaecologist who did abortions in his house. I said thank God, there are still doctors who are daring to do that. Even if they do it for money, at least they do it properly. But, once in a while, bad cases came in to the hospital, done by a butcher, not a doctor. Sometimes we had three or four deaths in a week. It was like having a serial killer in town when all of a sudden we had a cluster of horrible cases in the hospital.'

Sángeorzan saw a variety of DIY methods of abortion. 'The most popular method was to use a rubber catheter, which was regularly used in the hospital to catheterize the bladder. You could buy them from the pharmacy; it was not a problem. So that was introduced into the uterus, and they then injected into the uterus the most bizarre things like iodine, alcohol, glucose, camomile tea or boiled mustard.

'Gradually we learned that some of these substances were more dangerous than others because their gut absorbed it into the blood and provoked a sort of toxic abortion, which was the worst of the worst. If it went wrong a woman could die in two days.

'I remember once I found the tip of a thermometer containing mercury in one woman's uterus, which was very toxic, and a geranium stem which was popular in the countryside. Of course, when we found things like this we just threw them into the waste bin, carefully so that nobody noticed.'

Every day the gynaecological wards at Braşov were heaving with patients who had broken Ceauşescu's Decree 770, admits Sángeorzan. 'One of the largest wards in the hospital was reserved for septic abortions. Every morning we used to do the rounds of this very big ward; sometimes there were two or three women in a bed. We did the morning visit with two or three doctors who always had 30 or 40 patients. We used to call that place "Death Valley" because so many women died there.'

Every woman entering a gynaecological ward was viewed as a potential lawbreaker, suspected of having had an abortion, so a pregnancy test was routine. Without ultrasound machines, the hospital employed a more traditional method, using bullfrogs.

During pregnancy the so-called 'pregnancy hormone' is present in a woman's urine. When the urine of a pregnant woman is injected into a male bullfrog the frog's urine develops sperm cells, which are easy to detect. It's called the Galli-Mainini reaction. Pregnancy can be detected as early as two weeks. But it takes a while to get the test results. In the meantime, patients too afraid to confess to having had an abortion, and therefore not able to recieve the proper treatment, could bleed to death.

While the patients faced grave risks, clinicians faced punishment if they covered up an abortion. Doctors who chose to help their patients had to proceed with extreme care so they would not be discovered. It was forbidden to insert an IUD in a woman's uterus or to sterilize a woman by tying the Fallopian tubes together, although doctors like Adrian Sángeorzan would do this, usually during a Caesarean operation. 'Only if the women requested it, of course, but there was no paperwork. Everything was between you and that woman. Sometimes just a sign, a gesture, was enough.

'I like to deliver babies and for me everything was about life, giving life and happiness. Then I realized that everything was about lies. I really don't know how many women died. Ten thousand sounds reasonable to me. I am sure there are hundreds of thousands of women who were mutilated, and who survived.'

Of particular concern were the paid informers among hospital staff, recruited by the security forces. It was common for a policeman to arrive moments after a patient who was suspected of having an abortion, having been alerted by a nurse, housekeeper or, occasionally, a doctor.

Doctors like Adrian Sángeorzan felt under particular pressure from the militiamen who were a constant presence around the hospital, trying to uncover lawbreaking by either doctor or patient. 'We knew that there was always the man from the police who had us under surveillance. He would come, pop in at his own will. He used to wear a white gown as we did. And, of course, we were afraid of him.

'We were not allowed to tie patients' tubes, or use any kind of sterilization. And the militiaman could appear even in the operating theatre during surgery if he was informed about it. And that was really unbearable. Of course, it was inappropriate and, a few times, I felt his breath on the back of my neck when I was operating; he was right there watching.'

Sometimes, however, even members of the security forces needed assistance from Sángeorzan as their female relatives wrestled with draconian contraceptive laws. By 1989, with the country's economy in freefall, hospitals like Braşov were struggling to obtain the most basic of medical supplies.

The day after the Ceauşescus were executed, Decree 770 was abolished. 'Our hospital was completely invaded by pregnant women,' recalls Sángeorzan. 'At about 8 o'clock in the morning about four or five hundred women showed up to request an abortion and we could not cope. I remember some of them broke the glass doors. We tried to see who could be helped that very day and who could be helped the next day. After that first day we used to do about a hundred abortions in the hospital every day.'

VASILE PARASCHIV

IF CONTROLLING ROMANIA'S population growth proved futile, controlling dissidents by labelling them as insane proved to be more effective. What happened to Vasile Paraschiv illustrates how the false diagnosis of a mental illness was used by the Romanian Communist Party to suppress, torture and terrorize critics of the regime.

Born in 1928 into a poor family in a village called Ordoreanu, Vasile Paraschiv left to look for work in Bucharest at the age of 12. He joined the Romanian Communist Party in 1946 attracted by their promises to stop exploitation of the working class.

In November 1968, during a general assembly for party elections, Paraschiv stood up and said that he no longer wanted to be a member of the party because it had turned its back on the workers and trampled over the country's constitution and laws.

Soon afterwards, Paraschiv tried to set up an independent trade union, free from the control of the party. On 3 March 1971, Paraschiv sent a list of 11 proposals to the Central Committee of the Romanian Communist Party and the General Union of Trade Unions – of which he was still a member. Although he didn't get an answer he attracted the attention of the Securitate. 'In 1975 I sent a letter to Radio Free Europe (RFE). The letter fell into the hands of the Securitate. They arrested me and they put me in the Voila psychiatric hospital in Câmpina. Later, I sent another letter to RFE and I was arrested again and put into a psychiatric hospital for political reasons.

'Ceauşescu had declared in a speech in Timişoara that only a madman could disagree with the grand achievements of socialism.

And if there were people who disagreed, then they were mad and the straitjacket awaited them.'

Ceauşescu's statement was one of the justifications for committing dissidents to psychiatric institutions, and at least one decree was used to provide legal cover for such treatment. Those without any history of violent behaviour and without a prior medical diagnosis of psychiatric illness could be sent to a psychiatric hospital. They could be committed by a state prosecutor or the secret police as well as by a health authority. Such patients could be kept in hospital against their will for months or years. Electric shocks and mind-altering drugs would often be administered.

The first time Paraschiv was sent to a psychiatric hospital in 1976 he was diagnosed as suffering from 'paranoia'. The symptoms 'proving' this listed on his original admission file included 'writing a series of irresponsible complaints against the authorities in the country and abroad'.

On another occasion, Paraschiv was arrested at the home of the leading writer and dissident Paul Goma and taken to Sápoca psychiatric hospital in Buzău county. 'The director of the hospital was a tool of the Securitate and he subjected me for the first time to compulsory medical treatment. That hospital had a ward specifically designed for dangerous, violent, untreatable patients. That's where they put me.

'Every day they'd put six to eight pills in my hand. Two nurses forced me to swallow them. I'd put them under my tongue and they'd give me a glass of water that I'd drink and then they made me open my mouth. And I'd open my mouth, they'd see there was nothing in there and they'd say I was free to go. Then I'd go straight to the toilet where I'd spit all of them out. That's what I did from the first day to the last.'

There was no official diagnosis before Paraschiv was brought to Sápoca hospital. However, he overheard the director of the hospital say to the policeman who brought him in that, 'it was the last time he was accepting a patient without legal paperwork'.

In 1977 Vasile Paraschiv went to France where he was examined by independent psychiatrists who confirmed that he was not suffering from any mental illness. The following year, his case was one of 16 highlighted in an Amnesty International report. Paraschiv supported an open letter sent on 8 February 1977 by a group of dissidents, including the writer Paul Goma, to the 35 states that were signatories to the Helsinki Final Act (1975). The act, an attempt to improve East–West relations, included a section expressing support for basic human rights like freedom of expression and freedom of thought. He was subsequently isolated at work and bugged by the Securitate.

In 1979 Paraschiv supported the newly founded Free Trade Union of the Working People of Romania (*Sindicatul Liber al Oamenilor Muncii din România* or SLOMR). It advocated the right to free association and the legalization of trade unions not controlled by the Romanian Communist Party. This happened a year before the Solidarity trade union was formed in Poland. Predictably, its existence was short-lived – SLOMR was forcibly suppressed by the Securitate after only three months. Later on that year, Paraschiv received his most severe physical punishment yet, being kidnapped and beaten senseless in a forest.

Right into the final year of Ceauşescu's rule Paraschiv was subjected to brutal beatings and psychological torture. This time he also says he was irradiated durng his captivity. 'On 22 March 1989 I was arrested in the street by a uniformed militiaman without any reason. They took me to a chalet where they kept me for seven days and nights. They hit the soles of my feet with a rubber stick, they hit me in the face and stomach. Their boss would tell the man who was beating me, "Hit him in the liver, hit him in the liver". And my abdomen swelled up like a football. On the seventh day they put some machines in the room where they'd been tortuing me and they irradiated me. After about an hour they entered the room. They told me to stand up, but I couldn't. And then the Securitate officer who had tortured me said, "Perhaps you've been bitten by an adder". And he brought a glass jar into the room which had a snake in it. And he asked me, "What's this?" "A snake," I said. "No, it's not a snake, It's an adder. And from now on when you hear on the phone someone say, 'This is an adder,' you should know it's me and you must do exactly as I tell you. Otherwise you will be brought back here and you won't get out alive." Then they got hold of me, put me in the car and admitted me to the Voila hospital in Campina They didn't want me to die in their hands.'

Today, Vasile Paraschiv is glad about the greater freedom he enjoys in Romania, but feels people like himself have yet to receive justice for the treatment meted out to them under communism. Those who committed the crimes have not, he feels, been punished.

DR ION PÁTRAŞCU

OF ALL THE HEALTH issues associated with post-communist Romania, it is perhaps HIV/AIDS that looms largest in the public's imagination. Striking pictures of young children gaunt with AIDS and isolated in orphanages inspired an international aid effort. Yet while the effects of AIDS on the people of Romania is well known, the story of how the Ceauşescu regime tried to ignore and then hush up the existence of the virus has received less attention.

Dr Ion Pátraşcu is the man who first identified HIV/AIDS in Romania's children and discovered how it was transmitted. Now retired, Pátraşcu worked at the Virology Institute in Bucharest under the Ceauşescu regime. Before 1989 HIV/AIDS officially didn't exist in Romania because it was a 'capitalist disease' associated with prostitutes and drug users. Therefore there was no reason to allocate money for research.

'Politically, the existence of AIDS in Romania was not acceptable,' said Pátraşcu. 'Therefore the Health Ministry was under pressure from the Securitate and from the party. That's why the Health Ministry – through their staff, through their specialists – were taking the official line that there was no AIDS in Romania.'

In June 1989 18 patients from the Hospital for Contagious Diseases tested positive for HIV. Pátraşcu's institute asked for permission to do extra research. This was refused. Pátraşcu recalls, 'One day I met a professor from the Fundeni Children's Hospital and – as I was telling him about the difficulties I was meeting regarding my attempts to get blood samples for research – he offered to give me samples from the children in his own ward. He told me that many of them were very sick and he didn't know what they were suffering from. Next morning I received a sample taken from a 13-year-old girl. I tested it all day long and it turned out to be positive. The girl had full-blown AIDS. I asked the same professor to give us more samples and they sent us another 16. Eight of them proved to be positive.

'When we got those results, we asked for samples from all the children in the hospital. The hospital had 120 beds. In total 13 per cent of the 120 children tested were sick. They had AIDS, they weren't just HIV positive. We also received samples from another hospital. They had the same number of children (120) and – by coincidence – 13 per cent of them turned out to have AIDS, too.'

While the Health Ministry accepted these findings, the regime was concerned that they remain secret. Ceauşescu's secret police were now called in to ensure there was no leaking of the information. Despite the close attentions of the Securitate, Pátraşcu continued his work and discovered that AIDS was evident right across Romania. Having been forbidden to continue his research, Pátraşcu went to the European Parliament and delivered a speech about AIDS in Romania that had not been cleared by the authorities. Afterwards he was threatened with jail.

As the communists refused to accept that HIV/AIDS existed in Romania, there was no medical provision to control the spread of the virus. In particular, the virus spread through infected blood transfusions, carried out to assist the development of underweight, newly born babies. A blood bag containing 250 millilitres was typically distributed among 25 babies. Further, equipment shortages meant that children were given treatment with shared needles.

Of course, there were prostitutes and homosexuals in Romania, but infection rates among them were surprisingly low. Under communism it was HIV/AIDS among young children that mainly concerned Pátraşcu. He believes the real number of HIV-infected children between 1988 and the fall of communism was at least double the official figures of 10,000 or 11,000.

The weakest of the children infected with the virus died within six to 18 months. But the majority, 60 to 70 per cent, are still alive today and have started their sexual lives. Many, he believes, either still don't know they are infected or don't tell their partners.

MARTA PUŠKOVÁ

IF ROMANIA'S HEALTH system had to accommodate the megalomaniac notions of the 'Father of the Nation', communist Czechoslovakia also had plans to reshape the ethnic composition of its population. From the late 1950s until the Velvet Revolution, a significant section of Romany women in Czechoslovakia were sterilized, many of them against their will. This was usually done either without informed consent or with some form of coercion or financial inducement. Often the operation was performed after a Caesarean delivery or an abortion; alternatively it was presented as a bit of medical 'cleaning up' after a normal delivery.

It was all part of a programme conducted by the Health, Labour and Social Affairs Ministries between 1958 and 1989 to produce a 'healthy population'. They sought to regulate and reduce the birth rate of Romanys, describing them as a 'highly unhealthy population'. It was a strategy that was consistently applied for decades.

The communist government issued the sterilization guidelines in 1958, the same year it also outlawed those leading a nomadic existence. In 1971 it issued a directive allowing physicians to sterilize Romany women and offering financial incentives to those who underwent the procedure. In 1988, for example, over 1.5 million dollars was paid out to Romany women who were sterilized. While Romany people accounted for less than three per cent of the population, they represented over 20 per cent of all sterilizations carried out. Social workers used to pressure Romany women with threats about the forced removal of their existing children unless they were sterilized.

In 1978 Charter 77 denounced the policy of the sterilization of Romany women saying, 'In some areas the sterilization programme is carried out as a planned administrative programme and the success of employees is judged by the number of Romany women an employee has been able to talk into sterilization. In this way, sterilization is becoming one of the instruments of the majority aimed at preventing childbirth in a particular ethic minority.' But the practice continued in Czechoslovakia even after the Velvet Revolution of 1989. Cases documented under communist rule and after were condemned by the United Nations Human Rights Committtee in 2007.

Marta Pušková is a Romany woman now living in Ostrava in the Czech Republic. As a young woman she lived in the Slovakian part of Czechoslovakia, where 28 years ago she was the victim of a coercive sterilization. 'I was in hospital in Ružomberok, giving birth to my third daughter. After I gave birth the doctor came to see me and told me I was to have "sterilization" done. I didn't understand what it meant. Nobody talked about it. I was 22 years old and I thought that I would be able to have children again later. I wanted to have a son.

'After the surgery, when I left the hospital and went home, I was told to come back to sign some papers. I went there, signed and was told I would be given 2,000 Czechoslovak crowns. I remember it still. I was surprised. I asked them why I was given the money. They said because I went for surgery.

'I got to know what it meant a year or so later from older women who discussed it with me. In fact, none of us agreed to anything. I felt like I was forced to do it. Some of the older ones said the same thing happened to them, but they were not given any money. It was just the young ones who got paid.

'I'd had three children already but when the older women were talking about the consequences and I realized I wouldn't have the chance to have a son, I felt sad. I had to see a doctor, too, as I was feeling depressed, and my husband was angry with me because I didn't let him know what had happened. I told him I didn't know myself. He went to the hospital to complain about it; he told the doctor off and got kicked out for it.'

Pušková feels that Romany women were treated as second-class citizens by the communist authorities. 'In the hospital in Ružomberok they put all the Romany women in one room. What kind of rights did they have? They couldn't even lie in the same room with white women, only with the Romany ones, in one or two rooms with about six women in each room. They segregated us.

When they heard the surname Pušková, which was the most common Romany surname, I was sent straight away to the room with the other Romany women.

'The idea came from the authorities; I think they wanted the Romany people to stop "spreading"; they wanted us to disappear. I always felt the Romany people were unwanted.

'If you experience something like that you never forget it. You bear that in mind for the rest of your life. And it didn't happen only to me, it happened to many other women too. That is how it goes. I suffer to this day and haven't recovered yet. It will never be the same again. I have never felt good again since it happened; one remembers it and feels sick because of it. It is a kind of pain you suffer for the rest of your life.

'It's about the woman's choice. We didn't have the right to choose then, we had to do what we were told. There are many women like me. We were young and healthy, we had the gift from God to bring children into the world but, to the communists, we were "gypsies" without rights.

'I was a healthy woman, there was nothing wrong with me and I could have had a boy. I need help many times in my house; if I had a son I could have asked him to help me. Sons always come back to their mothers, or so they say.'

10
SOCIALIST SEX

'East [German] women had more fun, everybody knows that. Orgasm rates were higher in the East, all the studies show that. After all, it was a proletarian society. None of this bourgeois concern with chastity until the wedding night.'

Unidentified East German woman in her 40s talking during the 1990s quoted in *Sex After Fascism* by Dagmar Herzog

EAST GERMANY DEVELOPED a sexual culture all of its own. Initially, the sexual advantages of socialism were proclaimed – socialism meant better love and better sex. The idea of socialist sex was used in the SED's (Socialist Unity Party of Germany) propaganda war that began in October 1949 to help win over that majority of its citizens who had little appetite for socialism. Great play was made of the fact that under communism sex was not for sale and, indeed, prostitution and pornography were banned. It was claimed that socialism provided the best conditions for lasting love where women, because of state support, did not need to sell themselves into marriage to survive financially. Commitment to socialism and hence the future, it was said, would enhance any romantic relationship.

This wasn't always the case. The 1950s in East Germany was characterized by a strain of social and sexual conservatism that seemed characteristic of the Politburo's public prudery. Sex was seen as a distraction from socialist goals.

Yet even in the 1950s some East German doctors were enthusiastically endorsing premarital sex. Promiscuity was condemned but sex before marriage was seen as healthy and normal. This secular state was also keen to counsel against Christian notions of morality. Over time this encouraged a more relaxed attitude to sex among East Germans. The country's most popular advice book in the late 1950s, *The New Marriage Book*, endorsed premarital sex for 19- to 25-year-olds and advised 14- to 18-year-olds only against having 'regular' sexual intercourse. This advice stood even in the case of pregnancy outside marriage.

By the 1970s East Germans had decided that sex and the body were areas where they would carve out a degree of freedom for themselves. Nudity had long been a part of the German cultural scene and the FKK (*Freikorperkultur* or Free Body Culture) became an important element in East German society. From the mid-1960s nude bathing became acceptable for growing numbers of East Germans, and by the 1970s full nudity was the norm on beaches and at other holiday sites.

Nudity within the home for children and adults also became

more common, especially for the generation that had grown up with the East German state. For the children of these families, nudism was often standard. Homes in which family nakedness was routine tended to be those where parents advocated progressive attitudes about sex. This second East German generation was raised with far more liberal and tolerant perspectives towards all aspects of sexuality than the previous one.

East Germany witnessed sexual evolution rather than revolution. By the 1970s the SED expressed support for premarital heterosexual activity and unwed motherhood. Abortions on demand were legalized in 1972 and, simultaneously, the contraceptive pill was introduced. A move to end the culture of shame surrounding illegitimacy was an important government objective. This encouraged the more liberal attitudes towards sex that emerged in East Germany. By 1989 one in three children was born outside marriage.

The role of women in East German society was a key factor in the sexual culture that developed in the country. After the Second World War, women in the Soviet zone of occupation heavily outnumbered men, due to the heavy male casualties sustained during the conflict. Consequently, East German women were in great demand in the labour market.

Allied to this was a Marxist belief in the need for the 'emancipation' of women in accordance with collective aims. The equal status of women was established in the 1949 constitution, which said that men and women had equal rights, including the right to work and equal pay for equal work. In 1950 the Law for the Protection of Mother and Children and the Rights of Women introduced measures of practical support. The provision of crèches and various childcare facilities, improved hospital and medical care, and rights to work, along with increased financial support, all underlined state support for women.

In practice, this 'emancipation' of women in East Germany was only achieved to a degree. Nevertheless, the fact that some East German women found themselves in roles of responsibility and power at work and in public life, that men could accept women as their superiors at work, and that some men did stay at home and do housework, all helped redefine the relationship between male and female. This spilled over into the area of sexuality.

Sex advice became a growth industry in the mid-1960s as marriage and sex counselling centres were established. Great emphasis was placed on increasing a woman's pleasure during sex. For example one film, sponsored by the Dresden Museum of Hygiene and shown in schools, highlighted the question of the female orgasm and set out different positions to try during intercourse.

Experts claimed that East German women liked sex more and had more orgasms than their Western counterparts. It was said that East German women had more fun in bed generally. It is interesting that East Germany's joint top-selling book of all time in 1989 was Siegfried Schnabl's sex advice book, *Man and Woman Intimately*, with its advice for enhanced female orgasms and its enthusiastic endorsement of sex for sex's sake. It shared its exalted place at the top of the popularity list with a gardening guide.

Eventually, new outlets of sexual interest appeared. Nude photography, strippers and erotic dancers, centrefold pin-ups, soft-porn movies and pornographic animations emerged. By the 1980s East Germany's traditional reputation for small-town conservatism was at odds with the liberal sexual trends being experienced in its major cities. By the middle of the decade erotic dancing and striptease started to take off. Performers were supposed to obtain a licence for their act from the local authority but increasingly such controls were bypassed, overlooked or ignored.

HEIDI WITTWER

HEIDI WITTWER WAS a stripper and erotic dancer from Leipzig. She began her working life as a TV-store sales assistant then became interested in dancing and enrolled at art school. Although she joined the Free German Youth (FDJ), she was never a Communist Party member, even though that would have ensured fast-track promotion to shop manager. These days Wittwer runs a school for strippers and works as a photographic designer.

'In the early days, striptease wasn't well received in East Germany,' she says. 'It was regarded as beneath contempt. My involvement started when I was nominated Miss Leipzig Carnival – I was in every newspaper and some photographers asked me if I was prepared to do a few nude photographs. I was very scared at the beginning. At that time, I was so timid that I'd cross the road when guys walked on my side of the street.'

The photo-sessions gave her confidence and Wittwer decided striptease would be fun to try. She applied for an erotic dancing licence, a procedure that required her to perform in front of a city-government-appointed committee, and hit on the idea of stripping in the character of an Alpine girl called Edelweiss. 'I was asked about my motivation and purpose in playing this girl,' said Wittwer. 'They had never seen a strip like it. It was funny as well as sexy, but they were not too sure about it. They told me I was very welcome to re-audition, but I didn't and I thought that my goose was cooked. In the end, not one of us artists received a permit allowing us to perform erotic dancing. But we all ended up stripping on stage around Leipzig nevertheless.

'At the beginning we were invited to birthday parties, then town fairs, and so I went from village to village. I started with my "Edelweiss" striptease for which I wore a huge skirt and big, fake, stuffed-up breasts. I carried a bucket for milking, had a gap in my teeth and wore glasses. When I got on stage I looked very ugly, and then I started taking off my clothes piece by piece. Eventually I stood there in expensive lingerie and the ugly "Edelweiss" had gone. People laughed and were enthusiastic because they hadn't seen anything like it before. Striptease was not a common thing in the DDR. But then suddenly it started booming.'

Perhaps because of this, club impresarios never asked to see Wittwer's erotic dancing permit. Success forced her to quit her nine-to-five job and she began working seven nights a week, sometimes to marquee audiences of up to 1,500 people – including Stasi and party officials. The Leipzig Fair, where she performed nine ten-minute shows per night, was particularly gruelling. She noticed how the *Wessis* (West German) visitors seemed so much smarter and healthier than the *Ossis* (East Germans) who 'always looked so dull and worn out and pale'.

Wittwer thought the *Wessis* 'behaved as if they could buy us everything we wanted' and got the feeling she was 'everybody's girl'. She was not among the strippers who boosted their income by prostitution – lucrative though it was – but often wondered how she could earn more. Despite the strictures of communism, wealth and privilege somehow flourished in certain quarters, including the striptease clubs.

'It was clear that the Stasi was somehow involved and that similar things had always existed,' she said. 'At some events people arrived looking very "exclusive" in their capitalist cars. That was when I became aware of how things actually worked in the DDR. During my shows, I saw champagne in huge bowls, fruit like bananas and everything we didn't have. I started wondering what was going wrong, what I was doing wrong.

'I earned loads of money during the Leipzig Fairs – 250 East German marks per ten-minute performance, provided I worked with a manager. I was able to buy a Wartburg car from doing 50 shows in a single week. I was able to fulfil all my wishes – the best make-up, great clothes. That was no problem for me. It was inconceivable for an ordinary DDR citizen to afford these items.

'I never knew who was a party member and who wasn't, and I was never asked to adhere to regulations. I heard rumours that prostitutes had been forced to comply with these rules but such problems never occurred to us freelance artists. We registered at the revenue office and received a booklet where our income was entered. Everything was very accurate. Nobody ever put any real obstacles in my way.'

Before the emergence of striptease, public nudity was confined to beaches or the occasional risqué ballet performance at the Friedrichstadtpalast in Berlin. Suddenly there were striptease acts live on stage in your own village. 'The best time was when I performed in an old people's home. The youngest person watching must have been 90 years old. When I entered dressed as an Alpine girl everyone was very happy, but when I started taking off my clothes they covered their eyes with their hands. I stood naked in front of them and started thinking it might not have been such a good idea. But they hugged me and gave me flowers when I left. That was one of the best shows I did.'

Wittwer believes the emergence of erotic clubs and striptease took away a little of the country's innocence. Nudity was always considered healthy and normal; the problem for the state (at least publicly) and many East German citizens was when sex got 'dirty'. Clean eroticism, she concedes, is hard to find. 'I don't want to say that all porn is dirty,' she says, 'but there were many things that were out of reach for DDR citizens, and when they got hold of them everything got degraded a little. Back in the days of communist rule, people longed for sex and eroticism. It was something great. Nowadays, that longing has decreased. Striptease clubs are commonplace; you're free to go into any brothel or table dancing club.'

DIETMAR SCHÜRTZ

WITTWER'S PORTRAYAL OF a state apparatus concealing a 'grubby' secret was reflected in the East German army – once the most respected and feared military machine in the Warsaw Pact. On the face of it, a soldier's life was dour, predictable and unforgivingly strict. The reality, at least in some quarters, was very different.

Dietmar Schürtz was a cameraman, soundman and actor in the army's 160-man film unit. He helped set up the official unit in 1982 but was soon making erotic films for showing privately to army colleagues and high-ranking officers, and at selected film festivals. He also took nude photographs that appeared in official publications such as the NVA (*Nationale Volksarmee* or National People's Army) paper, which every soldier had to buy. His unit used locations such as military hospitals for its shoots and often chose female stars from among the army's civilian employees.

The films were made in secret but were partly sanctioned by Schürtz's superior officers. A cross between Benny Hill, the *Carry On* series and early Scandinavian photography, they featured humorous digs at the failings of communism and the public prudery of the regime's official face. Known as Filmgroup 82, Schürtz and his colleagues were sponsored by the NVA film studio and had previously worked there as assistants. Suddenly, they had their chance to explore new, edgy and erotic areas of cinema.

Schürtz, who today works in the reunited German army's media department, says senior officers were unsure quite how to deal with Filmgroup 82. 'It wasn't really allowed,' he said. 'We were looked at with critical eyes. However, it wasn't forbidden either. We got several warnings and were told to be careful with what we were doing.

'We made our first erotic film in 1983 or 1984. Actors were recruited from within our circle of acquaintances. We just asked and people were ready to participate because they wanted to test themselves. Nudity was something different from everyday life and illegal up to a certain degree. Consequently it was quite special for the actresses.

'One film we made was called *Heidi.* It was a weird story. A doctor was examining a woman with his stethoscope and then tuned her nipple on to a song, 'Heidi, your world, your mountains', as if her breast was a radio. Another erotic film was set in the East German army. It was based on the military command 'Chest out, stomach in'. A woman lined up with the soldiers and obviously she pushed her breasts forward when she heard the order 'Chest out' but one of her buttons fell off and she stood there with her naked breast. I played the inspecting officer.

'Once we realized that our films were going down well, we increased the erotic elements and were able to show them everywhere.

'Erotic topics weren't much disseminated in the DDR, at least not publicly. Only a few illustrated books, and from time to time some magazines, showed nude pictures. This presented a challenge because we had to think up our own plots. We got ideas from rude jokes and things we'd seen on West German television.

'One of our films featured a woman doctor's surgery. The plot reflected the fact that there was a constant shortage of replacement car parts in the DDR, and the patient, a mechanic, told the doctor, "Madam, I'm your mechanic and I've brought along the important spare part". She was so happy she took her blouse off.

'There were film festivals for amateur film-makers, which we always attended. We presented one film that was quite explicit and were told by an executive that it couldn't be shown to a socialist public. But a few weeks later the same man, who was a party member, approached us asking whether it was possible to get some of our films for "evaluation". I think he and his circle may have had other reasons for watching them.'

Schürtz knew that hard-core pornography was strictly forbidden. He had no interest in risking a prison sentence and regarded his 'soft-erotic' film-making as a big achievement in itself. However, it was often hard to know where to draw the line on socialist decency. One revealing photo of a model in the NVA paper for soldiers brought an angry backlash from a general, who wanted the entire publication pulped. He was too late – it had already been circulated – but Schürtz was told unequivocally, 'We don't tolerate images which make our soldiers wank'.

MICHAEL SCHMIDT

SOMETIMES EROTICISM could be used as a form of protest. Michael Schmidt taught himself animation as a 12-year-old schoolboy, using an 8mm camera and plasticine. Later, he worked as a state TV cameraman and eventually got a job with the animation studios at Mahlsdorf, where he began producing his own short stories for a series called *Hopla*.

The target audience was nursery-school children and Schmidt's films introduced them to people in everyday jobs, such as firemen or foresters. Most had a moral; the fireman, for instance, had to deal with a little devil who came out of a volcano to tempt children into playing with fire. In the end, the devil got punished. 'I wanted to do something in the *Wallace & Gromit* style,' said Schmidt. 'But I also wanted to represent a bit of East German reality.

'Another of my films was about the adventures of a policeman. I wanted it to become a series but was told it was too realistic. The management didn't want too much DDR reality, such as plaster falling off walls because skilled workmen couldn't be found, and consequently my film was rejected. I felt frustrated because I'd invested quite some effort into building the sets. So I decided to have some fun and make a slightly erotic movie to be shown privately to a few people.'

In Schmidt's new story a policeman helps a young girl cross the road only to discover that she's fainted from the smell in a nearby toilet. He buys her a chocolate-milk drink (then promoted in East Germany as good for growing children), and within seconds she has transformed into an adult woman. The policeman is aroused and tries to seduce her in a municipal park, but she hides behind a statue of Karl Marx.

'At that time we weren't allowed to make fun of Karl Marx; this man was sacrosant,' said Schmidt. 'But by then Gorbachev was leader of the Soviet Union and people started to think of Marx as old-fashioned. People knew that many things he'd written didn't work out. It was clear to us that it was impossible to achieve communism as professed by Marx; it was absurd. And that was why we made fun of him.

'So the girl hides and taunts the policeman. He doesn't know where she is hiding but he wants to get it on with her because she's very good-looking. He tears his service uniform into pieces because he doesn't want to be a policeman any more. Then she appears behind the Karl Marx monument and bells start to toll.

'Then the statue's eyes start moving and you realize the monument is alive. He follows the action with his eyes and when he sees the girl, a little bump – his erection – comes out of the pedestal. That's when you realize that even Karl Marx has urges and that his theories, which have grown abstract over the years, actually have some human traits.' The girl performs oral sex on the policeman in the film. At some point the theme music from the children's TV show *Sandman* is heard.

'People didn't get to see such things; films like this weren't on sale in East Germany. We knew there were porn movies in West Germany, and sometimes an elderly woman managed to smuggle them here and we got to see a third or fourth copy, usually of very poor quality.

'Of course, I didn't show the policeman film to my boss. He was a party member who stood up for our socialist country and defended it during his speeches at meetings. I didn't think he'd be able to understand the comic side of our films because he very strictly followed the guidelines of the party and would never make fun of it. I was a bit naïve. Of course, I only made such movies at home, but you never knew if one of your acquaintances would give you away. It was only afterwards that I realized the danger I'd put myself in.

'Later I made a secret film with the title *How Does Cheese get its Holes?* I worked on that film for two years although I knew I wouldn't be able to show it. It was about roadworks: in order to fill one hole, the digger opened up another one elsewhere. This summed up how things were in the DDR. There were never enough supplies or materials. I dubbed the film on the day of Honecker was removed from office. I realized I could get away with more than before. Honecker wasn't able to intervene any longer and eventually the film was shown on East German television.'

GÜNTER RÖSSLER

SCHMIDT'S FILMS used eroticism as an expression of private revolt. As a pioneer of nude photography in the DDR, Günter Rössler feels he creates art in capturing the female form through his lens.

Many of his photographs ended up in the country's only authorized nude-centrefold magazine, predictably called *Das Magazin*. It was licensed by the Ministry of Culture and was a mix of high culture, travel items, fashion advice, film star gossip, recipes, lonely-hearts club listings and advertisements. It had a wide readership, from schoolboys to construction workers and party members. Each issue had to be presented to, and approved by, the Central Committee of the Communist Party.

Eventually Rössler's work was noticed by the editors at *Playboy* – then and, arguably still, the definitive men's magazine. They wrote to Rössler with plans to use some of his photos and run a ten-page pictorial for which he'd receive 1,000 West German marks per page. To Rössler it seemed like the DDR equivalent of a lottery win. Even so, he didn't like the idea, regarding it as something of a sell-out to a decadent Western publisher.

'That was a period when my wife was happy if my parents, who lived in West Germany, left us some coins when they came for a visit,' he said. 'She was able to buy mascara with that money. Such was our situation. And then that letter came along offering me 10,000 West German marks. The more I reflected, the more I thought that I had to do it. Also, I had never had the chance to publish my work in the West before. The idea of my work being shown abroad was the decisive point.

'Dealing with the political offices here was a farce. I wasn't allowed to have any direct contact with *Playboy*; everything went through our political agencies, which had to be informed and give approval. I wasn't allowed to speak to, or correspond with the editorial office in Munich.

'Quite some time passed, probably six or nine months, then I received a postcard asking me to come to the Customs office. I was a bit surprised because I knew that the Customs office in Leipzig was in the same building as the Stasi. I had the impression that things weren't right. I didn't know what was going on. There was a very big room with just a table in the centre and two or three chairs. There were no cupboards or anything.

'One man was sitting at the table and I was asked to sit down. He said, "I'm not a party member. But didn't you know that DDR photographers are not permitted to publish their works in non-socialist countries?" I replied that I knew and wanted to know why he'd asked me such a thing. He started to say, "We have heard..." but I intervened and said, "So you have already heard that our agencies issued a permit for me". He replied, "You are not allowed [to keep a copy of the magazine]." But I reassured him that I didn't have any copies, I told him I had never even seen the pictorial.

'A copy of *Das Neue Deutschland* [*New Germany,* the official newspaper of the SED] was lying next to him on the table. He moved it and there was a copy of *Playboy* underneath. He said, "Here is a copy." I was allowed to take a look but I wasn't allowed to take it home with me. I jokingly told him that this wasn't necessary, and that certainly he and his colleagues would want to take a look too. It was quite funny.

'The pictorial had been given the title 'Girls from the DDR' and there was a short briefing on each girl's college studies or profession. I liked that very much although I hadn't expected it. *Playboy* had realized my work was a bit different and decided to put it that way.

'At one point I received another notification from our political office in Berlin asking how I wished to be paid. I could take cash or a cheque, but another possibility was to apply for a foreign travel permit because I owned Western money. An application had already been prepared for me so I decided on the latter. I drove to France taking 5,000 German marks with me – half the total I should have received.

'Later I spoke to the office in Berlin and asked why I had not received the full 10,000 German marks as agreed. I already knew that there was nothing I could do about it so I asked in a sarcastic voice. The man on the other end of the line replied, "Mr Rössler, you have been here yourself. Haven't you seen how much work my colleagues did in processing your case? They all need to be paid!" I was happy that he had the courage to at least say something like that.

'I was very satisfied with my life in the DDR. I just never made a lot of money. Because I was involved in fashion I always attended the annual Fashion Congress (*Modekongress*), which was arranged by a different socialist country every year. And that was how I travelled to all socialist countries and visited all socialist capitals and made contacts everywhere.

'During the whole of my career as a nude photographer I only ever had one difficulty with the publication of my work. A friend from university and I decided to put on an exhibition. We knew the only possible venue was in Ahrenshoop, a town where we used to go on vacation. We got to know a representative of the cultural institute there and convinced him to allow our exhibition in his building.

'We exhibited 30 to 40 works, all in a relatively large format and all framed. Everything was neatly done. After we had finished setting up in the late afternoon we strolled off for a coffee in the town centre. A man walked towards me and I realized we knew each other from Berlin. He was an editor or the like. But he was also a party member working in cultural politics.

'We told him about the exhibition. He sounded amazed and wanted to know when it was on. He said he really wanted to see it. The following morning, when we arrived to open up, everything was bolted and barred. He had banned the exhibition and we had to take all our photographs off. Some 20 years later, a photographer from Berlin told me she had met this man and that he had enquired about me. He told her to tell me that he now realized that his decision had been completely wrong.'

KURT STARKE

THERE ARE FEW BETTER qualified people to give an overview of sexual attitudes in the DDR's dying years than Kurt Starke, the leading East German sexologist. In 1984, together with Walter Friedrich, he published *Love and Sexuality before 30* – a book that drew on the results of a wide-ranging survey among young East Germans. Findings suggested that, on average, young East German women had their first orgasm at 16 or 17, that 70 per cent of 16-year-olds had had an orgasm, and that two-thirds of young East German women 'almost always' had an orgasm during sex.

The authors concluded that social conditions in East Germany played a key role in fostering sexual pleasure. While this may sound like classic communist propaganda, Starke insists that his view is supported by later research showing that DDR women liked sex more, and experienced orgasms more often, than their counterparts in West Germany. He believes there is plenty of evidence to support the claim that a socialist society produces good sex.

'There have always been two lines of thought within the proletarian movement,' he said. 'One was very stern. It held that love for the socialist cause meant that love for other things needed to be repressed or forgotten. If there was any doubt you had to choose the socialist cause. Party people who did this were the true revolutionaries. The second line was more relaxed, more liberal. It was for free love, abolition of religious or any other barriers, it was for the free being.

'In the early years of the DDR, in the post-war period, it was expected that married couples with children would not cheat on each other, otherwise the party would avenge such behaviour. The party was very rigorous and that influenced other areas. For instance in boarding schools – and I attended one of those – dating was prohibited. Those caught defying this ban, almost everyone in fact, would be publicly humiliated. I witnessed these humiliations and it made a strong impression on me. That was why my first analysis, in the early 1970s, dealt with this very topic, what happens when young people start a relationship and have sex at an early age.'

In the early 1950s at Kurt Starke's school, pupils caught dating members of the opposite sex – for instance, going to the cinema together – would be hauled up before the school board and were dressed down in the presence of the entire school. The state used an old German law about premarital relationships to justify this.

'The Honecker era began in the late 1960s, early 1970s. During those years a sexual liberation of unprecedented dimensions took place but in a gradual, undramatic way. It had several causes but chiefly it was related to the fact that the position of women within society, within families and within relationships had changed. Also women's attitudes had changed. When a woman went to bed with a man she also wanted to enjoy sex. And the more East Germany became a secular society the less the moral restraints of Christian faith mattered.

'Family structures changed when women started going to work and became financially independent. Women earned less than men but at least they didn't have to rely on breadwinning males. This produced new family structures in which people got married and became pregnant at an earlier age. Both partners would have a job and wouldn't have to fear unemployment. People couldn't always express preferences about the nature of their employment and studies, or the location, but it was understood that everybody would stay in work. This massively increased the self-confidence of both men and women.

'The second determining factor was that while standards of living were modest, nobody suffered from hunger. And, most importantly, once you had a flat – even if it might be in a deplorable condition – it was yours and nobody could take it away from you.

'The third factor was education. Over 50 per cent of students at universities were women, and at professional schools this rose to 90 per cent. This too shaped the structure of the family because the whole atmosphere within a family changed. It became more democratic.

'I believe that the events of 1989 and 1990 wouldn't have happened the way they did, or even at all, if this democratization within the family hadn't taken place. The most important family matters were now discussed with the children – themselves a generation of latchkey kids – including physicality. This also influenced the relationship between parents. Marriage, love and sexuality didn't depend on money, or only rarely. There was no market interested in the commercialization of the female body – that simply didn't exist. Naked women would be shown very seldom in public. Love and sexuality were topics that would be discussed with more openness in the family circle. I showed clear evidence of this in my analysis.

'The more respectful children were, and the more their questions were taken seriously, and the more warnings and bans on sexuality were dropped, the more people's capacity for love would grow. When they became 15 or 16 years old and fell in love, they weren't scared of sexuality. That was the DDR. People always forget that. When people think of East Germany they think about certain themes such as the Berlin Wall, barbed wire and dictatorship. But those ideas make it difficult to talk about delicate matters such as democratization of the family and sensuality.

'The so-called sexual liberalization wasn't an issue in the DDR. It had developed step by step and was taken for granted. Why shouldn't a 15-year-old girl who had fallen in love not engage in a proper, full relationship? Why shouldn't she touch or kiss the boy she loved?

'Curiously, it was women who seemed to take the initiative on sex. Honour and virginity were notions of no importance. Women were not judged according to their physicality, and that's why they felt free. People simply wouldn't talk about it; everything was so very self-evident. Two-thirds of girls were engaged in proper relationships at the age of 16, and thus 16 was the average age of first sexual contact, sometimes even earlier. Teenagers were free to decide about their sexual activity in East Germany.

'When I started my research at the institute in Leipzig in the early 1970s we discovered that 98 to 99 per cent of women aged 16 to 18 were able to have orgasms. The capacity to achieve an orgasm was linked to the engagement in proper relationships in the DDR. That is a difference that still persists today between East and West Germany. Men in the DDR were not brought up as macho individuals, because women were highly respected in society. Women were seen as the best and the greatest creatures. It was understood that father and mother stuck together. That is something people in the West cannot understand; they don't see that it is possible to forget about one's gender when you have joint tasks. In East Germany both partners used to do the shopping without any problems. If a man tried to impose his dominance he would have had to face discussions either with his wife or with the other people around him.

'Studies on the ideal partner showed that in the West it was social status, wealth, good looks and many other things that mattered, whereas being a loving father or a loving mother was the priority in the DDR. There was no double morality. Sexuality was not commercialized. Many factors influenced a person to feel free to talk about and exercise their sexuality.

'We studied the difference in orgasm rates among students in the East and West in the 1980s. It's still the case that East Germans more often engage in genuine relationships and sexual activity takes place mainly within these relationships; consequently they have more sex. This leads to relatively higher orgasm rates. But that doesn't have anything to do with the woman as such, or with something abstract, but rather with their situation.

'When abortion and the pill were introduced in the 1970s you couldn't say that women were more carnal because of these changes. You need to acknowledge the context; it was a big chance for working women to have access to free contraception pills legitimized by the doctor. So, while in West Germany fierce controversies took place because of the pill, this was not the case in the East.

'As for nudity in society, morals relating to nudity didn't exist.

East German men didn't know much about pornography; they didn't see a woman as somebody who jumped around naked in a porn film. In any case nudity in itself is not erotic. I have never heard of anybody seeing even one erect penis on a nudist beach. On the other hand it can be sensual. It is a matter of custom. If parents don't force their children to lock the bathroom door, or to put on bathrobes, nudity is perceived as normal.

'Today people want to distinguish themselves from others by means of status symbols. How many bodyguards do I have? What car am I driving? What's my salary? What clothes do I wear? Such things are thought to increase people's value. In East Germany young people and especially women found such things repellent. On nudist beaches it didn't matter if you were a party secretary or a concierge. Elderly women enjoyed being on nudist beaches because they were accepted as people in their entirety. They would not be excluded just because they were old. East German women replaced the fake normality of going swimming in bathing costumes with a natural normality. Normality really means that things are not questioned; they are considered as standard, a convention.

'Two other things need to be said about East German women. Firstly, they have always had a more positive ideological attitude than men. That might sound a bit antiquated but in all the analysed categories, such as attitude to the DDR, to socialism, to the Soviet Union, to capitalism and so on, women always showed more engagement. They also embraced social functions, like those offered by the Free German Youth, more and possessed a certain independence. In 1989 and 1990, as the country collapsed, the criticism that was voiced against the system appeared to be initiated by women. I believe that they massively contributed to those changes, and that even after the fall of the Wall they continued being the dynamic element.

'Secondly, although there were some attempts to create feminist groups in the DDR this wasn't warmly received. Western feminism emerged from a completely different background, and had different goals, some of which had long been achieved in the DDR. East German women didn't know what do to with the West German feminists. That's because the experiences and views of DDR women on emancipation are different. The merit of Western feminism is, for example, the acknowledgement of male dominance and behaviour and how this influences culture. But its basic error is the excessive emphasis on gender differences, and the idea that fighting against men is the means to solve all social problems.

'This idea of feminism is way too narrow for East German women because they had a Marxist education. They don't think of themselves primarily as women or men, but as personalities. That has been empirically proven. Apart from being male or female, they feel they have many other characteristics. When asked if they had ever found it to be an advantage or a disadvantage to be a woman, the percentage of West German women answering both questions with a yes is higher than the percentage of East German women. That is a very important difference, which still has not been completely overcome.

'The chance to travel, to study and to be informed has massively increased and DDR citizens have clearly benefited from that. What they have lost is probably not the orgasm during sex or demonstrations of tenderness, but rather the environment. People now take a long time before founding a family – 40-year-old men suddenly realize they still don't have a wife but don't worry about it. Women find they are made redundant or discriminated against in ways they didn't know existed before, or are branded worthless at the age of 16 because they can't find an apprenticeship.

'If you look at sexuality not as something isolated, but rather as part of the personality, a certain personality within society, you have to search for the existing love-friendly and love-unfriendly conditions. I am always looking for love-friendly conditions, which obviously exist en masse. Love cannot be forgotten, and young people often rebel emotionally against a certain society simply by falling in love. There's nothing you can do about it. Whoever is in love is less violent. But I also acknowledge the existence of many love-unfriendly, woman-unfriendly, parent-unfriendly conditions. It's a telling fact that one main difference between pregnant teenagers is that those in the old East Germany tended to keep their children whereas West Germans tended to terminate them.'

11
DISSENT

After the uprising of 17 June,
The Secretary of the Writers' Union
Had leaflets distributed in the Stalinallee
Stating that the people
Had forfeited the confidence of the government,
And could win it back only
By redoubled efforts. Would it not be easier
In that case for the government
To dissolve the people
And elect another?

Bertolt Brecht, 'The Solution', August 1953

MARXIST-LENINIST IDEOLOGY claimed that there was no reason for opposition to exist under socialism because the working class exercised power. Yet dissent still occurred in East Germany, Czechoslovakia and Romania both politically, in the form of insurrection, escape and spying, and culturally, in fashion and even pop songs.

The first major uprising against communist rule in Eastern Europe occurred in East Berlin on 17 June 1953. What began as a protest against pay and working conditions among building site workers developed into a political protest. Protestors demanded the resignation of the government and free elections. Estimates suggest that almost half a million people went out on strike and about 418,000 people took part in demonstrations throughout East Germany on that day.

It was three months after the death of Stalin, interpreted by many as a signal for change. But if the demonstrators believed they would receive support from the Allies they were disappointed. American intelligence was caught on the hop and failed to respond while in Britain there was a fear that a unified Germany could once again pose a threat. Loyal communists believed that the event had been whipped up by residue fascists.

Like the Americans, the SED (Socialist Unity Party of Germany) leadership in East Germany was caught off-guard and quickly lost control. Order was only restored after the intervention of Soviet troops stationed outside Berlin.

HORST KREETER

HORST KREETER FOUND himself at the centre of events on 17 June 1953. He was 22 years old and worked at a small petrol station owned by his parents on the outskirts of East Berlin. He was not a socialist and had been disaffected with the government for some time. 'Until 1945 Adolf Hitler was the greatest for us as Germans and I was extremely disappointed when I later found out what kind of person he really was. In the East German Zone Stalin was the greatest. There was no one bigger than Stalin, and I thought, "This is the same as before but with different symbols". So when I heard about the demonstration in Berlin, I knew I needed to be part of it.'

For Kreeter, participation led to a shadowy existence in espionage and, finally, a jail sentence. But at the outset the mood among protestors was jubilant. 'People were pouring in from every street. I was close to the head of the march. There were a lot of police trying to form barriers so that people could not go further but we always managed to avoid them. It was amazing how many people had gathered.

'At the beginning we marched quietly; later, we made demands. A free election was priority number one. When we reached Marx-Engels-Platz it was packed with people. Some strike leaders were trying to address the crowd from a little podium, but with the huge numbers of people we could hear very little.

'Then around midday from a distance we could hear the chains of tanks. When we realized that Russian soldiers were coming the crowd started howling. About a dozen tanks arrived. The commander of the first tank looked out and shouted something, which nobody understood. He was waving his arms but nobody knew what he wanted. The tanks slowly approached.'

The crowd began to get restive, booing anyone who begged them not to provoke the soldiers. When the soldiers started firing into the air, the crowd stampeded. 'It was total mayhem, and then the first machine guns started firing. It was deafening. We were all thinking we should scarper so as not to be hit by the bullets. That's when I saw the first casualty. A man had been squashed by a tank. We ran past the corpse. We were now boiling inside.'

The Russian tank officers retreated inside their machines when the angry crowd began pelting them with stones – and then began to respond with firepower. 'Even though the tanks fired in the air the sheer sound caused people to piss in their pants. When we realized that they were firing into the air we were a bit braver. You had to get used to it in order to be able to continue protesting.

'Then trucks arrived with soldiers in the back. You could see that they were young soldiers who did not really understand what was going on and it could be assumed that they would shoot if they received the order.'

Demonstrators began setting fire to cars, starting with those bearing government number plates. 'While we threw stones towards the police, the police would also throw stones in our direction. Sometimes protesters were caught by the police, but we would always try and get them released again by rushing towards them as a crowd.

'It was clear that we couldn't win this one. The Russians' power outweighed ours pretty quickly. They started controlling street after street. Those who didn't run fast enough were taken prisoner and beaten up. There was no order at all in our strike action so it ended up being total madness, with everyone acting for himself, trying to save his own neck.'

Kreeter and a friend slipped away and went into West Berlin to buy a sausage and potato salad from a kiosk. At the time there was still free passage from East to West in the city. When they heard there was to be a curfew enforced by the police and Soviet army they decided to make their way home. 'There was a blanket over a dead body and a wooden cross which said, "Killed by the Soviet Army"' remembers Kreeter.

'The following day, I saw that the Russians were hiding behind the church wall and were pointing their machine guns in the direction of Berlin. The Russians maintained this position for a few days. The curfew remained for another few days but we did not take it too seriously.'

Sixteen Soviet divisions, around 20,000 soldiers, stationed in East Germany had been involved in suppressing the revolt, supported by 8,000 KVP (*Kasernierte Volkspolizei* or People's Police). In particular, it was the active presence of Soviet T34 tanks that was so dramatic. For Kreeter the use of tanks confirmed his suspicions about the nature of the East German government.

The number of dead is still a matter of dispute, but it is estimated at least 50 demonstrators were killed and over 20,000 arrested; 1,400 people received life sentences and 200 were executed. From then on, security and control of the people became the SED's top priority.

The aftermath of the protest did nothing to diminish Kreeter's opposition to the communist regime. By chance he met another like-minded man in Berlin who put him in contact with the American army, specifically the Counter Intelligence Corps, and he became a covert radio operator. 'I was already a media technician and they said they would train me to become a radio operator. I thought it would be a good opportunity to work against the communists. My parents had been accused of not resisting the Nazi rule and I thought if I did not do it I might be accused of not resisting the communists. I did not want to be a coward. If you want to be considered as an opponent of the system, you need to have the courage to say "yes".

'Once or twice per week I travelled to Berlin. My contact was Captain Walther and I requested that he would be the only person I was in contact with. He was a German.'

When he got married, Kreeter leased a summer house outside Berlin, where he had no neighbours. It proved ideal as a base for radio equipment that was no bigger than a box of matches. 'As far as I understood, the Americans wanted to build radio communication routes from West Berlin to Moscow. They wanted a team of radio operators to deliver information as fast as possible. Since we were still dreaming about satellites, radio communication was the way to deliver information. It's also why they wanted to test their UKW (*Ultrakurzwelle* or ultra short wave) radio devices in my summer house.

'I had one device at home, a so-called Morse code training device, to learn the different Morse codes. The Americans paid me 100 West German marks every month for expenses. I also received 200 cigarettes per month from the American army – they took off all the labels and packaging and put the cigarettes into a plastic bag. Also, I received 500 grams of coffee per month. I had to sign a statement to confirm that I worked as a radio operator for the American army. I think they needed that paper to explain to their superiors where the money was going.

'They were generally interested in what the mood was like among East Germans and the general climate in the DDR. Even if I wanted to, I could not tell them any state secrets because I only saw the Russian army compounds from the outside.'

Kreeter knew the risks he was running in a country where a political joke could merit a three-year prison term. He was eventually arrested on 10 January 1956, a few days short of his 24th birthday. Sentenced to ten years in prison, he was released after nine and left East Germany for good.

Although he considers 17 June a day of glory, it has sunk from view. 'We immobilized the system through peaceful demonstrations. I am surprised that the day is not properly highlighted in German history; but it simply does not fit into today's politics. I always thought I did the right thing. Even though people died or went to prison, I never regretted it. Socialism did not really exist; it was brutalism that existed at the time.'

JUTTA GALLUS FLECK

ANOTHER PARTICULARLY POPULAR form of dissent against the communist regime in East Germany was escape. Before the Berlin Wall was erected around three million citizens voted with their feet by fleeing the country. Afterwards escape became more difficult and dangerous. During East Germany's 40-year existence over 800 people died trying to escape from the country: 250 at the Berlin Wall, 370 along the border dividing East from West Germany and 189 trying to escape across the Baltic Sea. Others died trying to escape across the Czech and Polish borders. Of those that tried unsuccessfully to escape, and survived, on average seven people a day were imprisoned.

One punishment for captured escapees was the forcible adoption of their children by the state. In these cases, the state became the children's guardian, and sometimes the parents were not permitted to see their children again, or even to know where they were. Jutta Fleck was helpless when her two daughters, Claudia aged 11 and Beate aged 9, were forcibly adopted after she was given a 36-month jail term for trying to escape.

In the summer of 1982 Jutta was recently divorced, her mother had died of cancer and her 12th application to emigrate had been turned down. Determined to raise her children in a free society, Jutta tried to escape from the DDR with her two young daughters but they were picked up in Romania en route to Yugoslavia. They were handed over to the East Germans and flown back to the DDR. Police and Stasi boarded the plane and separated mother and children immediately. Jutta remembers: 'It was the worse day of my life. I wasn't given the chance to say goodbye to the girls. I could only wave them goodbye from the aeroplane window as they left.'

The girls were shipped off to a children's home. Beate said, 'We were not able to imagine the extent of what was actually about to happen. Suddenly, our mother was gone. All I had left was my sister.' Meanwhile, Jutta was taken to Dresden in a *Minna*, a small van with four cells. 'I was told nothing about my children. Not a thing. It was night. I felt like I was in a film… The cell door was opened and I saw a wooden plank bed and a loo. Then the door closed and that was it.'

On subsequent days she was photographed and fingerprinted, but otherwise abandoned in her cell. Only when the Stasi interrogated her did she discover her children were in a home and that she would be allowed to write to them in return for good conduct. 'It was wonderful when I received the first letters from them. They wrote that they supported me and they drew pictures. The Stasi knew about it, of course. You weren't allowed to keep your post. After you had read it, you had to sign and then hand it over to them again. All I was allowed to keep was one photograph in which I was pictured with my girls but I had to cut off my head from that picture. I wasn't allowed to preserve any identity; to them I was just a number. At first I thought [the prison warden] was joking when she gave me the scissors. What was I supposed to do? I wanted to keep that picture of my daughters with me and so I did what she said.'

Jutta was sentenced to three years for her attempted escape and sent to Hoheneck prison, a notorious destination for East Germany's female political prisoners. The prison, built in the precincts of a medieval castle, was renowned for its poor food and hard labour. However, Jutta found a gratifying level of solidarity among the inmates. 'Mine was no case apart; thousands of people experienced the same in the DDR. I built up a close relationship with one or two detainees and we used to discuss everything and tried to comfort one another. The letters from my daughters sustained me immensely. And so did visits from my brother Klaus, who came every other week if they let him.'

Meanwhile the children were living in a children's home, not knowing what had happened to their mother. Beate recalls, 'For a long time she was simply gone. Also, we were just a number in that children's home. The paradox was that we, too, were treated like criminals although we were only children. We had to give up our personalities, our identity. We were given uniforms. That was horrible. Sometimes they wouldn't even call us by our names.'

Eventually they were let out and allowed to live with their father. Although they were still unable to visit their mother the girls were delighted to resume ballet lessons. Nonetheless, they had to endure constant attempts at re-education. 'We had meetings with the headmaster or our teacher on a weekly basis almost, and they tried to somehow brainwash us into thinking how good the DDR system was, that we were given every chance to succeed, that West Germany was evil with its capitalism, that what our mother had done was very, very bad and consequently we wouldn't want to stay with such a person voluntarily.

'I just went deaf when they said such things. Every day we would write letters to our mother. We didn't know if she received them, but we didn't want any gaps to be created over that long period of time. We wanted to give her the impression that she was spending every single day with us.'

In 1984 Jutta was freed by West Germany as part of a regular trade of political prisoners for hard currency. But while she was in custody awaiting deportation she was stripped of her rights as a parent. However, once free, although there was little hope of a reunion through conventional channels, she began three years of dedicated campaigning to get her daughters back. 'I wouldn't have had any rights, because once you lose your right of child custody you're not allowed to approach your child and I had a criminal record. I thought that the authorities in West Germany would be the only ones able to help me to be reunited with my children, but they couldn't help.

'You feel powerless. You're helpless. I kept on thinking what to do and talked to many people. That's how I got to the International Society for Human Rights (ISHR) and they told me that the only way was to make it public. I summoned up all my courage and began to demonstrate at the border.' Jutta stood on the western side of the Berlin Wall at the Allied border-crossing point known as Checkpoint Charlie.

'I went there every day for almost half a year. You grow strong because you are on the free side of Germany. I would wear placards I'd made myself with photos of my daughters and, pointing at the pictures of my children, I would shout, "They are what I want! Honecker, give me my daughters back!" I later found in my file some photos that the East Germans had taken of me.' The vigil earned her the nickname 'The Woman at Checkpoint Charlie'.

For their part, the children were filled with anticipation after Jutta's release. 'We thought we would join her in a short time. We never had a doubt about that. We were very happy that she was out of that prison and that the hard time was over for her. Actually, we already imagined being on the other side. I think that the most important thing we wrote was that we missed her, that we loved her more than anything in the world and that we were always with her.'

Jutta maintained contact by sending regular parcels, often covertly so they weren't intercepted. 'A packet contained food and candy and, of course, clothes, which were trendy but trendiness didn't exist in the DDR. The girls would tell me about their likes and wishes in their letters.'

The letters were censored as Beate recalls. 'In our letters we would draw things we knew about in West Germany. It was our way of showing opposition. For example, Mickey Mouse didn't exist in East Germany. We weren't allowed to draw Mickey Mouse because it was Western propaganda; it was forbidden to draw such things.'

The gifts from the West helped to brighten otherwise dreary lives in East Germany. 'Candies like Haribo or Nutella didn't exist there,' explained Beate. 'You had to queue for bananas. You could get those things only if you were privileged or if you were the first one in the queue at the supermarket. It was a sort of double freedom, to put on clothes that others didn't have. There used to be standard clothes so that you couldn't distinguish yourself from the others, but we could do that. It wasn't always easy because many at school would envy us. Children make the worst enemies. There was a lot of bad blood at school, a lot of envy and they accused our mother of being a criminal.'

On 25 August 1988, following a six-year separation, Jutta was reunited with her children after a political deal involving the East German lawyer Wolfgang Vogel and the West German government. Remembering that emotional time, Jutta said, 'Embracing my children for the first time was incredible. No one will ever be able to take that away from me, and I'm very thankful to all the people who contributed so it could happen. I am very proud that we managed to make it happen before the Wall came down.'

Beate recalls, 'We asked ourselves, how it would be, had she changed much? But, of course, she hadn't. She deliberately remained the way she was when we left her. That made it much easier for us because she looked exactly like she did when we last saw her and the way she looked in the photos. Of course, it was a bit strange and new, but also old. That mix of feelings was crazy.'

VÁCLAV HAVEL

VÁCLAV HAVEL IS one of communism's most famous dissidents. A playwright by profession, he was a founding member of the human rights group Charter 77 and became the figurehead of anti-communist opposition in Czechoslovakia. He played a leading role in the Velvet Revolution of 1989 and ultimately became the tenth and last president of Czechoslovakia. Afterwards, when Czechoslovakia split in two – against his wishes – he became president of the Czech Republic for ten years, leading his country into a system of multiparty democracy.

Havel was born into an affluent and influential bourgeois family in Prague in 1936. When communists seized power in 1948 he was identified as a class enemy and was not allowed to complete his secondary education for political reasons.

After military service he worked as a stagehand in Prague and studied drama by correspondence course. His first publicly performed full-length play was *The Garden Party* in 1963, which won him international acclaim; this was followed by *The Memorandum* in 1968 before his plays were banned in Czechoslovakia.

Havel himself was also barred from the theatre and forced to take a job in a brewery.

His political activities resulted in several prison sentences in the 1970s and 1980s, and he was also subjected to persistent government harassment and surveillance outside prison. Apart from his plays, he is famous for writing letters to his first wife, Olga, that crystallized his opposition to communism.

Despite his achievements he still feels handicapped by missing out on a formal education. 'I have to say I have never been a communist and have never been attracted to communism either. However, I have always wished for some kind of social justice. I tended towards social democracy. But I have never been inclined to any party and have never been a part of one.

'I just don't like any ready-made, self-contained or enclosed ideologies with which one does or does not identify. I can be interested in an idea and I can accept it, but that's all. And that is the difference between an ideal and a utopia. Ideals are always on the horizon; they are a part of life, of course; they exist around us, they surround what we try to do, but as soon as they start to turn into a utopian vision, into a definite ideological project for the world, it starts to be dangerous.'

Havel's first public criticism of the communist regime in Czechoslovakia occurred in 1956 when, as a young author, he spoke at a conference in Dobříš focusing on jailed writers and censorship. But he maintains that it wasn't so much political opposition as a defence of literature. However, he had disturbing first-hand experiences to draw on after the Warsaw Pact invasion in 1968. 'When the Russians invaded I was with my wife and my friends in Liberec, in the north of Czechoslovakia. We were visiting all our friends there, and at about 11 p.m. somebody called saying that we should switch on the radio. They were announcing that the Warsaw Pact army had crossed our border.

'We ran out and could hear the tanks in the streets already. So from there we watched it, there we went through it, and joined immediately the non-violent resistance in protest against the occupation. I spoke every day on Radio Free Czechoslovakia and on television and provided a commentary on what was happening, and I wrote various announcements about the invasion. We had a group that advised the mayor of Liberec and we wrote different texts for him. I can remember those days very clearly.

'The worse thing in Liberec was the deaths. The tanks came to the main square in Liberec; I was there, watching. I saw a house falling down, then a commander from one of the tanks started to shoot all around and there were more victims everywhere else. It was probably because of those deaths that the Russians were more restrained later on.'

As there was no permanent military post in Liberec he and his colleagues had a relatively free hand to put up posters because the streets were often free of soldiers. However, becoming a politician was still not his burning ambition. 'I took one step that forced me to make another step, and so on. It wasn't about a decision to become a dissident or a fighter. I got into politics by a kind of logic. It was my destiny to become a politician.

'Czechoslovakia was a morally devastated country under communism in the 1970s and 1980s. The constant presence of the totalitarian system, which watches and sees everything and destroys any inclination to think differently – all this, of course, destroyed characters.

'Everybody went to vote, and voted for the official candidates; people were threatened with punishment if they didn't come to vote. It all created a climate of fear. People were scared to talk out loud or candidly; society became introverted. People did one thing but thought another. This all went to create a morally devastated environment in the country, which we will have to deal with for a long time to come. Two new generations will have to grow up to wash away the footprints of communism.'

JOSEF JANÍČEK

ALTHOUGH THEIR MUSIC had minority appeal, a rock band called the Plastic People of the Universe inadvertently furthered the cause for freedom in Czechoslovakia after forging a bond with Havel. The communist authorities put members of the band on trial in 1976 some of them received jail sentences. Their arrest and incarceration inspired the organization of Charter 77, a group of writers and artists led by Havel who challenged the regime. Yet the Plastics describe themselves as 'dissidents against their will'. They just wanted to play their music, not overthrow communism.

Czechoslovakia was going through two decades of 'Normalization', a restrictive process that imposed state standards and abhorred nonconformists like the Plastics. The band was known for wild dancing, make-up, bizarre costumes and psychedelic light shows, and echoed hippy rock bands popular in Britain and America.

Keyboard player Josef Janíček described the slow-burn assault on their right to self-expression that took the band and Havel to the centre of the political arena. 'At the time bands were not able to play just like that,' he explained. 'They had to pass an exam and a committee had to decide whether the group could perform in public or not. We attempted to pass this exam at some point around 1970. We were, however, not granted the right to perform. In spite of this we performed from time to time. But without a licence you couldn't get paid for your performance.

'I think our last "official" performance was when we played at a high school leaving party in Písek. The headmaster of the school got upset. But to be honest the main reason he was upset was that there were ten people with long hair and they started to dance in their own way. After this there was one half-official concert on a steamboat in 1973. When the steamboat moored there were police officers checking the people taking part in the event.

'Another time we played in front of a committee and they were split in their opinions of us. One member of the administrative staff said, "Cut their hair, send them down the mines or put them in jail"; the others said, "Let them play". In the end, the group in our favour prevailed, so we were granted the right to perform. But after two weeks we received a letter from the cultural centre in Prague stating that they could not promote us due to the negative impact of our music. Later, when we called them, they told us our lyrics were morbid. I think they were just looking for an excuse.

'They must have seen that we were not willing to meet the criteria which were imposed on an artist at this time, who was supposed to be dressed reasonably and play reasonable music. I can remember that one of us was criticized for his long hair and so he brought up an argument that his ears were too big and he had to cover them. We were not really that concerned about it.'

The band subsequently went 'underground' and organizing a concert became a clandestine operation. The exact location was only revealed at the last minute, and fans would travel long distances to reach some remote farmhouse. Often police would arrive and break up the concert. After a while a whole underground subculture built up around the Plastics. 'It was getting tougher and tougher to perform. The secret police presence was increasing. When people were bussed to our concerts, they checked on those getting on and off the bus. Then they were checking the school attendance of the audience. Those who were still at school who came to our concerts had a lot of problems. The idea was that they were getting education from the state and were misbehaving like this. So the audience was worse off than us.

'In March 1974, there was České Budějovice where we and other musicians were arrested. It was a bloodbath. The fact was that people with long hair were messing around in the town and, because it was quite hot, they were having fun close to a fountain. This terrified the Communist Party of České Budějovice and the response was brutal. The secret police ordered us out using loudspeakers. They were beating people. The people who went to the train station were beaten really hard over their heads. Police were confiscating their cameras and escorting them in the train.' The Plastics never performed that day.

On 21 February 1976, the Plastics held a music festival in Bijanovice (a village near Prague). The following month the secret police arrested all the members of the band and a number of other musicians. Many of the Plastics fans were interrogated. Band members' houses were searched and some of their possessions were seized.

The case came to court six months later. Some said it was rock and roll on trial. The prosecution claimed that the Plastics were guilty of producing vulgar and anti-social music, and were corrupters of Czechoslovak youth. Four band members were found guilty of 'organized disturbance of the peace'. They were given sentences ranging from eight to 18 months. 'I did not have a trial,' says Janíček, 'and I was released after five months. Only those in the group who had attended a university were given a prison sentence.'

Among the band's champions was Havel, who said they were defending 'life's intrinsic desire to express itself freely, in its own authentic and sovereign way'. The Plastics used Havel's country home in Hradecek for the Third Music Festival of the Second Culture on 1 October 1977, an attempt to re-launch rock music in Czechoslovakia in the face of repression. There was an imposing police presence surrounding the event but, on this occasion, unlike at České Budějovice, the Plastics did perform. They also recorded their album, *Leading Horses*, at Hradecek in 1981. By 1982 two members of the band had been forced to leave Czechoslovakia and the others were still in and out of custody.

Havel explains how the band became a primary focus for him. 'The Plastic People of the Universe played an important role for me and my journey to the centre of politics. It was a kind of dead period in the mid-1970s; people were just hiding away. The Plastic People were arrested not because they were performing against the government and against the regime, but simply because they behaved the way they wanted, and the regime hated that. They arrested them thinking nobody would notice that the long-haired ones were there, somewhere, on trial and afterwards condemned.

'However, people had already started to feel the need to speak out, to step out from the "era of forgetting" and they woke up. We created a kind of wave of solidarity among musicians, and many people then performed publicly for the Plastics' defence.

'Of course, you wouldn't have read about it in the newspapers outside the country, but people got to know about it by word of mouth. And then we came up with an idea to create something more permanent and not focus just on that one case. In that atmosphere Charter 77 was born.'

VÁCLAV HAVEL

HAVEL REMAINED IN THE spotlight long after the Plastics had stopped playing. House arrest and surveillance were both unpleasant experiences, Havel remembers, and his home was often ransacked and his car smashed. 'Put simply, I was under constant guard. They were not spying on me secretly; it was a blatant way of hounding a person, limiting his freedom of movement and so on.

Sometimes I really couldn't leave the house; I couldn't even do a shop for groceries. When talking about it today it might sound funny, but back then it wasn't pleasant at all.

'One day they were surrounding the house and there was a policeman in uniform who kept following me all the time and was always one metre behind me. I decided to walk the dog round and round in the garden and the policeman was following me round and round too; a friend of mine recorded that for the BBC.'

In August 1985, Havel and his wife went on holiday to a friend's home but they were followed there too and were arrested. 'They were with me and around me all the time, and my holiday journey kept tens of policemen and quite a number of their cars busy. It was quite absurd. I had to go to Bratislava on the way and they arrested us for 48 hours, then they released me and I continued on the journey; I thought I wasn't going to give up once I set off on this holiday.

'Of course, they wanted to make life unpleasant for the "Chartists" and for anyone who expressed themselves in opposition to communism, but at the same time, by treating us in this way they were sending a message to the whole of society; because everybody knew about it and people were scared; everybody had got something to lose. And they wanted to construct a kind of fence around us, to drive us back in to a ghetto so that people would avoid us and wouldn't want to have anything to do with us. So it was about a constant threatening of society and of freedom of speech.'

Havel still finds it difficult to talk about his incarceration. But during that time he distilled his political beliefs in letters to his wife,

Olga, often written in coded language to escape the attentions of the censor. 'I had gone to prison a few times; the longest time I spent there was about three and a half years. I do remember certain bad moments; for example, when they transferred me from the cell in Ruzyn to one in Ostrava. I had to go through a 40° difference in temperature, as inside the cell was 20° and I was working outside there at minus 20°. We didn't have any proper clothes and we were doing hard manual labour. I got a fever of about 39° and I got pneumonia for the first time. Since then I suffer from pneumonia all the time and have problems with my lungs today. That was a nasty moment.

'I can't say, though, that I have any regrets about my actions. I had the opportunity to end what was happening at any time; the communists were offering me emigration, which I wouldn't take out of principle. But there were moments when I was forced to hesitate a little, as they were threatening that if I refused to go they would arrest my brother and my wife. And at the same time they were saying that if I accepted the offer they would help others, that there wouldn't be any trials and that the destinies of both those in prison and those outside were in my hands. But I agreed with my then wife, Olga, that there was no way I would do anything like that.

'I definitely wouldn't put all Czechoslovak communists in one bag; in the 1970s and 1980s, both decades of the era of "Normalization", typically there were more cynics in the party; they were those who didn't care about an ideology or a class struggle. Simply, there were people who entered the party and were loyal; they did so in order to be able to travel and to have a professional career. And the ideology wasn't based on any belief any more but on a mere borrowed word, "communism".

'The most characteristic thing about this totalitarian system was that it obliged everyone to do things and at the same time it made them victims. The extent to which this hapened differed and the general secretary of the party was more responsible for what happened at that time than a worker, but ultimately both were responsible and both were victims. To a greater or lesser degree, everyone participated in the system and that was the new factor, which wasn't there during Nazism. Nazism also didn't have an attractive and understandable ideology that appealed to intellectuals. We know very well how many coffee-house-style communists and "left-wing intellectuals" there were; but I haven't heard of any Nazi coffee-house types.'

Following four months' detention in 1989, Havel detected a change in Czechoslovak society. 'At one time people from the officially approved group of artists and actors who were allowed to perform and put on exhibitions couldn't have anything to do with me. They couldn't even be seen with me. Then they suddenly started to sign petitions for my release. Somehow they had stopped fearing the pressure, even though all of them risked something.

'Serving my sentence in Pankrác prison I could sense something even from the censored TV programmes. Many demonstrations had started happening to mark different anniversaries. Of course, you had to "translate" from "their" language to understand what was going on. It works on the principle of a snowball: at the beginning a small ball is rolling and you think it is not important, but gradually more snow sticks to it and it becomes bigger and bigger, and suddenly there is an avalanche. And we couldn't know when the ball started to roll; but it probably started earlier than I could imagine, or I expected.'

Havel was also behind the Civic Forum, a political movement that embraced all opponents to communism during the Velvet Revolution. 'The Civic Forum was successful because it gave an opportunity to all those who wanted to express themselves publicly. We didn't know it would develop that fast and, of course, we ourselves couldn't found branches of the forum everywhere. It happened of its own accord; it grew like mushrooms after the rain. Branches spread around the factories, companies and offices, and they all were relatively autonomous as they weren't founded from the centre. And then the turning point happened during the general strike, in which really everyone participated. And at that time the regime started to give up.'

Despite the liberation won by Havel and his cohorts there are things he misses about life under communism. 'I miss the atmosphere of cohesion and solidarity that was inside the dissident ghetto, where there were people with different opinions – those on the left, those on the right. Basically, they were "pulling the same rope" because they wanted the same thing. That started to fall apart later and doesn't exist any more.

'And the atmosphere of the solidarity, even the happiness of life under those awful conditions with the police's outrageous behaviour, beating people up or hauling them off to some distant forest to deal with them… despite all that, and because we pulled together, there was a kind of solidarity; people helped each other.'

DOWNFALL

'Poland ten years, Hungary ten months, East Germany ten weeks, Czechoslovakia ten days.'

Prague graffiti, December 1989

WHEN THE END of communism in Eastern Europe came in 1989, it was swift and unexpected. In October, Gorbachev arrived in East Berlin to celebrate the 40th anniversary of the Workers' and Peasants' State. On 9 November, the Berlin Wall was breached. In Czechoslovakia, the communist regime of Miloš Jakeš was still refusing to talk with opposition groups in late November. On 29 December, Václav Havel was elected president after what became known as the 'Ten Day Revolution'.

Also in November, Nicolae Ceauşescu was re-elected leader at the Romanian Communist Party's 14th Congress, officially known as the 'Congress of the Great Socialist Victory'. Ceauşescu's six-hour speech was famously interrupted by 125 standing ovations.

On Christmas Day, he and his wife were shot dead by a military firing squad.

CONSTANTIN LULCIUC

THE SEAT OF revolution in Romania was the western city of Timişoara. On the night of 15 December a crowd surrounded the home of a Hungarian priest, Laszlo Tokes, to stop police from evicting him. Tokes was an outspoken member of the Hungarian Reformed Church and it was his own Church authorities who sought his removal.

During the early evening the crowd had grown, bringing nearby traffic to a standstill. During the night their mood had intensified and the target of their anger was changing. Cries of 'Freedom' could be heard.

Joining the crowd the following day was Constantin Lulciuc, an assistant in a food shop in the city. In his late 20s and married with one child, Lulciuc had no previous involvement with politics; he says he got involved in the Romanian revolution 'by mistake'. On his way to have a beer with some friends he heard that there was trouble in Timişoara 's central town square. He and two mates decided to take a look. He recalls the scene on Saturday 16 December. 'There was already a strong crowd shouting "Down with Ceauşescu". There were about a thousand people – perhaps even more. And it was dark so we weren't that scared. We were apprehensive, of course – but also they [the security forces] couldn't see us clearly.'

The blackness of midwinter Timişoara cloaked the activities of both demonstrators and security forces. Unseasonably clement weather also meant more people were prepared to spend longer periods outdoors despite the arrival of special forces and uniformed troop reinforcements, who came with fire engines to hose down the demonstrators. When it inevitably began, violence between the restive crowd and the security forces quickly escalated. When he saw things turning nasty, Lulciuc and others headed towards the university to rally the students.

By early afternoon the next day more than 2,000 people had gathered in the city centre. Guarding the local Communist Party headquarters were security troops, two rows deep, supported by fire engines. By the late afternoon the security forces, now issued with live ammunition, moved to crush the demonstrations. 'They started to shoot. I took cover behind a wall,' remembers Lulciuc. 'We were all afraid. I saw two young boys fall near me. A car appeared out of nowhere. We stopped it. We put the boys in the car – one was shot in the leg and the other in the shoulder. I asked where they were taking them and these men replied "To the county hospital", but I can't be sure whether they were telling the truth or not.

'When I think about it now, it must have been a Securitate car. There were also state-owned taxis – there was a rumour that the drivers worked for the Securitate – and they would take the victims to an unknown destination. Who knows where they were taking the people?

'After that a man told us, "You know what's going on at the ONT (National Tourism Office) building? It's been broken into and they're giving away whisky and Kent cigarettes." In those days that sort of thing wasn't available, so I thought I'd like to get my hands on a whisky bottle. Later on, I heard that the people who went there were shot – it was a trap set by the Securitate.'

During a tumultuous day in Timişoara the local party headquarters was ransacked. Protestors in front of the Hotel Continental threw petrol bombs and stones. Away from the town centre, an angry crowd captured five tanks and tried to set fire to them. But, by the evening, the authorities had partially regained control; more than 60 civilians lay dead, 200 more were wounded and 700 were under arrest.

At 8.30 a.m. on 18 December, Ceauşescu flew to Iran to finalize an arms deal. He kept in close touch with developments in Timişoara and authorized the use of force. Mistakenly, he believed foreign elements were behind the disturbances. Troops now patrolled the streets of the city and another six people were killed. The following day wildcat strikes took place at the Elba factory, and there were two more civilian deaths. On 20 December, in the face of overwhelming public force, soldiers stopped their resistance and representatives of the protestors prepared to negotiate with members of the regime, who had arrived from Bucharest.

The next day witnessed a large meeting in central Bucharest. It had been organized by the Communist Party at Ceauşescu's behest to demonstrate the wide support he believed he still commanded within the country. It was to be televised live to the nation. Groups were bussed to the centre of the city where they were handed pro-communist placards. They marched to Piata Palatului where a large, apathetic crowd awaited the arrival of the Ceauşescus. It had been vetted for troublesome elements by the security forces

Meanwhile, Lulciuc and some of his colleagues had decided to take news of the events in Timişoara to the Romanian capital. As Timişoara was cordoned off with no trains in or out, Luluic went by car to Lugoj and caught a train there to Bucharest, arriving in time for the demonstration. Their aim was to infiltrate the crowd. 'The first time we ran into the crowd we shouted "Down with Communism", "Down with Ceauşescu". And everybody was looking at us – they didn't understand. And then we explained what was happening in Timişoara and first the people at the back of the crowd started to shout "Timişoara, Timişoara" and everybody was turning their heads to see what was going on. And the information was passed forward that a group had arrived from Timişoara and saying that people had been killed there. But we said we'd arrived to bring the news that Timişoara was a free town.

'Of course, at first people were in two minds: should they join in or not? I felt a cold shiver. People were afraid. But they were pushing each other to get closer. And then they started to shout "Down with Ceauşescu" first in weaker voices, then stronger. Then they started to boo. It was like a shock wave.'

After some introductory speeches from the balcony of the Central Committee building, Ceauşescu came forward to address the crowd. After only a short while he was interrupted by a disturbance in the crowd. He looked startled. After a few moments of confusion, he resumed his speech and spoke for about 20 minutes to a background of jeers and whistles. In the crowd the Securitate and soldiers moved in on Lulciuc and his friends. The Timişoara contingent ran and hid at the railway station, fearful of reprisals, and eventually made their way back home. But

Ceauşescu's expression of bewildered apprehension signalled the vulnerability of his regime.

In the aftermath of the meeting in Bucharest there were clashes between the crowd and the security forces, claiming the lives of 49 demonstrators. The following day, 22 December, military units protecting the Ceauşescus inside the Central Committee building were ordered to withdraw. This removed a key protective barrier around the two leaders and allowed the crowds to storm the building later that morning.

Just after midday a helicopter carrying Nicolae and Elena Ceauşescu took off from the roof of the Central Committee building. By late afternoon the couple had arrived at a military garrison at Târgovişte, north of Bucharest, where they would remain until their execution three days later.

DAN VOINEA AND IONEL BOERU

EARLY ON CHRISTMAS DAY, Major Dan Voinea, a military prosecutor in his early 30s, took a call from Mugurel Florescu, a military lawyer at the Ministry of Defence, asking for a prosecutor. 'I offered to go. And, armed with the reference number of the penal file, I went to the MoD headquarters to see what the trial was about. There I met the president of the military tribunal, Colonel Magistrate Gică Popa, a colleague of his, Colonel Nistor, and a military court clerk called Tánase. They told me that we were to take part in the trial of the Ceauşescus.

'I wrote down their two names in the file. I wrote an indictment.

The indictment was handwritten because we were afraid that if we had it typed the typist might divulge the secret, and we were afraid of terrorists and of the people who were still loyal to the dictator who might have attacked us. So the indictment was handwritten to eliminate any potential leaks.

'I looked into the penal code to see what offences we could charge them with. We thought that for a dictator of Ceauşescu's stature we had to opt for the most serious offences. We accused him of genocide and of sabotaging the national economy. Even today we feel how economically backward we are, compared to other countries, and that's due to Ceauşescu's policy that he pursued for decades and which destroyed the economy and our society.'

Voinea added further evidence, both from the recently arrested interior minister Tudor Postelnicu and official minutes, which pointed the finger at Ceauşescu. However, the lawyer was concerned about procedural shortcomings. 'I spoke with Gică Popa about the case and the problems raised by it. It wasn't an ordinary trial and it was difficult in those days – under the pressure from the streets – to follow procedure. Popa said that it was important to start the trial straight away, and at a later stage witnesses and evidence could be brought in front of the court to correct any potential procedural errors. He stressed that it was essential to start the trial of the two dictators immediately. That was the original thought. Nobody had told us that they were to be executed after the first court session.'

Later that Christmas morning Voinea climbed on board one of two helicopters destined for Târgovişte. The front helicopter was adorned with a yellow scarf for identification purposes. Also on board were General Victor Stănculescu and Captain, now Colonel, Ionel Boeru. Stănculescu, a senior figure in the military high command, was well known to both the Ceauşescus. A key orchestrator of the trial, he was to be present throughout the proceedings that followed and was caught on camera during the filming of the trial. He was the object of many of the Ceauşescus' bitter references to treachery from close associates. Built like an ox, Boeru was part of an elite paratroop unit and was one of those chosen to execute the Ceauşescus.

Waiting to meet them at Târgovişte was the commander of the garrison unit, Colonel Andrei Kemenici, who'd had Nicolae and Elena Ceauşescu in his care since 22 December. The situation inside the barracks was tense, as soldiers feared an attack from Securitate sharpshooters. Romania seemed poised on the brink of civil war.

When they landed, Boeru recalls, an armoured personnel carrier pulled up. 'Nicolae Ceauşescu was brought out from the vehicle. He was handed over to me, according to General Stănculescu's orders. My orders were not to hit him, not to insult him, not to have any kind of words with "that person"... I didn't recognize him. He took his hat off, he ran his fingers through his hair and he was very pale. But as soon as he got some fresh air in his lungs he regained his normal colour and I recognized him as Nicolae Ceauşescu. He was looking around, frightened. When he saw so many people around him he wasn't sure what was going on.

'Elena Ceauşescu was then brought out. She smelled embarrassingly badly. She behaved normally though. She walked without having to be pushed, or forced in any way, towards the place where the medical check-up was done.

'I was supposed to take him to the room where he was going to be seen by a doctor. As the door was ajar, I witnessed the medical check-up. He had his blood pressure checked. He was unhappy, saying that his blood pressure was usually lower than the doctor had just recorded.'

Before the trial began General Stănculescu selected the precise spot where the execution would take place. It was on one side of the barracks square, against a wall.

Meanwhile, military prosecutor Voinea was still wrestling with the technicalities of the trial. He remembers a misunderstanding between Stănculescu and the trial team. 'General Stănculescu told Gică Popa, the main judge, to fit the session into one hour. Initially, we agreed to that because we weren't quite sure how to proceed. And thinking that it was going to be a lengthy trial we thought it was a good idea. Little did we know that, in fact, Stănculescu wanted an hour for the whole trial, having in mind the execution of the two defendants immediately afterwards.'

A small lecture room in the barracks had been selected as the most secure and appropriate place for this military tribunal. The chief prosecutor, Voinea, sat on the left of a five-strong panel. To the panel's left, beyond Voinea, sat the two defence solicitors, Nicolae Teodorescu and Constantin Lucescu. Ceauşescu was dressed in a dark overcoat, Elena in a coat trimmed with fur on the lapels. Beside her was a white package containing insulin for her husband's diabetes and her handbag.

There were four main charges: genocide (under article 357 of the penal code), undermining state power (article 162), acts of sabotage (article 163) and ruining the national economy (article 165).

Ceauşescu appeared reasonably dignified. He refused to recognize the court and denounced the trial as part of a *coup d'état*. His wife, though, was nervous, as Ionel Boeru recalls. 'She wasn't calm. She was agitated. At some point she even argued with the two judges and the prosecutor Dan Voinea, but Nicolae was trying to calm her down by patting her slowly on the hand and on her leg. He behaved in a dignified manner, if you ask me. He didn't have any harsh verbal exchanges with the other people in the room, with one exception. The prosecutor then asked him if he suffered from any mental disease. Ceauşescu was upset and told Voinea he'd be punished for that question once he got out of there.'

The case for the prosecution, by Voinea's own admission, wasn't based on credible facts. 'I used the data and the information that I had at the time – not from evidence, but from the mass media. For example, TVR (Romanian TV) and the press were giving the figure of 60,000 deaths [in Timişoara], and – as we used to believe everything that the mass media told us – we didn't question the honesty of those who gave the figures. And we used this information, along with lots of other information in the indictment, without checking it.'

Given his reliance on press cuttings, it is unsurprising that some of the accusations Voinea made in court – that the Ceauşescus had stashed 400 million US dollars in a secret Swiss bank account, for example – were wide of the mark. Voinea also admits that he was a relatively junior figure to be handling such an important trial. 'I was nervous. After the session, I was asked by Gică Popa to draw my conclusions. Bearing in mind the seriousness of the offences, I asked for the death penalty. That was the only proper sentence to ask for at the time for the two dictators.'

Voinea couldn't help noticing that one of the Ceauşescus' own defence team was more critical of Ceauşescu than the prosecution, as several quotations from the trial's transcripts bear out:

> Defence lawyer on Elena: *The defendant here, the renowned scientist, used to bug even the dignitaries' toilets. This was the defendant's main occupation.*
>
> Defence lawyer on Nicolae: *Your honour, allowing the defendant to speak further is an insult to the Romanian people and to justice.*
>
> Defence lawyer to Nicolae: *You are exactly like Ayatollah Khomeini, someone who killed his own nation.*

The judge was scarcely more objective:

> Judge on Elena: *She is more talkative [than her husband] although I witnessed on many occasions how she was simply reading out her speeches. She is the scientist, engineer and member of the academy who was barely able to read. The illiterate had become an academy member.*
>
> Judge to Nicolae: *You never had a dialogue with the people. You always had a monologue and expected people to applaud as*

> *in an African ritual. You have behaved in exactly the same manner today. You have not changed; you have learnt nothing, like a megalomaniac.*

The trial had barely begun when the death sentence for Nicolae and Elena Ceauşescu was pronounced. Nicolae Ceauşescu was recorded shouting defiance. Still reeling from Stănculescu's involvement, Elena remarked, 'That's how it goes. Treason happens right next to you, where you least expect it.'

In fact, in opting for an immediate execution, the tribunal was breaking a Romanian law that stated that death sentences could not be carried out within ten days of their pronouncement, regardless of whether the accused had appealed or not. Fifty-five minutes after the proceedings in court had started, Nicolae and Elena Ceauşescu were facing death by a firing squad headed by Ionel Boeru. He remembers how they asked to die together. 'She insisted "No! We die together!" And then I asked an officer to grant them their last wish. And indeed the soldiers who accompanied me entered the courtroom and tied their hands, and we took them one by one to the place where they would be executed together.

'After their hands were tied, I went out first with Nicolae Ceauşescu. Other members of the firing squad got hold of Elena. A soldier had a heated exchange with her on her way to the execution site. He told her, "Your time is up Leano!" and she swore at him, saying, "Go back up your mother's fanny".

Voinea walked outside to the execution site and saw soldiers rush the Ceauşescus into position, though they were not keen to be filmed by the official cameraman during the actual execution. There was considerable fear of reprisals among all those involved even at this stage of the proceedings.

Captain Ionel Boeru and another paratrooper held on to Nicolae Ceauşescu as they approached the execution site. 'We walked by the wall. He – Nicolae Ceauşescu – shouted, "Long live Romania!" "Down with the traitors!" and sang a few lines from the International Socialists' hymn. We got to the execution site. I was thinking all the time that my gun must work properly; I wanted to avoid having any problems.

'I ordered my colleagues to walk back approximately six paces. Then we turned to face the two of them. I ordered my colleagues to set their machine guns on automatic fire to make sure we wouldn't miss. At that moment I yelled at a colleague who was standing frozen between the two. I shouted at him to go away, otherwise he'd be shot too. Also, there was a soldier at the window of the toilet to the right of the execution site. I waved at him to go away, which he did.

'I was thinking all the time that if I don't shoot them properly, then I'd be shot myself because I was sure that there was a back-up squad behind us. I was also sure that if we hadn't done it, we'd have been considered to be traitors and – probably – we'd have been executed too, on the spot.

'Then I ordered them to fire and we executed them. I shot 29 cartridges in three bursts of automatic fire. The first one hit Nicolae in his knees and the second in his chest. The third hit Elena Ceauşescu in the chest.'

Boeru had been given a very specific order to shoot from the hip earlier that morning, despite the fact that he wasn't used to firing in that way. None of his group had received training as a firing squad. Consequently, the results were somewhat chaotic. 'I was scared – it's difficult to kill two people from a distance of three or four metres. One doesn't look where the bullets go. One looks through things. That's what I did. I was like a robot. All I could think about was that the gun must not jam, that it must work properly.

'There were also shots fired from behind us – the firing squad – from the top of an armoured personnel carrier. That's when I got very scared. I turned towards the machine gun that I felt was shooting above our heads and I shouted, "Stop firing!" At that moment somebody else yelled, "Stop shooting! Nobody shoots any more!"'

A military doctor then inspected the two corpses. The bodies were carried to one of the waiting helicopters. Returning to Bucharest with the bodies were General Stănculescu and Virgil Mágureanu.

When the helicopter landed at Bucharest's Steaua football stadium, home of the army football team, the two corpses were left there for over 12 hours before being transferred to the Central Military Hospital. They were eventually buried in the Ghencea civilian cemetery in the city.

When Major Voinea returned later that same day to the Steaua stadium the helicopter he was in came under fire. Now concerned for his own safety, Voinea took precautions about his whereabouts in the aftermath of the trial, unsure where the greatest threat now lay. 'I went home, took my family and we lived for two weeks with my sister-in-law in a block of flats in Olteniţei district [in Bucharest] – nobody knew her address. They looked for me at night at my mother's home. There were four soldiers. They had an altercation with the people who were guarding the entrance to the building. That's how I found out later that they were looking for me. But since then I have never asked for anything; I had no dialogue – if you like – with anyone after that. I just pursued my career as a prosecutor.'

On 1 March 1990, the chairman of the tribunal at the Ceauşescus' trial, Colonel Magistrate Gică Popa, committed suicide, adding to the speculation already surrounding the speed of the trial and execution. Eventually, for his own safety, Voinea decided to talk about his part in the trial for fear that he and others involved would 'disappear'. Gradually information emerged about the decision taken to kill the Ceauşescus. Voinea recalls. 'I learnt afterwards that before the trial General Stănculescu, Petre Roman, Ion Iliescu and Silviu Brucan met at the MoD headquarters, and they decided that the Ceauşescus should be tried and sentenced to death. The people I've just mentioned cut this deal in a public toilet there, to prevent the conversation from being overheard.'

Today, Colonel Boeru has no second thoughts about executing the Ceauşescus, despite the unpleasantness of the task. 'I got over it! I don't wish it for anybody. But there are situations in life when one must do such things, thinking that otherwise one might take their place. I did it for the people who died in Timişoara and for my friend Livache who died in Bucharest.

'Nicolae Ceauşescu wasn't only the leader of the party. He was the president of the country. He played many parts. He was the supreme commander of the army. I didn't have a problem with this. It wasn't a problem at the time and it still isn't. I think that he got exactly what he deserved.'

Today General Dan Voinea also remains convinced that the execution of the Ceauşescus was the right outcome despite procedural shortcomings. 'What happened then, happened under the pressure from the streets – because the people asked for Ceauşescu to be tried. If you remember, the trial was imposed on us, and when that happens one forgets about details and there's no time to argue.

'I think that even if the trial had lasted for three years he would still have been executed for what he did. It's just that normal procedure was not followed – but the laws at the time allowed for that to happen.

'For a dictator, no matter what kind, left or right, there cannot be a punishment other than the death sentence. No matter how you describe this trial – kangaroo court or whatever you want to call it – he was the only dictator of the time who paid for what he did with his life. And he wasn't killed in a bloody manner. If the crowd had caught him in the Central Committee building he would have met the same fate – but it would have been carried out more savagely.'

MILOŠ JAKEŠ

MILOŠ JAKEŠ WAS general secretary of the Communist Party of Czechoslovakia from 1987 until 1989. He joined the party at the end of the Second World War and sided with the wing that ousted the reformer Alexander Dubček after the Warsaw Pact invasion of August 1968.

Jakeš was a key figure in the purges of party membership that followed, and in re-establishing authoritarian communist rule during the period of 'Normalization'. He still believes the 41 years of communism in Czechoslovakia were a golden age for his country. 'I joined the party in May 1945 as soon as the Soviet armies arrived. I was attracted to communism because of the social injustice and the economic inequality, particularly where I lived in Šumava.

'My father was a joiner but there was almost no work and almost no income. We relied on what we made from picking and selling mushrooms, raspberries and blueberries, and with that money we could buy shoes or clothes to go to school and so on. It was a Czech–German area and I attended a Czech minority school.

'I had excellent assessments and marks, so I applied for work at Bata's shoe company and was accepted. The acceptance procedure was interesting. I had to have my teeth seen to and I had to have certain personal items, such as pyjamas, which I never had before in my life, and another suit in addition to the one I already had. I travelled to Zlin; we passed a power station on which there were large signs with slogans, such as, "Let the machines take the strain". I'd say they were socialist slogans in essence. That was very impressive and so was the town of Zlin itself, so I settled in and stayed for four years at the Bata School of Work.'

Following further schooling in Moscow, and by the time of the Warsaw Pact invasion of August 1968, Jakeš had become a party official in Prague. After the Velvet Revolution in 1989, he stood trial for treason for his behaviour in 1968. He was accused of trying to form a 'workers' and farmers' government' at Moscow's behest to replace the Dubček regime and so legitimize the invasion.

He was acquitted of the charge, but there is no doubt about his concerns over Dubček's reforms and his hard-line pro-Moscow approach to communism. Nor did he regard the 'fraternal aid' offered by the Soviet Union and the 500,000 strong force of the Warsaw Pact that entered Czechoslovakia in 1968 as an invasion. 'If a socialist society starts questioning the decisive and fundamental aspects of socialism and its theory, one becomes alert and starts paying close attention to the situation, to its development and features. And gradually I became seriously concerned.

'If we wanted to be a socialist country the Soviet Union could never be our enemy. Never. I did not consider the Soviet Union to be an occupier in the strict sense of the word. I had different ideas about that. I have experienced German occupation. It wasn't the same.'

After the invasion, Jakeš played a key role in the purges of the party that followed. During his period as general secretary, between 1987 and 1989 one of his main tasks was handling the effects on Czechoslovakia of Mikhail Gorbachev's changes in the Soviet Union. While ostensibly promoting the virtues of *perestroika*, it was clear that he was not a convert to Gorbachev's reforms. 'During my talks with him I found him very likeable. He was slightly different to the rest of the Soviet leadership, who were stiff and older. He was young; he was from a different generation. He is almost ten years younger than me.

'What he was telling me I found appealing. But it all took a different course. His fundamental idea was to rid the party of the day-to-day decision-making, and to emphasize the significance of the soviets, the local and regional assemblies. And on that basis more people would be involved in decision-making.

'Over time I had doubts. I was not opposed, but I had doubts about where this would lead. And I said to myself, this is a destructive process, not a constructive one. Gorbachev was too enthusiastic about his acceptance in the West, especially in Britain. He was making false assumptions based on that – that they really were his friends, and friends of the Soviet regime. He became slightly lightheaded and he was in that respect similar to Dubček. He loved fame, which allowed him to become an instrument of the West and to make concessions over fundamental issues.'

Jakeš looks back with some bitterness at one conversation he had with Gorbachev in the summer of 1989. 'On 12 August 1989 I was on holiday in the Soviet Union at the summer resort of Youzhnyi in the Crimea. Gorbachev was staying there too. It was my birthday at the time. The telephone rang and they asked me to pick it up. So I ran upstairs to the telephone in my room. They said it was Comrade Gorbachev on the line. He asked me how I liked it in Youzhnyi, how was my health etc., and he said he had a lot of problems but he would solve them. I thanked him for his card and his present. Suddenly, he said, "Miloš, I am telling you that I will not let socialism go." I replied, "I'm sure about that. Thank you for such a nice wish." And we finished on that.'

Jakeš sees parallels between Gorbachev's *perestroika* reforms of the late 1980s and Dubček's reforms during the Prague Spring of 1968. Both he regards as disastrous. 'The events that took place in Czechoslovakia in 1968 also happened in the Soviet Union, though the events were unrelated and their timing was different. And what was the result of the politics of *perestroika*? The result was the most significant geopolitical change in the map of Europe that has taken place in recent centuries – when you look at the Soviet Union, it used to have a population of 280 million; Russia now has 147 million. The destruction of socialism, of the whole socialist camp, that is the result of a political development similar to that which took place in Czechoslovakia.

'Therefore, this gives me an answer to the question of what would have happened in Czechoslovakia if the political development in 1968 had not been stopped, and had prevailed.'

Despite claiming to be a reformer, Jakeš was resolutely opposed to talks with the opposition group Charter 77 or with their leading figure, Václav Havel. 'Well, I did not know much about him. I merely knew who he was and that he worked primarily among artists, and was in a way their standard-bearer. Only gradually, as I received more information, I began to think what I still think today – that he is a man whose statements cheated Czechoslovakia and who from the beginning intended nothing else but to renew capitalism in this country. That was not the wish of the majority of our people. No, it was not.'

Jakeš also admits that he underestimated the strength of the growing opposition in Czechoslovakia. 'Of course, we had discussions about how we should react, how we should deal with what they were doing. One thing was clear to us – their goal was not socialism, but a substantial change of regime. But we did not consider them important enough to endanger socialism and have the public on their side. Only the events in the surrounding countries and in the Soviet Union, and the pressure from the West, enabled them to become a force.'

Jakeš' decision to use force against a student demonstration in Prague on 17 November 1989 was a colossal error. Instead of intimidating the opposition, it galvanized and united them. Strikes and ever larger demonstrations followed. Jakeš went on national television threatening to introduce order; the official cry went up to 'defend socialism' and the workers' militia were put on standby. The regime, however, seemed to have lost the will to use force.

On 24 November the Communist Party held an emergency congress at the party's political college near the airport on the outskirts of Prague. During a stormy meeting Jakeš was replaced as general secretary of the party. On 1 December Czechoslovak communists condemned the very act that gave them legitimacy: the invasion of 1968. Before the end of December, Václav Havel was elected as president of Czechoslovakia.

For Jakeš, the low point was being thrown out of his own party for 'gross political errors' connected to his handling of the demonstrations of November. 'It was then that I realized it was over, because the congress did the worst it possibly could for the party. Nobody, no force or enemy, damaged the party as much as this congress. I did not attend it, and Central Committee members in general did not attend. I was expelled so that the party could breathe more easily and so that a culprit could be identified. And the culprit was Jakeš. When my aide called me to inform me of this, I got into the car and made my way to the Central Committee. I reported in and requested a hearing. I said I wanted to be present at the discussion concerning me. Nobody called me but, as they were leaving, they shook hands with me and said they were sorry about what happened.'

Jakeš was a figure of ridicule for his verbal clumsiness and symbolized the atrophied mediocrity of the regime. Chants of 'Jakeš to the trash' were a frequent cry during the demonstrations of November 1989. He reflected, 'Any person becomes an object of mockery if there is a will for this to happen. This fitted with the events that took place, when it was necessary to show the leading officials of the party and government as nitwits or illiterates who did not understand anything and who achieved their positions in questionable ways. They was done by people who didn't know about our lives and what we had accomplished.'

Yet, despite all the evidence to the contrary, Jakeš maintains that the communist era was a golden age for Czechoslovakia. 'Even though communism was defeated, it succeeded. All the main problems were resolved. Firstly, we had real people power. Secondly, communism removed unemployment, the horrible scourge of the majority of the earth's population. Thirdly, it created conditions under which all people could have access to education. Fourthly, it developed cultural life; this cannot be denied by anybody in this country. Fifthly, all the people enjoyed the social guarantees. Nobody was on the street, the social security in the country was perfect in comparison to the present day, and crime was not at the high level it is today. Hundreds of thousands, millions of flats were built for people who gradually had a place to live; transport was accessible in every village.

'Unified farmers' cooperatives – a miracle – became reality, they changed the character of villages into towns. The country people started living like people in towns and, like other workers, they would go on holiday, even during the harvest time. Agriculture production proved successful, it kept growing. The system secured permanent growth of the economy and everything that was handed out, stolen or sold later on was created in the socialist period. We took over and transferred only a few things from capitalism, only a small percentage, so everything that happened speaks in favour of the socialist regime.'

Today Jakeš is not a member of the Communist Party, but he still believes in communism. He can be seen at some party events like May Day parades and rallies. 'I would say, I miss – and I use the word carefully – the comradely relationship among people. Today there is hatred everywhere, deceit, smear campaigns, dirty tricks, the pursuit of money regardless of its impact. It is individualism and I would say individualism without restraint. This is my main complaint. I am a man of a collective cast.'

GÜNTER SCHABOWSKI

THE LAST WORD on the downfall of communism in Europe belongs to Günter Schabowski, the East German politician who thought that bringing down border controls would save socialism. But both he and his associates discovered that a change of personnel in the Politburo, some rousing rhetoric and even the scrapping of border controls would not be enough to prevent public opinion winning the day.

It was just before 7 p.m. on 9 November 1989 and East Germany's first televised news conference was drawing to a close. Schabowski, the most senior government figure present, suddenly remembered he had one further announcement to make. 'I realized I still had to announce the decree on freedom of travel, that the press conference was about to end and I had almost forgotten about the announcement – and that if I didn't make it the government would be in even more trouble. For me, it was just one item among several other items. I said, "I can tell you that the cabinet has passed a decree on travel regulations today. I will read it out to you." And that's what I did.

'There was a breathless silence. And all of a sudden lots of questions. Some asked, "When will that happen?" Because they hadn't really understood it at that moment. So I said, "As far as I know immediately."'

The key word that the press and East Berliners picked up on was *sofort* (immediately). At 7.05 Associated Press ran this sensational sentence: 'According to information provided by Politburo member Günter Schabowski, East Germany is opening its borders.' West German television stations now began broadcasting the story. By 8.30 several hundred East Germans had started gathering at checkpoints like Bornholmer Strasse wanting to cross into West Berlin.

It has been called one of the greatest PR gaffes in history. Schabowski hadn't realized that the new regulations didn't come into effect immediately. 'What was wrong was not the decision but the fact that there had been a provision, which I hadn't been told about, which stated that there would be an embargo. In an appendix to the decree it said that the border guards at the checkpoints throughout the DRR, from Berlin Mitte to Leipzig and Schwerin, needed to be notified. That ought to have been done by 4 a.m. the next day. Then at 4 a.m. a radio announcer was supposed to read out the decree. I still think that was a very sneaky gambit because at 4 o'clock in the morning the whole country would have been sleeping. But I didn't know about it. So I said, "As far as I know, immediately."'

As Schabowski recalls, 'Hundreds, thousands of people flocked to the border checkpoints, where they were blocked by the guards, who didn't know about any of this.'

At 9 p.m. the Bornholmer Strasse checkpoint began stamping 'no right of return' on the papers of people crossing to West Berlin. Two and a half hours later the pressure from the huge crowd was such that the colonel in charge decided to stop checking papers, open up completely and let the crowds stream across.

At the Brandenburg Gate people climbed the Wall and danced on top of it. A few minutes after midnight all the checkpoints between East and West Berlin were opened. Just six hours after Schabowski's comments the Wall had effectively come down. Over the following four days, a quarter of the population of East Germany crossed the border. A bloodless revolution had occurred. Schabowski and the whole Politburo had been caught unawares. 'To say that the Wall came down is a metaphor. It stands for everyone's right to unconditional travel,' Schabowski declared. 'I hadn't foreseen anything. For certain, I took part in the Politburo's decision that had started it all, but the people and the border guards who opened the border played a major role in avoiding a bloodbath. One of those guards could have very easily fired some warning shots, for all border guards were SED members. And the people might have reacted by attacking the guard and he then might have shot into the crowd.'

AFTERWORD

'What is communism? It is the longest road from capitalism to capitalism.'

East European joke

TWO DECADES AFTER the fall of communism in Eastern Europe, a rose-tinted view of the past persists in certain quarters. In today's unified Germany such Ostalgia (*Ostalgie*) – nostalgia for East Germany – is even experienced by those too young to remember life under communism. Such feelings were reinforced by the success of films such as the 2003 comedy *Goodbye Lenin*. As a result, a whole industry devoted to exploiting memories of the communist past developed.

Erotic dancers like the Magdeburger Models stripped off East German army uniforms. Singing groups like the Easty Girls performed communist songs to a techno beat interspersed with rap-style clips from Erich Honecker's speeches. At one time there were plans for a mini East Germany theme park, Ossie World. Travel agencies ran, and still run, Ostalgia tours. There is a cachet about East German design and communist kitsch – communist condoms, Vita Cola (East Germany's answer to Coca-Cola) and the canned aroma of Trabant fumes have all been marketed by the purveyors of Ostalgia. An East-German-themed youth hostel, Ostel, opened in Berlin in 2007.

More significantly, immediately after the raising of the Iron Curtain there emerged a host of difficulties for former communist countries, in respect both of coming to terms with the past and adjusting to the future. This was especially the case in Germany, which faced the challenge of unification. It soon became apparent to many East Europeans that capitalism too, with features like unemployment and its emphasis on individualism, was a flawed system. And many people didn't accept as accurate the harshly drawn pictures of their previous existence. East German actress Corinna Hartfouch put it like this: 'I cannot recognize my country from the way it is depicted in the press and media. We didn't just have autumn and winter. We had spring and summer too. Life wasn't just about the Stasi.'

East German singer Chris Doerk, who, like many others from the DDR, still feels at heart an East German, puts it just as strongly. 'It makes me angry when the DRR is often reduced to the Stasi and I don't know what more. Sometimes I have a feeling they think we lived in clay huts. Some people talk about the country in such a strange way: "In the DDR the bigwigs feasted and the people starved to death in the streets." I ask myself, "Did I live in a different country?" Because where I lived such things didn't happen. I am not immersed in nostalgia, I live in the here and now, but there are many things I miss about the DDR. The social network, the day-care centres; working mothers could leave their children in kindergartens, art and culture had a much higher value then. Many people say they are worse off nowadays. All right they can travel, but when you're on the dole and don't earn money you cannot travel. These are the things that make our people angry. I didn't lead a bad life in the DRR.

Although few want a return to communist rule, some people miss aspects of their lives under communism. Walter Womacka, a renowned Socialist Realist artist in East Germany, rues the loss of subsidy for the arts that was typical of the DDR. 'Art was a big concern in East Germany. A lot of money was spent on it, and the effects of that investment were clearly visible. Nowadays, East Germans used to seeing public art, paintings, sculpture, concerts, theatre, are very disappointed with what has happened. For example, today theatre tickets are very expensive and so only an elite few can afford them. And that's to say nothing about art funding.

'Look at my area – the fine arts. In Dresden, every four years there used to be a big exhibition in the Albertinum where contemporary art in general was on display. At the beginning, trade unions would bring people to the exhibitions but later that wasn't necessary any more, art became a matter of interest to everyone and visitors started attending voluntarily. At the last exhibition we had more than a million people turn up. Today people constantly ask why such things don't happen any more. Also, there were many individual exhibitions organized by museums. Amateurs were promoted. These were the great achievements that people still bear in mind, but they have disappeared.

'Nobody was happy about the Wall. But it was a means to an end. No one expected it to disappear the way it did, and so fast too. It was one of those moments in history, which can either be used to one's advantage or to one's disadvantage.

'I certainly miss the way people used to live together. Living side by side was good in the DDR. Most former DDR citizens miss that today. Money matters were of no importance back then, whereas nowadays they are more important than anything, because everything depends on money. The good thing about East Germany was the way people trusted one another, and even told their competitors about their business. That would be impossible today. These are the things that I miss.'

ACKNOWLEDGEMENTS

THERE ARE MANY PEOPLE to thank who helped me with this project. It originated as a television series and I am grateful to Karen O'Connor and Roly Keating of the BBC for commissioning the programmes. Thanks also to BBC executive producer Lucy Hetherington for her support for this book.

For the sections on Czechoslovakia, I am especially indebted to the peerless Vit Kolar OBE, formerly with the BBC World Service. His knowledge, journalistic and linguistic skills were as indispensable as his trenchant mind and good fellowship during the course of this journey.

For the sections on East Germany, I would like to thank Kerstin Fischer, head of the BBC Berlin office. She shared the journey from the early stages, and her personal experience and professional expertise proved essential. Patricia De Mesquita also made an important contribution.

For the sections on Romania, I am grateful to Anca Toader of the BBC World Service for her indefatigable approach and her sedulous research. Thanks are also due to William Treharne Jones, the producer of the Romanian episode of the BBC series, for the important part he played in the project.

Cameraman Ian Kennedy and film editor Bob Hayward gave, as ever, their wholehearted support and I benefited greatly from their sound judgement and creative input.

The BBC production team also helped enormously, especially film archivist Barry Purkis, production manager Libby Hand and production assistant Luciano Piazza. Thanks are also due to Marcella Gasche, Tatiana Bednarova, Rosie Goldsmith, Renata Clark, Mary Moss and Boyd Nagel.

I am also indebted to the many authors I have read who have written on post-war Eastern Europe. I only regret I don't have the space here to acknowledge their work individually but I am most grateful to them.

My editors, Karen Farrington and Julian Flanders, provided wise counsel and strong support during the sometimes frenetic composition of this book. Thanks also to Albert DePetrillo for believing in the project and to his colleague, project editor Christopher Tinker.

There are many others too numerous to mention, as they say, but I especially wanted to thank the many interviewees who agreed to share their experiences of life during communist rule. Over fifty of them appear in this book; others are featured in the television series. To all of them, I am most grateful.

Finally my love and thanks to Fran, Beth and Ben who shared the dark days with me.

INDEX